D0445000

The State and Political Theory

JC
474
.C37
1984

MARTIN CARNOY

The State and Political Theory

Princeton University Press — Princeton, New Jersey

WITHDRAWN
Fresno Pacific College - M. B. Seminary
Fresno, Calif. 93702

101869

Copyright © 1984 by Princeton University Press

Published by Princeton University Press, 41 William Street, Princeton, New Jersey 08540
In the United Kingdom: Princeton University Press, Guildford, Surrey

All Rights Reserved

Library of Congress Cataloging in Publication Data will be found on the last printed page
of this book

ISBN 0-691-07669-3   ISBN 0-691-02226-7 (pbk.)

This book has been composed in Linotron Times Roman

Clothbound editions of Princeton University Press books are printed on acid-free paper,
and binding materials are chosen for strength and durability. Paperbacks, although
satisfactory for personal collections, are not usually suitable for library rebinding

Printed in the United States of America by Princeton University Press
Princeton, New Jersey

CONTENTS

ACKNOWLEDGMENTS

THIS BOOK grew out of an all too short year in Paris. There I became a student again and learned about the theory of politics from one of its masters, Nicos Poulantzas. I owe a great debt of gratitude to Poulantzas and his then-teaching assistant, Isidoro Cheretzky, for their patience with, and inspiration of an American economist who asked many naive questions inside and outside their seminar at the Ecole Pratique des Hautes Etudes.

Yet, even with their inspiration, this book would have been impossible without the urging and support of my friend, Manuel Castells. Castells convinced me of the need for a survey analysis of neo-Marxist theories of the State, and helped me work through the many problems in my original drafts. My thanks to him here can never fully express my appreciation for his empathy and time.

My thanks also go to other readers: Mark Blaug, Christine Buci-Glucksmann, Carol Colgan, Fernando Henrique Cardoso, André G. Frank, Herb Gintis, Bob Jessop, John Manley, Adam Przeworski, Carlos Alberto Torres, Victoria Woodard, and Erik Olin Wright. They all gave me valuable and constructive comments. The comments of David Abraham and Peter Evans as external readers for Princeton University Press were particularly helpful. Their wisdom corrected many errors and omissions. To my editor at the Press, Sanford Thatcher, for his support, and to my copyeditor, Elizabeth Gretz, for her careful attention to details, special notes of gratitude.

Finally, an acknowledgment of the unknowing help provided by my students at Stanford in class discussions, and the knowing help of my children, to whom this book is dedicated. In a very conscious way, these two young men understood that all that time their father spent at the typewriter and word processor was important to him, even though it detracted from many of their needs.

Menlo Park, 1983

The State and Political Theory

THIS IS A BOOK about politics. It is a book about the increasing importance of politics in shaping social change in today's world. The primary problem of advanced capitalist societies, after two centuries of economic growth, is no longer the adequacy of resources or their "efficient" allocation for maximum output. The *way* that output is produced, the definition of what constitutes output, *what* is produced, and *who decides* development policy are the significant "economic" problems today. These problems are settled as much in the political arena as in production.

There is another reason for the importance of politics: as economies throughout the world have developed, the public sector—what we call here the State—has grown increasingly important in every society, from advanced industrial to Third World primary-good exporter, and in every aspect of society—not just politics, but in economics (production, finance, distribution), in ideology (schooling, the media), and in law enforcement (police, military). Why this occurs, and how the growing State is shaped, has become for social scientists a crucial issue—perhaps *the* crucial issue—of our times. The State appears to hold the key to economic development, to social security, to individual liberty, and, through increasing weapons "sophistication," to life and death itself. To understand politics in today's world economic system, then, is to understand the national State, and to understand the national State *in the context of that system* is to understand a society's fundamental dynamic.

Naturally, capitalist development and the State have always been intimately entwined. In the nineteenth century, however, the State's role in capitalist societies, while significant, was usually relatively limited. This was, in part, a reaction to the strong mercantilist State that preceded the industrial revolution, but it was also due to the great dynamism of private capitalism. Until the 1930s, the driving energy of capitalist societies resided in private entrepreneurial production. The private production sector, not the State, was the source of this energy, and the private sector economy was the center of social change. Thus, Ricardo, Marx, Weber, Durkheim, and Marshall could all discuss the State as an important but certainly not central element in their social analyses.

That can no longer be the case. The traditional nineteenth-century (and pre-nineteenth century) views are anachronistic, even though they continue to dominate much of the way we think about what the public sector is and should be. In the United States, we are particularly tied to certain of these traditions, as if little has changed during the last two hundred years. But the issue of the State has become much more complex, and with this increased complexity, we need theories that deal with it adequately and accurately. Indeed, the growth of the State *has* been accompanied by a burgeoning of diverse and sophisticated analyses of its "new" social role.

In this book, I do not attempt to review all theories of the State, but rather concentrate on taking a new look at the whole concept of the State from a class-perspective view, particularly the nature of recent debates in that intellectual context. To develop the setting for this discussion, I show how social scientists have analyzed the State in the past, including those who wrote about the State from a classical and utilitarian philosophy. The task of presenting both past and present views is not an easy one. It requires summarizing "objectively" a subjective choice of principal State theories, especially those theories that are not well known to American readers. The general purpose of presenting the recent debate among class-perspective views automatically limits the authors chosen for summary, and produces notable omissions of other State theories: for example, Max Weber's work is discussed only in terms of its considerable influence on certain versions of pluralist and Marxian theory; the institutionalists like Michel Foucault or the historical humanists like Henri Lefebvre also do not appear except in references and footnotes; the recent discussions in American pluralist circles are only referred to in the context of a very general (and brief) analysis of pluralism and corporatism; and the lengthy discussion of corporatism among political scientists is only mentioned as a contrast to classical and Marxian theories.

My principal purposes in this book, then, are: (1) to draw attention to the State as an object of investigation; (2) to demonstrate that there *are* discussions about what the State is, what it does, and how it functions; (3) to show that disagreements inherent in these discussions reflect different views of society and the role of the State in society; and (4) to show how different views of the State imply different politics of social change, in both their means and ends.

I argue that traditional classical "common good" and Marxist views of the State remain fundamental to understanding their present-day offshoots, but that in fact the more recent theories—and this is particularly true of those with a class perspective—only have a relation to their traditional predecessors in the broadest terms. Yet, even though modern Marxian analysts of the State have profound disagreements, they continue to provide, as a whole, a totally different approach to the subject than modern "common good" conceptions (which are also characterized by internal divergence). These differences among and between broad groupings of

State theory, I contend, are the basis for understanding different political-economic strategies for social change and control in advanced capitalist societies and the Third World. Theories of the State are therefore theories of politics.

With these purposes in mind, I have organized the presentation in a fairly straightforward way. The first chapter discusses "mainstream" American political theory and its origins. It is suggested there that pluralism and corporatism have a particular philosophical foundation which, in turn, leads to particular interpretations of democracy, the State, and the relation between the State and civil society, including the economy. Chapter 2 presents what might be called "traditional" Marxist political theories, showing how these theories are based on a different view of State and society than mainstream American views. Furthermore, it suggests that there are at least two different interpretations of the relation between the State and civil society in Marx, and that each leads to different views of class struggle and social change.

In the context of these interpretations, Chapters 3, 4, and 5 discuss five major post-Leninist contributions to Marxian political theory.

Gramscian views pose the State as a key to understanding the acceptance by subordinate classes of a class society. Marx, Engels, and Lenin had attributed this acceptance to a "false consciousness" developed in the relations and nature of capitalist production. But for Gramsci, acceptance is the result of capitalist-class "hegemony" (the dominance of that class's norms and values), and the State, as an ideological apparatus, helps legitimate this hegemony and is therefore part of it. In building a consensus for capitalist development, crucial responsibility is placed on intellectuals for this legitimation function, both inside and outside the State. So the principal crisis of capitalist development for Gramsci is not economic but hegemonic. It is only when the "consensus" underlying capitalist development begins to crumble that society can transform itself. Revolutionary politics is thus the struggle against hegemony, including the development, as part of that struggle, of a "counterhegemony" based on working-class values and culture.

The structuralism of Louis Althusser and of the early writing of Nicos Poulantzas considers the form and function of the capitalist State as determined by class relations inherent in the capitalist mode of production. The function of the State is ideological-repressive, but its class nature is "structured" by economic relations outside the State. At one and the same time, the State is necessarily "relatively autonomous" from these economic relations (civil society) in order to fulfill its class role, and is also the site where the dominant capitalist group(s) organizes the competitive fractions of the capitalist class into class "unity" (hegemony). Politics in the struc-

turalist view is principally the politics of the dominant class in establishing
or maintaining its hegemony over subordinated groups; the dominant fraction of the ruling group must—through the State—constantly create and
extend capitalist hegemony over an inherently antagonistic working class.
The State and politics itself (parties, legislative action, etc.) are the crucial
factors in hegemonic rule. Thus the class struggle is relegated to civil
society; the State and politics are the arena of capitalist–class fractions
attempting to mediate that struggle.

The German "derivationist" view, represented by Joachim Hirsch's
work, deduces the form and function of the State from the capital accumulation process. In particular, the tendency of the rate of profit to fall
requires the capitalist class to organize a State that counteracts this tendency
with State expenditures on physical and financial infrastructure and investment in human resources. Although in part the direct result of class
conflict, capital accumulation crises are more "inherently logical" aspects
of competitive capitalist development; hence the historical role of the
capitalist State can be analyzed in terms of this inherent logic. "Derivationist" politics are also relegated to capitalist-class efforts to use the State
to counteract capitalist crisis.

Claus Offe's[1] "political" view of the State draws heavily on Max Weber's theories of bureaucracy. Offe argues that the capitalist State is "independent" of any systematic capitalist-class control, either direct or structural, but that the State bureaucracy represents capitalists' interests anyway,
because it depends on capital accumulation for its continued existence as
a State. At the same time, however, the State must be *legitimate*. It mediates
workers' demands in the context of reproducing capital accumulation.
Politics, and contradictions in capitalist development, are fundamentally
intra-State. The State is a political "subject" in the sense that it organizes
capital accumulation and is also the site of the principal advanced capitalist
crises. Politics is primarily inside the State.

The "class struggle" analysis of the State, first suggested by Pietro
Ingrao in Italy and incorporated in Poulantzas's later work, argues that the
capitalist State itself is an arena of class conflict, and that whereas the
State is shaped by social-class relations, it is also contested and is therefore
the product of class struggle *within* the State. Politics is not simply the

[1] An American, James O'Connor, writing at the same time as Offe and Hirsch and like
them, deriving his views of the State and social change from the concept of capital, developed
in the late 1960s a theory of the State that includes "automatic" elements and an emphasis
on capital accumulation similar to Hirsch's, but focuses primarily on the contradictions
inherent in the dual role of the capitalist State: stimulating accumulation and remaining
legitimate to the voters (the working class). This latter formulation has many elements in
common with Offe's work.

organization of class power through the State by dominant capitalist-class groups, and the use of that power to manipulate and repress subordinate groups; it is also the site of organized conflict by mass social movements to influence State policies, gain control of State apparatuses, and gain control of political apparatuses outside the State. Politics, in this view, also takes place in the economic structures themselves: these are struggles for greater control of the work process and for power over surplus.

The remaining chapters present particular developments of class-perspective views related to these five new political analyses and crucial to their recent extension and deepening as theories of the State.

In Chapter 6, we review the debate on socialism and democracy, emanating principally from Italy and France because of Socialist and Communist Party electoral strength in those countries. This discussion is particularly important in serving as the basis for a reformulation of the nature of the "bourgeois" State, and poses a clear challenge both to Althusser's and Poulantzas's structuralism, as well as to Lucio Colletti's reinterpretation of Lenin. The debate therefore represents the clearest break with Leninism since Gramsci and postwar French humanism. The distinguishing feature of the very different positions represented by Norberto Bobbio and Pietro Ingrao, however, is that rather than breaking with economic determinism in general, they specifically focus on the State as a place of working-class "victories"—a site of conflict in capitalist society where the working class has been able to make both material and political gains. So-called "bourgeois" democracy, seen by Lenin as a manipulative facade, is both bourgeois *and* working-class. It "belongs" as much to subordinate groups as to the dominant classes. The Bobbio version pertains to the independent-State category of theories, and the Ingrao version, to the class struggle view. The importance of the discussion, however, lies in its application to democracy itself—a return, it might be added, to some of Marx's earlier writing, when he also considered democracy a crucial element of social justice (Draper 1977).

Chapter 7 deals with the State in Third World societies, and in doing so, reviews extensions of theories of the State from their usual focus on the national State to the State within a world system. At the same time, the discussion shows that the State in the Third World develops in a different set of conditions than those faced by the advanced industrial countries, largely because of the historical role of foreign capital in the periphery and the resultant weakness of local bourgeoisies. This weakness, in turn, makes the establishment of local hegemony difficult and creates the conditions for highly coercive, bureaucratic authoritarian regimes. There are a number of different dependency theories, and their differences correspond to some of the five contributions discussed in Chapters 3, 4, and

5. The debate is primarily between a structuralist view of the world (Frank 1979; Amin 1980) and a more historical, class struggle view (Cardoso and Faletto 1979; O'Donnell 1979), with important methodological as well as political overtones. For us, the most important of these is whether there is a "tendency" to a coercive, exclusionary corporatist form for Third World States (this would imply that armed revolution against the State is the most correct political strategy for democratic forces), or whether the bureaucratic authoritarian form is inherently fragile in the face of mass movements. In the latter case, bureaucratic authoritarianism would be subject to important democratic "openings," the reestablishment of democratic institutions, and would represent a State form characterized, as in the industrialized capitalist countries, by social struggle.

We return in Chapter 8 to American social thought. But recent U.S. class-perspective theoretical discussions of the State and politics are quite different from the traditional "mainstream" theories discussed in Chapter 1. American attention to class-perspective views of the State even in recent years goes back to Paul Sweezy's work in the early 1940s and to Paul Baran's and Baran and Sweezy's studies of the 1950s and early 1960s. Yet G. William Domhoff's power structure research (continuing the earlier tradition of C. Wright Mills) in 1967, and James O'Connor's research on the fiscal crisis of the State in 1969-1973 signal the beginning of a rich and varied literature emerging from the American scene. The contribution of this literature to the understanding of the State from a class-perspective view is now so important that it stands on its own as an innovative force in the theoretical literature. It is in the United States, for example, that we can find a highly developed debate between those who argue that the advanced capitalist State is "independent" of both capitalists and labor (Block 1977; Skocpol 1981), and those who view the State as a site of struggle between a capitalist class and social movements (minorities, women, community groups) emerging from a fragmented working class (Castells 1980; Wright 1978; Bowles and Gintis 1982).

The contrast between the analyses in Chapters 1 and 8 allows us to discuss, in Chapter 9, the differences in political visions emerging in the United States and their implications for political futures, strategies, and further research. It is these implications, after all, that are the raison d'être of State theories and our better understanding of them. With that understanding, the present crisis of the welfare State and the neoconservative response become much clearer. What is less clear is the nature of the State itself, and, therefore, which of these political futures and strategies is "correct." Now that the State has become so important in most national economies, do the principal contradictions of capitalist development take place in the private production sector (competition among capitals, and between capital and labor) or in the State? Is the crisis of hegemony primarily a State economic (fiscal) crisis or one of ideology? Is the State an independent political-economic force posed "against" both capitalists' direct interests *and* those of labor and mass-based social movements? Will the State in advanced capitalist societies and in the Third World inevitably take an increasing economic and social role until struggles between traditionally defined classes are minor compared to everyone's relationship to the State? Or do traditionally defined class relations shape the nature of conflicts within the State to such a degree that the State and State policies cannot be viewed separately from those conflicts? And what *is* the nature of "class" conflict? How are they changing?

There are two important themes that emerge from our review of these recent debates, and both represent significant recastings of traditional Marxist theory.

First, the literature has moved in the direction of arguing that it is the State, rather than production, that should and will be the principal focus of class struggle. This is not simply the result of a worldwide tendency for the State to become increasingly involved in the economy. Rather, *politics* in recent Marxist thought has itself taken on a primacy that it did not have in the past, a politics that reflects as much the reality of the Soviet experience and of capitalist hegemony as the relative absence of a theory of the State in traditional Marxism.

This increasing primacy of politics produces a second theme: Marxist theorizing on the State has moved increasingly toward the position that the political struggle for the transition to socialism must be essentially *democratic*, in the sense of combining an expansion of parliamentary and electoral struggles with social movements, worker control, and other forms of direct democracy. Extending democracy into new forms and, through these forms, breaking down the logic of capitalist social relations, is a dramatic change from traditional Marxist-Leninist "smash the State" strategy, and, again, reflects the reality of postwar history. The "discovery" of Gramsci, the attack of structuralism, and the recasting of the class struggle represent a new understanding among Marxists of the shortcomings of deterministic political theories for radical change.

The review suggests, therefore, that recent theories of the State represent a significant step toward revising class-perspective social change theory and political strategies. The different views have not been completely resolved intellectually, but the contribution of this book is to show the considerable distance that this intellectual quest has already gone and where it can continue most fruitfully into the future.

CHAPTER ONE

The State and American Political Thought

IN AMERICA, the typical citizen would probably describe the government as a pluralist democracy in which competing interest groups and the public at large define public policy. The State is seen as a neutral arena of debate. Elected representatives and appointed bureaucrats lead but simultaneously reflect public wishes, at least for that public which is interested in the issues at hand. And although the State bureaucracy may develop a life of its own, the general public assumes that, through elections, it has ultimate power over government decisions.

Pluralist political theory is, in some sense, the official ideology of capitalist democracies. On the basis of its central tenet of individual liberty, pluralism claims an exclusive right to democracy itself. But, as we shall show, there are problems with this claim, and they emanate from the fundamentals of classical political theory. The theory makes certain assumptions about economic and social relations among individuals—specifically, about the relationship between individual liberty in the market and individual political power. In light of the history of capitalist development and the capitalist State, those assumptions are highly questionable—so questionable, that non-Marxist political analysts from Max Weber to Joseph Schumpeter to recent writers such as Philippe Schmitter, Alfred Stepan, and Leo Panitch have questioned whether the liberal democratic State is in fact democratic. There are some who suggest that democracy as such is inherently compromised under twentieth-century industrial capitalism, and others who argue that what is described as pluralism is really corporatism.

Nevertheless, pluralist theory continues to be dominant ideologically in the United States. Pluralism's pervasiveness and its claims on democracy demand that we explore its intellectual bases before going on to analyze an alternative class-perspective tradition. That alternative, as we shall see, not only challenges the fundamental classical and pluralist premises about the relationship of State and civil society, but also challenges their theories of democracy and the democratic State. More recent debates between Marxist theories of the State focus on the meaning of individual liberty in a class State, and the deepening and extension of capitalist democracy. The class-perspective analysis of the State in America, to be discussed in

Chapter 8, brings the views we describe in this chapter into sharp contrast with the Marxist theories of the State that are the theme of the rest of the book. It is that contrast that best reflects the underlying political divisions between contemporary social scientists with traditional and class-perspective views. And it is the challenge to the pluralist claims on democracy that represents the most serious move toward a new Marxist politics.

"COMMON GOOD" THEORIES OF THE STATE

Implicit in analyses of the State that are couched in the pluralist view is the idea that the government intends to serve mass interests even if, in practice, it does not always do so. Government is the servant of the people placed there by the people to perform that function. The concept that individuals collectively should be able to determine the laws that govern them is as old as the ideas of human rights and democracy themselves. Yet, for a long period of history, divine law defined relations between individuals, including who was to govern them and how they should be governed. Divine law came from a higher authority, a superhuman force that was both above and beyond the comprehension and control of the individual and yet within each person, giving him or her the possibility of complete knowledge and understanding. Authority was derived from interpretations of this law, interpretations provided by the hierarchy of organized religious institutions and the struggle within the political hierarchy itself. In Europe, this meant that landed nobility (who had acquired their land through conquest during and after the fall of the Roman Empire) and the Catholic Church established and enforced a set of "divine" laws. These laws came not only from religious texts but from economic and social relationships directly established by the conquerors of Europe as they replaced Roman rule. Nevertheless, religious precepts served to legitimize all these relationships, including economic ones, for more than a thousand years.

It is difficult to say when the feudal system and the legitimacy of divine law began to break down. Although the development of alternative economic patterns in Europe can be found in the thirteenth-century Adriatic city-states, where merchants trading between Europe and the Orient accumulated vast sums without owning land or using serfs (they even established banks), when capitalism arose depends largely on the definition of capitalism itself. Some authors have stressed that the rise can be dated by the accumulation of capital as the prices of grains rose over a long period of time in the sixteenth century (Wallerstein 1974); others argue that it was a new concept of man or a new rationality in the conduct of economic and political affairs that defined the rise of capitalism (Foucault

1970; Weber [1904] 1958); others that it was the integration of national markets; and still others that it was the emancipation (or forcing off) of the labor force from the land (Marx [1867] 1906). Although it would be foolish, then, to try to date the decline of feudalism and the rise of capitalism, it is clear that by the sixteenth and seventeenth centuries, there were important transformations taking place in the old social formation. And although divine law was still fundamental to hierarchical legitimacy even in the 1600s, the Catholic Church (as the single interpreter of that law) had been split asunder by religious wars that reflected the gradual economic decline of the nobility as the dominant class supporting the enormous economic and political power of the Church.

Thus, the sixteenth and seventeenth centuries were a period of drastic change in European history. As we have suggested, the reasons for this change is a subject of continuous debate among historians, who have developed a variety of historical theories to explain the transformation. We are not going to discuss the merits of these ideas here, despite their importance for a theory of the State. The crucial point for our purposes is that there was a drastic change, and because of that change it was possible for new forms of government to develop. Along with those new forms came new concepts of what governments should be like. The spread of these ideas, in time, served as the basis for further changes.

It is toward the end of the seventeenth century that we see a redefinition of the state of nature (man's natural condition), and the final systematic presentation of individual rights replacing divine law as the foundation of political hierarchies.

Classical writers such as Hobbes and Locke developed their ideas in the throes of political changes already taking place in England. Indeed, the basic concept of representative democracy had existed since the thirteenth century in their country (the Magna Carta and Parliament—including a House of Commons—date from that time), and can be said to be rooted in nobles' protesting their feudal rights against attempts to centralize power in the hands of a king. Nevertheless, although it is definitely not obvious that representative democracy is a concept whose origins lie with the rise of a bourgeoisie, in practice its spread and institutionalization are identified with the growth of capitalism and bourgeois economic and political power.

The Classical Doctrine

The classical theory of the State emerged from the changing conditions of economic and political power in seventeenth-century Europe. As the feudal system—already transformed by the development of centralized,

authoritarian, national monarchies—declined further, the existence of nar-
rowly based State and quasi-State apparatuses (like the Catholic Church,
for example) were not only questioned but attacked. The result was a series
of civil wars which racked Europe in the end of the sixteenth century and
throughout the seventeenth.

Hirschman (1977) discusses this change in terms of the history of ideas.
He points out that although Machiavelli tried to improve the art of statecraft
by teaching his prince how to achieve, maintain, and expand power by
providing a scientific, positive approach to governing in the real world,
political philosophers of the seventeenth and eighteenth centuries based
their theories of the State on human nature, on *individual* behavior and
the relationship between individuals. And, at the same time, a profound
change took place in the approach to human behavior: "A feeling arose
in the Renaissance and became firm conviction during the seventeenth
century that moralizing philosophy and religious precept could no longer
be trusted with restraining the destructive passions of men" (Hirschman
1977, 14-15). Coercion and repression, as Foucault (1978) has shown us,
gradually were replaced as the principal means of restraining passions, by
a State and society that harnessed the passions instead of simply repressing
them. Again, it was the State that was called upon to accomplish this—
to act as a civilizing medium.

It is in this context, then, that the theory of the liberal State based on
individual rights and the State acting in the "common good"—to harness
men's passions by allowing their interests to overcome those passions—
developed. As we shall see, the particular version of that theory that
eventually became dominant in England and America was that men's
interests—especially their insatiable desire for material gain—would themselves oppose and control their passions; and the role of the State that
would best serve humankind was one that relied on and guaranteed the
operation of a free market in civil society.

The theory of the liberal State went through a series of important changes.
They reflected the political struggles taking place as English and French
capitalism developed. There is no truly appropriate way to divide the
discussion of that State, since any change in theory has its roots in previous
writing and reaction to political reality. Nevertheless, I have taken the
often-used categories of classical and liberal doctrine for the purposes of
the analysis.

The new political philosophy that came on the heels of these enormous
disruptions stressed individual over divine rights and in that sense legitimized new bases of power, new relationships among human beings, and
the human soul itself. No longer were power and knowledge inherited

through birthright; they were acquired (although, as we shall see, this was not quite as egalitarian as would first appear). Now a new version of human rights was the birthright. Furthermore, the classical theorists retained a "divine" basis for exercising power: the "common good."

I say "divine" basis for power because, although the classical doctrine overthrew divine rights in favor of a redefinition of natural and, from it, individual rights, the origin of all rights was still a "higher authority"— human reason itself came from God. Thus, the basis for new forms of the State was still divine reason and rationality inculcated in human beings from above. The "common good" was inherent in the divine rationality of human beings; it was God in man; but rather than being revealed, its understanding could be acquired.

The religious foundations of classical doctrine stem from the moment in time in which the doctrine was formulated. Political struggles in the seventeenth century were still enmeshed with interpretations of divine law. It is perfectly logical, then, that the origins of bourgeois legitimacy and the theory of the bourgeois State should be couched in theological terms, and that intellectual differences among classical writers revolve around theological interpretations.

Is it contradictory to stress the relation between feudal divine concepts and a classical doctrine that was supposed to be such a sharp break with those concepts? At that point in history arguing that man was rational— that God gave him reason in the state of nature and that from there he was on his own—explicitly broke with the divine order of feudal society and specifically with the idea that people were put on an earth whose workings were totally out of their control. But from the perspective of the twentieth century, the religious aspects of the doctrine are striking. As historian Carl Becker has argued:

We are accustomed to think of the eighteenth century as essentially modern in temper. . . . Surely, we say, the eighteenth century was preeminently the age of reason, surely the *philosophes* were a skeptical lot, atheists in effect if not by profession, addicted to science and the scientific method, always out to crush the infamous, valiant defenders of liberty, equality, fraternity, freedom of speech, and what you will. . . . But, if we examine the foundations of their faith, we find that at every turn the *philosophes* betray their debt to medieval thought without being aware of it. . . . In spite of their rationalism and their humane sympathies, in spite of their aversion to hocus-pocus and enthusiasm and dim perspective, in spite of their eager skepticism, their engaging cynicism, their brave youthful blasphemies and talk of hanging the last king in the entrails of the last priest—in spite of all of it, theirs is more of a Christian philosophy in the writings of the *philosophes* than has yet been dreamt of in our histories. (Becker 1963, 28-30)[1]

The other fundamental aspect of classical doctrine is its revolutionary character: classical philosophers were, to different degrees, deeply committed to political change in particular directions. They were concerned with finding a new organization of the State based on a *new* concept of man. Although this may seem contradictory to the theological elements of the classical doctrine, we can well imagine that revolutionary ideas, like new social formations, contain important elements from the past—and in the case of political ideas trying to "persuade," must indeed contain past elements in order to convince people of their worthiness. Thus, while drawing on God for men's reason, the classical philosophers broke sharply with divine law in placing all political and economic power in the hands of reasonable men, not God.

Understanding these general features of classical theory, we now turn to Hobbes, Locke, and Rousseau. These three "representative" classicists are analyzed primarily because of their influence on American political thinking.

Hobbes's *Leviathan* (1968), originally published in 1651, was one of the first attempts to systematize human political behavior according to deductive logic and the laws of motion, the seventeenth-century concepts that had so revolutionized scientific investigation. In its very method, then, Hobbes's work was a break with the past on two counts: first, he applied a scientific methodology to individual behavior—instead of making the operation of the State itself more efficient (like Machiavelli)—as the basis of his political theory; and secondly, he argued that appetites and aversions are what determine a man's voluntary actions (as opposed to the medieval view that man's appetites, or passions, had to be curbed by an external source), and that the only way for men to satisfy their appetites and simultaneously avoid the most important aversion (death) was to acknowledge a perpetual sovereign power, against which each of them would be powerless.

Hobbes could have argued his case for giving up individual power to the sovereign by showing that the omnipresent struggle for that power would lead to the breakdown of any society and to an increase in the probability of violent death. Reasonable men could be expected, without

---

[1] It is not by accident, then, that religious elements, especially the divine foundation of nature and reason (and from them, the "common good") are part of American political ideology. The fact that God is behind capitalist relations of production and the American State ("one nation, created under God"; "in God we trust"; "God bless America") give a divine standing to national purpose and destiny (see Schumpeter 1942).

any further discussion, to understand the need to hand over whatever power necessary to a sovereign who could prevent this breakdown. Instead, to make this case, Hobbes introduces the logical abstraction of the *state of nature*, a hypothetical condition wherein there is no common power to restrain individuals, no law, and no law enforcement. Civilized man would want to get out of this condition, but at the same time, he also has—in the state of nature—natural rights which he wants to preserve, particularly "the Liberty each man hath, to use his own power, as he will himself, for the preservation of his own nature; that is to say, of his own Life; and consequently, of doing anything, which in his own Judgment, and Reason, he shall conceive to the aptest means thereunto" (Hobbes 1968, 189). Therefore, there is a tension between preserving the liberty available in the state of nature and the fear of violence and war which that state so logically produces. This leads to an individual's giving up power to a sovereign. Men should in their own self-interest acknowledge full obligation to the sovereign. This sovereign (either an individual or a body of men) would reduce all subjects to impotence, but Hobbes countered that argument with two points: first, subjugation is better than civil war (death), and second, it would not be in the interest of the sovereign to do this to his (or its) subjects because the sovereign's strength consists in the vigor of those subjects.

There are a lot of problems with this conception of the State: why, for example, should individuals who love their liberty give *all* their power to a sovereign, in the hope that the sovereign would be just and fair, or at least represent their best interests? According to Macpherson, the English bourgeoisie never accepted Hobbes's model of the State because he stipulated that the sovereign, whether a single person or an assembly, should have the power to name its successors (Macpherson, in Hobbes 1968, 54). This rejection makes complete sense in terms of individual or group interest: no one who wants to maintain control over a government could be satisfied with giving the government itself self-perpetuative powers.

And, as Hirschman (1977) points out, Hobbes's concept of the social contract only appealed once to the strategy of interests taming passions, for the purpose of founding a State so constituted that the problems created by passionate men are solved once and for all. Men seeking peace would give up to a sovereign the control of their passions in the interest of taming themselves; they would give up their individual power, in order that no one of them could diminish any other one's power by force. But many of Hobbes's contemporaries, and certainly those who followed him, did not embrace this solution, believing that a countervailing strategy was needed on a continuing day-to-day basis. Eventually, such a formulation emerged and developed: it centered on the free-market exchange of goods, in which men's passions would be contained by the maximization of their economic interests, a sublimation of violence into the quest for economic gain in the peaceful context of the market. Physical power would be overcome by the civilizing force of this market. Hobbes's theory was not inconsistent with such a market (Macpherson, in Hobbes 1968, 48-51), but it did not at all rely on it for opposing interests to passions, that is, for social control.

Unlike Hobbes, who developed a whole new way of looking at political society, John Locke, writing forty years later (1692) and coming out of the same historical period of English civil wars and the emergence of the bourgeoisie as a powerful force opposed to feudal structures and political forms, was, in the words of one analyst, "not an original thinker, but rather a synthesist or popularizer," who "endeavored to harmonize the findings of seventeenth-century science with the Christian tradition" (Kirk, in Locke [1692] 1955, v). For Locke, as for Hobbes, man's original political condition is a remarkably unprimitive "state of nature"—the state of perfect individual freedom, in which man has a title to all rights and privileges of the law of nature equally with all others—where man could not only protest and preserve his property, but be both judge and enforcer of natural law. But this state of nature can degenerate into a state of war: one man can attempt to get another man into his absolute power.

> Men living together according to reason, without a common superior on earth with authority to judge between them, is properly the state of nature. But force, or a declared design of force, upon the person of another, where there is no common superior on earth to appeal to for relief, is the state of war; 'tis want of such an appeal gives a man the right of war even against an aggressor, though he be in society and a fellow-subject. (Locke 1955, 14)

In order to defend themselves against a state of war, Locke argues (still agreeing with Hobbes) that men join together in political society, with a body of laws which govern power relations among them. In that political society, men give up the rights of self-preservation of property to the community (the State):

> But because no political society can subsist without having in itself the power to preserve the property, and, in order thereunto, punish the offenses of all those of that society, where every one of the members hath quitted this natural power, resigned it up into the hands of the community in all cases that exclude him not from appealing for protection to the law established by it. . . . Wherever, therefore, any numbers of men so unite into one society, as to quit every one of his executive

power of the law of nature, and to resign it to the public, there, and there only, is a political, or civil society. (Locke 1955, 61-63)

Yet, Locke diverges completely from Hobbes on the nature of the sovereign: in this definition of political society, *absolute* monarchy is inconsistent with civil government. The monarch has no authority to appeal to but himself, and so is in a state of nature, not in civil society. Locke excludes absolute monarchy from any acceptable form of government. Men may have at one time been willing to give power to a single "good and excellent man . . . to a kind of natural authority," but then finding that his successor could not keep their properties secure in the same manner, insisted that power be placed in "collective bodies of men" (Locke 1955, 67-68).

Locke's political society does not really define the form of the State, but rather, defines only its underlying principle of individual rights. And he is quite specific about in whom these rights reside. What is important for Locke is that individuals give up their "natural" political power to someone else—to a legislative power, a group of men or a single man who will make and enforce the laws that keep each individual's property and person secure. But this national political power still resides in the individuals making up the civil society—those who delegate it to others to govern them. Whether this "other" is a monarchy, or an elected legislature, power is given to them only as long as they fulfill the protective function, equitably governing the individual members of the civil society.

Political power is that power which every man having in the state of nature, has given up into the hands of the society, and therein to the governors whom the society hath set over itself, with this express or tacit trust that it shall be employed for their good and the preservation of their property. Now this power, which every man has in the state of nature, and which he parts with to the society in all such cases where the society can secure him, is to use such means for the preserving of his own property as he thinks good and nature allows him, and to punish the breach of the law of nature in others so as, according to the best of his reason, may most conduce to the preservation of himself and the rest of mankind. So that the end and measure of this power, when in every man's hands in the state of nature, being the preservation of all his society—that is, all mankind in general—it can have no other end or measure when in the hands of the magistrates but to preserve the members of that society in their lives, liberties, and possessions; and so cannot be an absolute, arbitrary power over their lives and fortunes which are as much as possible to be preserved, but a power to make laws, and annex such penalties to them as may tend to the preservation of the whole, by cutting of those parts, and those only, which are so corrupt that they threaten the sound and healthy, without which no severity is lawful. And this power has its original only from compact and agreement and the mutual consent of those who make up the community. (Locke 1955, 126-127)

As Macpherson (1977) has pointed out, this is not an argument for democracy as we think of it today, but for *individual rights* in a classless society. But Locke *constructs* classlessness, excluding everyone from civil society who does not own property (for example, all women and wage laborers). In Locke's view, the individuals who have political rights are all property owners, a relatively homogeneous group. The State (legislative and executive power) is *given* power by these individual owners to protect their property and person. If the State does not fulfill its mandate, the members of civil society have the right and the power to dissolve that State. Legislative and executive have political power as long as they reflect the will of individual (property-owning) members of civil society, in whom real political power resides.

It is in his concept of civil society that Rousseau differs most from Locke. For Locke, civil society is a new means for men to regulate themselves—he viewed existing monarchies as not civil society, as not reflecting his construction of how men *should* govern themselves in an extension of their reason and perfection. Locke saw the state of nature as degenerating into war and strife, and men forming a naturally just and equal society to protect their naturally acquired property from the state of war possible in nature (since every individual could take the law into his own hands). Thus we have the reason and perfection of civil society posed against the chaos and inequality of the state of nature.

For Rousseau, to the contrary, and in contrast with other social contract theories of that time, civil society is a description of the way men are actually found in society, not as an ideal or a hypothetical construct but as a reality. Hence, he postulated exactly the opposite dichotomy between nature and civil society: Rousseau saw man in nature as without morality but at the same time without evil; man is corrupted not by nature but by the ownership of property and the forming of civil society itself. It is civil society that is corrupt and nature a prehuman ideal.

Given such differences, it is not surprising that Rousseau and Locke should also view the process of *forming* civil society and the fundamentals of that society—particularly property and the market—as different: first, Locke viewed property ownership as the basis of a just and equal civil society; Rousseau claimed it was a source of evil and inequality:

The first man, who after enclosing a piece of ground, took it into his head to say, *this is mine*, and found people simple enough to believe him, was the real founder of civil society. How many crimes, how many wars, how many murders, how many misfortunes and horrors, would that man have saved the human species, who pulling up the stakes or filling up the ditches should have cried to his fellows: beware of listening to this imposter; you are lost, if you forget that the fruits of the earth belong equally to us all, and the earth itself to nobody! (Rousseau 1967, 211-212)

Second, Locke argued that men formed civil society in order to protect themselves from conditions in the state of nature. They gave up the natural freedoms of that state to gain collective security for property and life. Civil society was a move to perfect relations among men—it was a product of man's rationality and desire for improvement. Rousseau, however, sees the formation of civil society as the product of man's *greed*: "from the moment it appeared an advantage for one man to possess enough provisions for two, equality vanished; property was introduced; labor became necessary; and boundless forests became smiling fields, which had to be watered with human sweat, and in which slavery and misery were soon seen to sprout out and grow with the harvests" (Rousseau 1967, 220).

Furthermore, contrary to Locke's formulation of the civil society as an agreement among equals banding together with full knowledge of their rights and obligations, Rousseau constructs civil society as the work of the more wealthy and powerful forming such a society in their interests, not necessarily in the interest of the masses. In an unequal society, the rich found it necessary to preserve order, to control attempts to usurp them, and to legitimize the exploitation of the poor. It was therefore the rich who conceived of civil society, of a civil society that protected *their* interests:

the rich man, thus pressed by necessity, at last conceived the deepest project that ever entered the human mind: this was to employ in his favor the very forces that attacked him, to make allies of his enemies, to inspire them with other maxims, and make them adopt other institutions as favorable to his pretensions, as the law of nature was unfavorable to them. . . . "Let us unite," said he, "to secure the weak from oppression, restrain the ambitious, and secure to every man the possession of what belongs to him. . . ." . . . All gladly offered their necks to the yoke, thinking they were securing their liberty; for though they had sense enough to perceive the advantages of a political constitution they had not experience enough to see beforehand the dangers of it. Those among them who were best qualified to foresee abuses were precisely those who expected to benefit by them. (Rousseau 1967, 227-228)

Rousseau therefore saw the State of his time as the creation of the rich to secure their position as the dominant class, a State presented as benefiting all but designed to preserve inequality. He argued that it was impossible to separate social from political inequality, but at the same time believed that men *wanted* to be free and equal—that it was their ignorance that led them to accept the civil society in which they lived. Rousseau could thus conceive of a State that would guarantee this freedom and equality. It was this State that he described in his later work, *On the Social Contract* ([1762] 1978).

What is the basis of this social contract? Here Rousseau and Locke are much closer, since both are speaking of ideals. For Rousseau, like Locke, the power of the State resides in the people who give up their freedom to the State and the State in turn is the *general will*:

If, then, everything that is not of the essence of the social compact is set aside, one will find that it can be reduced to the following terms. *Each of us puts his person and all his power in common under the supreme direction of the general will; and in a body we receive each member as an indivisible part of the whole.* (Rousseau 1978, 53)

What man loses by the social contract is his natural freedom and an unlimited right to everything that tempts him and that he can get; what he gains is civil freedom and the proprietorship of everything he possesses. (Rousseau 1978, 56)

The State under this social contract treats all citizens equally because it is acting as a State under the direction of the general will: "every authentic act of the general will, obligates or favors all citizens equally. . . . As long as subjects are subordinated only to such conventions, they do not obey anyone, but solely their own will; and to ask how far the respective rights of the sovereign and of citizens extend is to ask how far the latter can engage themselves to one another, each to all and all to each" (Rousseau 1978, 63).

In this sense, then, we have a State that is the general will, much as Locke saw State power residing in the citizenry and only in the citizenry. The two also agree that while the general will treats people equally, not all citizens are equal: the law considers citizens as a body and actions in the abstract (never a man as an individual or a particular action), but there can also be classes of citizens—that is, legal categories of citizens—defined by the State in abstract terms without defining the specific people who are in each class (Rousseau 1978, 66). The implications of this position should be clear: there could be classes of citizens but not social classes—no classes to which individuals were assigned by virtue of birth or property.

Since he organized the dangers to this social contract from man's greed, Rousseau went much further than Locke in discussing the conditions under which the State (the general will) could be expressed and maintained. While upholding property as the "most sacred of all the rights of citizens, and more important in certain respects than freedom itself" (Rousseau 1978, 224-225) he insisted on the need to limit property rights so that there would be no extremes of wealth and poverty: "With regard to equality, this word must not be understood to mean that degrees of power and wealth should be exactly the same, but rather that with regard to power, it should be incapable of all violence and never exerted except by virtue of status and the laws; and with regard to wealth, no citizen should be so opulent that he can buy another, and none so poor that he is constrained to sell himself" (Rousseau 1978, 75).

Nor was Rousseau an advocate of laissez faire. He saw the State as intervening directly to ensure a certain degree of equality. He argued that if "you then want to give stability to the State. . . . Bring the extremes as close together as possible: tolerate neither opulent people nor beggars. These two conditions, naturally inseparable, are equally fatal to the common good" (1978, 75 n). This followed directly from his view that the general will was the State. For if men were divided into classes with opposed interests, they would be guided by those opposed interests rather than the good of society as a whole, and if they were guided by those interests, the general will would cease to be acceptable to the whole. Strife would follow (Macpherson 1977, 17). Intervention by the State was therefore necessary to preserve the State.

In his *Discourse on Political Economy* ([1755] 1978), Rousseau spelled out the nature of this intervention. Besides providing enough money for administrators and legislators so that they would not be tempted to be corrupt, he continued that it was "one of the government's most important tasks to prevent extreme inequality of wealth, not by taking treasures away from those who possess them, but by removing the means of accumulating them from everyone; nor by building poorhouses, but by protecting citizens from becoming poor." This would be accomplished by State education for the population.

> And as each man's reason is not allowed to be the unique arbiter of his duties, it is even less appropriate to abandon the education of children to the enlightenment and prejudices of their fathers. . . . Public education, under rules prescribed by the government and magistrates established by the sovereign, is therefore one of the fundamental maxims

of popular or legitimate government. If children are raised in common in the midst of equality, if they are imbued with the laws of the State and the maxims of the general will, if they are taught to respect them above all things, if they are surrounded by examples and objects that constantly remind them of the tender mother who nourishes them, her love for them, the inestimable benefits they receive from her, and what they owe in return there can be no doubt that they will learn from this to love one another as brothers, never to want anything except what the society wants, to substitute the actions of men and citizens for the sterile, empty babble of sophists, and one day to become the defenders and fathers of the homeland whose children they will have been for so long. (Rousseau 1978, 223)

Rousseau, like Locke before him and Jefferson after, argued that the success of the social contract in which the general will could be exercised depended on a society of small proprietors; in Rousseau's case, this meant a State that was actively involved in preventing inequality from developing.

Rousseau more than Locke seemed to be aware of the pitfalls of the social contract. If the State had to act to preserve the equality necessary to have a legitimate, functioning social contract, how was the system—both public and private—to be kept from degenerating into a class-based, strife-ridden society? Rousseau ultimately counted on education and the fundamental rationality and good will of men to achieve balance and social over individual interest. As men were more aware and informed they would *choose* to be free—to be committed to the general will and its sovereignty—and would ensure that there would not be excess wealth or poverty. If they did not, Rousseau argued, tyranny would be the rule.

The Liberal Doctrine

It is difficult to divide the "classical" from the "liberal" doctrine—to the point that the terms themselves may be arbitrary. I have placed the break-point at Adam Smith, not so much chronologically (he was a contemporary of Rousseau), but rather because Smith, in Hirschman's words, "establish[ed] a powerful *economic* justification for the untrammeled pursuit of individual self-interest, whereas in the earlier literature . . . the stress was on the *political* effects of this pursuit" (Hirschman 1977, 100). The new theory still took the individual as the focus of the analysis, and individual behavior as its basis, but, at the same time, made several important and very influential changes in classical views of social relations.

First, Smith argued that men were actuated entirely by the desire to better their condition and that increasing their fortune (material gain) is the means by which the majority of them achieved this better condition (Smith [1776] 1937, Bk. III, ch. 4). Smith eliminates the competition among various desires or aims of human existence that had existed in previous political economics, by collapsing all other motives into the economic. As Hirschman suggests, Smith does this by showing that since man's bodily needs are limited, the principal economic drive is to seek glory, the administration of fellow men, etc. The motive for economic advantage is "no longer autonomous but becomes a mere vehicle for the desire for consideration" (Hirschman 1977, 109).

> What is the end of avarice and ambition, of the pursuit of wealth, of power, and perseverance? . . . From whence . . . arises the emulation which runs through all the different ranks of men and what are the advantages which we propose by that great purpose of human life which we call bettering our condition? To be observed, to be attended to, to be taken notice of with sympathy, complacency, and appreciation, are all the advantages which we can propose to derive from it. It is the rarity, not the ease or the pleasure, which interests us. (Smith, in Hirschman 1977, 108)

Second, Smith not only claimed that men's various motives are translated into the single desire for economic gain. He added the fundamental axiom that each individual acting in his own (economic) interest would, when taken together as a collectivity of individuals, maximize collective well-being. This continues the Lockean model, yet puts primary emphasis and responsibility on the free and unfettered operation of the market for social well-being. It is commerce and manufactures that introduce order and good government (Smith 1937, 385); moreover, the free market is such a powerful force for bettering the human condition that it can even overcome poor laws and an "interfering" government.

> The natural effort of every individual to better his own condition, when suffered to exert itself with freedom and security, is so powerful a principle, that it is alone, and without any assistance, not only capable of carrying on the society to wealth and prosperity, but of surmounting a hundred impertinent obstructions with which the folly of human laws too often encumbers its operations; though the effect of these obstructions is always more or less to encroach upon its freedom, or to diminish its security. (Smith 1937, 508)

Third, Smith stressed that the achievement of collective well-being through individual action was an unwitting result of individual motivation for economic gain. Individuals striving for personal enrichment were not necessarily aware that their efforts were resulting in a better society. This was an unintended effect of what might seem at first to be (and certainly was treated as such by many of Smith's predecessors) the undesirable human trait of avarice. Smith's theory showed, at one and the same time, that human passions were subjugated to the overriding motive for material gain, and that this motive was actually desirable because it resulted in the greatest good for the greatest number.

In this sense, Smith appeared to have "solved" the problem posed earlier by Rousseau, and by Bernard Mandeville in *The Fable of the Bees*: Rousseau, as we have shown, believed that civil society based on competition and trade, on exchange and personal interest, necessarily leads to the corruption of that society unless there is a countervailing force of a social contract (a State committed to regulating such competition and trade, or at least controlling the necessarily corrupt outcomes of competition); Mandeville argued the paradox that though each individual pursues his own selfish passions, the total result is national prosperity and the well-being of society as a whole. Smith incorporated Mandeville's argument, which anticipated Smith's "invisible hand," but countered that there was a fallacy in it: not every passion, particularly that of acquisition (avarice) is necessarily vicious.[2] Since these passions are not necessarily vicious, there is no reason *not* to expect public benefits from their individual pursuit. Yet Smith never proves, or even argues persuasively (in *The Theory of Moral Sentiments*, where it is posed) that individuals seeking material gain *in competition with one another* is not a vice, in the sense that it tends to injure others.

> Wherever there is a cohesive community . . . individual interests and passions, far from harming anyone, can be turned to the advantage of others. But they inevitably become quite another thing when this community no longer exists and *competition* is dominant. Personal interest has a loud voice in each case, but as Rousseau points out, *"it does not say the same things."* In the one case, individual interest, solidarity and homogeneous with the interests of others, is in fact only *one* aspect, or a specification, of the *common interest*; but in the other, where such a "community" does not exist, it is an interest which collides with that of others and can be achieved only by harming them: only if it operates, in effect, as immorality and injury. (Colletti 1972, 211)

Thus, Smith's solution to Mandeville's paradox of negative factors producing a positive result is to eliminate the paradox, by contending that the positive result arises from the sum of partial factors which *in themselves are already positive*.

[2] See the discussion of this issue in Colletti (1972, 208-216).

It appears from these three elements that for Smith, the role of the State was at best peripheral to the principal social dynamic—the "invisible hand" of the free market—a dynamic that not only should not be interfered with, but would require rather extreme human "folly" to set back significantly from its inexorable ability to provide for collective material gain (and therefore overall social betterment). "In this view . . . politics is the 'folly of men' while economic progress, like Candide's garden, can be cultivated with success provided such folly does not exceed some fairly ample and flexible limits. It appears that Smith advocates less a state with minimal functions than one whose capacity for folly would have some ceiling" (Hirschman 1977, 104).

Generally, this interpretation of Smith's view is correct. In *The Theory of Moral Sentiments* ([1759] 1976), published almost twenty years before *The Wealth of Nations* ([1776] 1937), he had argued that the basic foundation for society is man's love for it and the order it implies. But, more important, this society (and its order) are possible for Smith because the moral sentiments that govern human behavior are generally conducive to positive interaction among individuals. This is the larger meaning of what we discussed above in regard to the pursuit of material gain: Smith considered the configuration of human sentiments such that society could exist without the direct intervention of "the general will"; indeed, the general will was an unintended result of the generally positive relations among individuals. To pose this as "social control" (Samuels 1966) is misinterpreting Smith's view, for social control means control from the outside by some overshadowing force or power. Smith regarded control as coming from within; his general rules of conduct (what he calls "a sense of duty") come from inside each individual and make his behavior compatible with the social whole.

> Without this sacred regard to general rules, there is no man whose conduct can be much depended upon. . . . But upon the tolerable observance of these duties depends the very existence of human society, which would crumble into nothing if mankind were not generally impressed with a reverence for those important rules of conduct.
>
> Upon whatever we suppose that moral faculties are founded . . . they were given us for the direction of our conduct in this life. They . . . were set up within us to be the supreme arbitrars of all our actions, to superintend all our senses, passions, and appetites, and to judge how each of them was either to be indulged or restrained. (Smith 1976, Pt. III, ch. 5)

Yet, there is a reward for this kind of behavior, even though Smith also invokes cooperation with the Deity by "acting according to the dictates of our moral faculties'' (Smith 1976, 166): ''What is the reward most proper for encouraging industry, prudence, and circumspection? Success is every sort of business. . . . Wealth and external honors are their proper recompense, and the recompense which they can seldom fail of acquiring'' (ibid.). Again, he melds morality with motivation to gain, with gain itself, and again, we have the affirmation that striving for material gain is the morality that acts as a social cement.

We can see in this analysis the elements of the Marxist discussion of superstructure and structure, of Smith's theory of production and economic development (in this case the invisible hand) and a theory of social reproduction. For Smith, the very morality inherent in capitalist production (free enterprise) is the social cement for society. Individuals are generally moral and in pursuing individual gain do so as moral individuals: ''It can seldom happen, indeed, that the circumstances of a great nation can be much affected either by the prodigality of misconduct of individuals; the profusion or imprudence of some, always more than compensated by the frugality and good conduct of the others'' (Smith 1937, 324). The honesty, sense of duty, love of nation, and sympathy for fellow human beings that are essential for social reproduction are therefore inherently part of the majority of individuals in a free enterprise, competitive society. In this society, based on the ''natural rights'' of individuals, it is the individual who is the bearer of the unintended betterment of the social condition, and also the intended social cohesion. Smith's individuals are inherently social beings.

Why, if free-market economic activity produces the best of all possible societies, and if Smith saw as the greatest danger to the maximization of welfare the corruption of government officials or their restriction of commerce in favor of particular interests, did he argue for any State at all?[3] Underlying all of Smith's writings is a tension between social cohesion emanating from civil society itself (the invisible hand/individual moral sentiments) and the existence of a State with juridical and educative power. Indeed, for Smith, the general rules of morality fluctuate between being an inherent part of human behavior and an object of promulgation and dissemination by some decision-making body that has this morality. How invisible is the invisible hand? How moral is the mass of mankind? It seems that Smith is never able to resolve these issues, although his tendency

---

[3] ''Great nations are never impoverished by private, though they sometimes are by public, prodigality and misconduct. The whole, or almost the whole, public revenue is in most countries employed in maintaining unproductive hands. Such are the people who compose a numerous and splendid court, a great ecclesiastical establishment, great fleets and armies, who in time of peace produce nothing and in time of war acquire nothing which can compensate the expense of maintaining them, even while the war lasts'' (Smith 1937, 325).

is, as we have shown, to rest his case on the inherent and unwitting morality of men who engage in the pursuit of wealth. Yet he is never quite sure. When he argues that "the great secret of education is to direct vanity to proper objects" (Smith, in Samuels 1966, 67), he is, in effect, falling back on the existence of a power over individuals to develop their morality in a particular way.

The existence of a State, furthermore, is not only never questioned by Smith, loyalty to it as long as it "benefits mankind" is one of the highest virtues man can have:

> The love of country seems, in ordinary cases, to involve in it two different principles; first, a certain respect and reverence for that constitution or form of government which is actually established; and secondly, an earnest desire to render the condition of our fellow-citizens as safe, respectable, and happy as we can. He is not a citizen who is not disposed to respect the laws and to obey the civil magistrate; and he is certainly not a good citizen who does not wish to promote, by every means in his power, the welfare of the whole society of his fellow-citizens. (Smith 1976, 231)

As long as the government maintains the "safe, respectable, and happy situation of our fellow citizens," it should, according to Smith, be supported, but when it fails to do that, each citizen is thrown into the anxiety of deciding whether to support the old system or try something new. Smith gives no guidelines for that choice, nor the exact conditions that define the failure of the State to maintain the happy situation.

But we can infer from this later work that the proper role of the State is to provide a legal framework in which the market can best maximize the "benefits to mankind." At the moment in history when he was writing, the principal objective in this regard was for the State to use the legal process to create a market economy out of the landlord-dominated, semi-feudal, and mercantilist status quo. The State he railed against was the "interventionist," mercantilist State; what he called for was a body of laws and State action that would allow the free market more freedom. Of course, this involved a paradox: the state had to interfere in order to clear out the existing, mercantilist framework. This interference not only involved new laws and their enforcement, but the educational function of creating a new morality (Samuels 1966). According to Samuels, classical economists, including Smith, were quite aware of this paradox, and acknowledged that it was an important facet of their view of the State, a facet that was manifested in their discussions on the relation of law to rights in general and to property rights in particular.

The importance of Smith's writings to current American thinking (and for that matter, to the debate over the State's role in all advanced capitalist countries) cannot be minimized.[4] In many ways, it is he who defines the way Americans look at the relationship between structure and superstructure—that is, the relation between production (the invisible hand) and the cohesive forces that bind society. The concept that each individual pursuing his or her own economic interests unwittingly provides the best possible formula for the collective good still holds a great deal of sway. The very assumptions that *individuals* are the source of power, both in their pursuit of wealth and their control over their passions, and that social corruption, if it exists at all, is much more likely to emerge from the public than the private sector, underlie much of American political philosophy of this day. Yet, it should be clear from our discussion that Smith never answered satisfactorily either Rousseau's or Mandeville's positions on the connection between individuals' economic pursuits and the public good. Furthermore, Smith subtly dropped Locke's and Rousseau's construction of a classless society as a basis for political theory. The earlier writers counted on the existence of such classlessness—an economy founded on small proprietors, none too wealthy to gain enough power to "enslave" the others (wage labor being included in the notion of slavery)—in order to assure cohesion in bourgeois society. Smith rejected the necessity of this construction: cohesion came from the provision of maximum benefit to mankind, and this could occur only when men as individuals pursued their economic interests unbridled except for the moral sentiments that bound them together in the first place. Thus, for him, there was no contradiction between the unfettered accumulation of wealth and social cohesion. A class society existed in each generation, but there was no conflict between the existence of such a society and the achievement of the greatest good by the greatest number. At the same time, Smith completely avoided the issue of the perpetuation of classes from generation to generation and its implications for the public welfare, particularly the effect that it could have on the definition of morality, the control and use of the State's legal apparatus, and the very development of the virtues that he regarded as so important to man's social functions.[5]

Smith's ideas formed the framework of discussion for utilitarian thought

[4] We could even argue persuasively that Marx incorporated Smith's (and Mandeville's) view in the materialist theory of contradiction—capitalism unwittingly creates its antithesis: inherently antagonistic classes.

[5] Smith was well aware of the dangers that capitalism and particularly the division of labor posed for the "heroic spirit" and the desire for education and self-elevation. If the same groups in society were to work at the simplest, most demeaning jobs from generation to generation, this danger, in Smith's terms, would only be accentuated (see Hirschman 1977, 105-107).

(the liberal doctrine) in the nineteenth century. Some thirty to forty years after *The Wealth of Nations*, Jeremy Bentham and James Mill developed the political continuation of Smith's ideas, but in a new context: by the beginning of the century, England was not only in the throes of industrialization, but also in a period of considerable violence—workers were resisting the factory system and demanding political rights not available except to those who owned property (Thompson 1963). Bentham and James Mill were necessarily responding to this real historical situation, essentially defending Smith's free market-centered society in the face of working-class assaults. What would the liberal State have to be in a society racked by the beginnings of class conflict? Bentham and James Mill concluded that the bourgeois State was all the more necessary to provide equality and security for the system of unlimited property and capitalist enterprise. As Macpherson has written,

> society is a collection of individuals incessantly seeking power over and at the expense of each other. To keep such a society from flying apart, a structure of law both civil and criminal was seen to be needed. Various structures of law might be capable of providing the necessary order, but, of course, according to the Utilitarian ethical principle, the best set of laws, the best distribution of rights and obligations, was that which would produce the greatest happiness of the greatest number. This most general end of the laws could, Bentham said, be divided into four subordinate ends: "to provide subsistence; to produce abundance; to favor equality; to maintain security." (1977, 26-27)

Yet, the State is not necessary, according to Bentham, to produce either subsistence or abundance—these emerge from capitalist production itself, from the fear of hunger and the desire to accumulate. He makes an argument for equality of wealth based on the law of diminishing marginal utility of wealth; in the end, however, it is security of property that becomes the most important function of law (the State). What sort of State would fulfill this function? In Bentham's (and Mill's) view, the State had to nurture the free market system and protect citizens from corrupt and rapacious government itself—essentially Smith's original position. For this second reason, elections and freedom of the press were crucial, for it was only under conditions where voters could change government officials that the populace could protect itself from the government.

Thus, power was assumed to be still in the electorate—in the citizenry—as in the classical theory of the State. The difference became one of admitting that all citizens were not equal in their political power and *should not be equal*. The only way to prevent the government from turning against the interest of its constituency was to make officials frequently removable by a majority of people other than the officials themselves. According to Macpherson, this was the "protective case" for democracy, in which democracy has the objective of securing society's members against oppression at the hands of government functionaries. Meanwhile, the free market system would take care of maximizing economic and social welfare (Macpherson 1977, 36). But for protection, all that was necessary was to have some set of voters who could control the government and keep it from abusing the citizenry. The discussion boiled down to who that set should be.

In any case, Macpherson argues, Locke and Rousseau had asked for a new kind of man, while Bentham and James Mill took "man as he was, man as he had been shaped by market society, and assumed that he was unalterable . . . that model did fit, remarkably well, the competitive capitalist market society and the individuals who had been shaped by it. . . . they did not question that their model of society—the hard-driving competitive market society with all its class-division—was justified by its high level of material productivity, and the inequality was inevitable" (Macpherson 1977, 43-44).

With the growing militancy of the working class in the middle of the nineteenth century, this model changed. Without giving up the idea that the people had to protect themselves from the government that ruled them, John Stuart Mill saw the democratic process as contributing to human development, as leading to a free and equal society not yet achieved (Macpherson 1977, 47). The exercise of power under democracy promoted human advancement more than any other system. Inequality existed, J. S. Mill argued, and it was incompatible with his developmental democracy, but inequality was *not* inherent in capitalism; rather, it was accidental and could be remedied. Thus, the younger Mill returned to the classical idea of the ideal society, defining this ideal as a community of hard workers and developers of their human capacities (Macpherson 1977, 51). Rewards in that society would be proportional to exertion, even though he found the actual system of rewards, operating under the same capitalist principles, unjust. He put the blame for this unjust inequality on the feudal distribution of property; capitalism, he believed was gradually reducing inequality of income, wealth, and power.

At the same time, J. S. Mill was not confident in the capability of the mass of working people to use political power wisely. He was aware of the opposing interests in society and of the greater numbers of working-class voters, but he was not in favor of giving the same number of votes to each member of society. He wanted the extension of suffrage to overcome the rule by a narrow, wealthy segment of the population, but voting power to be based on the contribution that various individuals would make to a democratic society.

The liberal vision of the bourgeois State, therefore, was a representative democracy, with power residing in a small group of the citizenry, largely because of a past precapitalist distribution of property. The ideal State was one in which political power was expanded to a larger group, letting the free market take care of the distribution of wealth and income. Inequality in property was increasingly acceptable to bourgeois theorists as a necessary price to pay for increasing production, with "equality" expressed more and more in political terms. With Bentham and James Mill, there was the first formal separation between the organization of the State as a political democracy and the organization of the economy as class-based, unequal, capitalist production. The issue was shifted from the role of the State as a guarantor of equality in production (in order to preserve the democratic State) to the issue of the class-based franchise—that is, who should be allowed, among the different classes of producers and nonproducers, to participate in electing (and thereby controlling) a government that would provide a limited set of services and enforcement of the laws. The economic system, unfettered, was "perfect" in the liberal model; it was the necessity of government that could create problems. Democracy no longer was the means of controlling the economic excesses envisaged by Rousseau; rather, for Bentham and James Mill, democracy was only necessary to limit the innate excesses of government officials by giving the citizenry power to change those officials at the general will.

The necessity to create the classless society in order to have a workable social contract disappeared, although the problem that economic inequality posed for the liberal model continued to plague its theoreticians, especially those like John Stuart Mill, who saw the need for some sort of organization of capitalist production (producer cooperatives) that would allow workers to become capitalists. This was closely related with the whole issue (left over from the classical theorists) of whether non-property holders, if allowed suffrage, would support a bourgeois State. According to Macpherson, it was the political party system that made it possible to have universal suffrage and simultaneously contain working-class hostility to capitalism (1977, 64-76). Political parties "tamed" the class divisions that might have led to the overthrow of bourgeois governments through the vote. But there are other possible explanations for the failure of universal franchise to overthrow capitalism: Przeworski (1979) argues that the industrial working class never had a numerical majority in any country; hence it had to make compromises to develop a position acceptable to the majority. In that view, political parties did not tame the working class, but rather it was the necessity of combining with other groups that forced the working class to take a more moderate stance to get any reforms. Przeworski and Wallerstein argue elsewhere (1982) that capitalism's success in providing higher incomes to workers, as well as the system's capability to emerge from crisis to continue on a growth path, were also both important reasons that the working class did not seek to overthrow the capitalist system, choosing instead to work within it for reform.

The defense of Smith's free market economy as optimal within a class society (where classes are perpetuated from generation to generation) did, however, require the abandonment of Smith's reliance on individual morality as the principal cohesive social force. The State came to play (in liberal theory) an increasing role as an expression of social will and individual equality. This was a particular role: since the State was to guarantee the smooth functioning of free enterprise, citizens whose economic positions were not equal were to be called upon to verify the reproduction of their own inequality under the assumption that in the long run this would result in the greatest good for the greatest number. The utilitarians had considerable doubts that the working class would go along with such verification, but gradually accepted the possibility that they might. Why the working class, granted suffrage, does not uniformly oppose the bourgeois State is, of course, a fundamental issue not only for utilitarians, but for Marxists as well. In any case, the liberal doctrine and its outgrowth, pluralism, never felt comfortable with universal suffrage and majority rule, largely because those theories view the ideal function of the State as one of smoothing the operation of the market system, but at the same time recognize clearly the inequality of that system and the power of the State to alter it if workers ever come to control the legislative and legal apparatuses. Pluralism was the twentieth-century "answer" to that difficulty.

REINTERPRETING THE "COMMON GOOD": PLURALISM

Writing in 1942, Joseph Schumpeter profoundly criticized the classical and liberal theories of democracy (Schumpeter 1942). Schumpeter's analysis seems heavily influenced by Max Weber's theory of the development of Western culture and social action (Weber 1958), and, in turn, Schumpeter's analysis influences pluralist theory. Weber describes cultural development as the progress of collective "rationality": a nation passes through stages of development from certain attitudes and behavior to others, from one "kind" of rationality to another. The affective-emotional end of Weber's spectrum is incompatible with modern capitalist society, while the purposive-rational is compatible; the implication is that the latter is more rational than the former. However, even though purposive-rational attitudes allow a nation to achieve systematically particular goals within a legal-rational framework, the question of who is to set these goals still remains. Weber argues that it should be a single charismatic leader, although he admits that this argument does not—indeed cannot—stem from any scientific theory of goal setting.

Schumpeter and the pluralists interpret Weber's analysis by implicitly applying his rationality categories and concept of development of entire societies to individual differences *within* societies: individuals are implicitly placed on a continuum of social-psychological development from "traditional" to "modern." This means that not everyone in a society is as "rational" as everyone else, contradicting the liberal assumption of rationality as a universal human characteristic. In sharp contrast with "modern" capitalistic individuals, the norms and values of "traditional" individuals are viewed as nonrational on utilitarian grounds. Secondly, applied in this context, Weber's value-based theory of action implies that traditional members of society would not be able to function as "rational" political citizens. Hence, their nonparticipation in a functioning democratic system is actually a positive contribution to the system. Schumpeter contends that direct democracy is not possible because not everyone in the society is at the same stage of cultural development. There are leaders and ratifiers; and those who are not interested and those who are misinformed. According to him, the purposes of society must be formed by leaders—by an elite that is politically involved, can devote itself to studying the relevant social issues, and is capable of understanding them.

Schumpeter made some specific points about political participation and democracy. First, there is no such thing as a uniquely determined common good that all people could agree on or be made to agree on by the force of rational argument; to different individuals the common good is bound to mean different things (Schumpeter 1942, 251). Second, "even if the opinions and desires of individual citizens were perfectly definite and independent data for the democratic process to work with, and if everyone acted on them with ideal rationality and promptitude, it would not necessarily follow that the political decisions produced by that process from the raw material of those individual volitions would represent anything that could in any convincing sense be called the will of the people" (1942, 254). Third, citizens are typically misinformed or uninterested in political issues except for those that affect them directly and economically. In those cases, rather than acting in the common good, they will act out of individual self-interest. "Thus, the typical citizen drops down to a lower level of mental performance as soon as he enters the political field. He argues and analyzes in a way that we would readily recognize as infantile within the sphere of his real interests. He becomes a primitive again" (1942, 262).

Furthermore, citizens are easily influenced by political advertising, which can shape their views. Although in the long run the people may be wiser than any single individual, "history however consists of a succession of short-run situations that may alter the course of events for the good. . . . If all the people can in the short run be 'fooled' step by step into something they do not really want, and if this is not an exceptional case which we could afford to neglect, then no amount of retrospective common sense will alter the fact that in reality they neither raise nor decide issues but that issues that shape their fate are normally raised and decided for them" (1942, 264).

Given this critique, Schumpeter posed an alternative model of how the modern, democratic, capitalist State does and *should* function. The classical theory argues that power resides in the "people" and that the State is composed of legislators, chosen by those people to represent their inter-ests—the general will. Selection of representatives is made secondary to the primary purpose of vesting power in the electorate. Schumpeter reverses these roles; he makes the deciding of issues by the electorate secondary to the election of representatives who are to do the deciding: "The role of the people is to produce a government, or else an intermediate body which in turn will produce a national executive or government. And we define: the democratic method is that institutional arrangement for arriving at political decisions in which individuals acquire the power to decide by means of a competitive struggle for the people's vote" (1942, 269).

In this theory, then, the State gains a certain power of its own—it is the decider of issues, of legislation, of the course of economic and social development. The electorate is left with the power to decide *which* set of leaders (politicians) it wishes to have carry out the decision-making proc-ess. Although it can be argued that this still implies power in the electorate (voters can dismiss a government and replace it with another set of rep-resentatives), choices are limited to those politicians who present them-selves to be elected. Nor do voters decide issues; it is politicians who decide these issues and present themselves to the voters as believing that certain issues and not others are important and as having a particular set of views on the issues at hand.

For this type of State (the democratic model) to be a "success," certain conditions have to be fulfilled: (1) the human material of politics must be of sufficiently high quality; (2) the effective range of political decisions must not be extended too far—that is, many decisions should be made by competent experts outside the legislature; (3) democratic government must command a dedicated bureaucracy that must be a power in its own right; (4) electorates and legislatures must be morally resistant to corruption and must exhibit self-control in their criticism of the government; and (5) competition for leadership requires a large measure of tolerance for difference of opinion.

Schumpeter's theory of the democratic State is therefore an empiricist theory that conforms to neoclassical economics in its amorality and its problem-solving approach (Popper, 1945). For Schumpeter, the principal issue, as he poses it, is whether the democratic State can work; whether it is an *efficient* governor in terms of democratic principles. Macpherson contends that the pluralist model makes democracy a mechanism for choosing and authorizing governments, not a kind of society or a set of moral ends; it empties out the moral content that the classicists and nineteenth-century liberals had put into the idea of democracy and the State. "There is no nonsense about democracy as a vehicle for the improvement of mankind. Participation is not a value in itself, nor even an instrumental value for the achievement of a higher, more socially conscious set of human beings. The purpose of democracy is to register the desires of a people as they are, not to contribute to what they might be or might wish to be. Democracy is simply a market mechanism: the voters are the consumers; the politicians are the entrepreneurs" (Macpherson 1977, 79).

Once the political system is posed as a market, and voters' decisions are based on a political version of neoclassical utility theory, the issue becomes one of the degree of consumer sovereignty in the market.[6] In a pure, competitive market, power over State behavior still lies in the hands of the voter. Even though the politicians may decide what issues or decisions to produce, it is the voters who have to buy those issues—political consumers decide what they want to buy. Furthermore, not every voter wants to buy every issue, and there are many functions of government— many decisions to be made—that the consumer is not interested in. These are the details of the production process that Schumpeter wants to leave to special agencies and the bureaucracy. Dahl argues that this does not contradict the concept of voter (consumer) sovereignty. He goes even further to argue that even though elections rarely reflect the will of the majority, they are

> crucial processes for insuring that political leaders will be somewhat responsive to the preferences of some ordinary citizens. But neither elections nor interelection activity provide much insurance that decisions will accord with the preferences of a majority of adults or voters. Hence we cannot correctly describe the actual operations of democratic societies in terms of contrasts between majorities and minorities. We can only

---

[6] See Dahl (1956) on polyarchal democracy, for a detailed application of utility theory and consumer preferences for public goods to political choice.

distinguish groups of various types and sizes, all seeking in various ways to advance their goals, usually at the expense, at least in part, of others. . . . Elections and political competition do not make for government by majorities in any very significant way, but they vastly increase the size, number, and variety of minorities whose preferences must be taken into account by leaders in making policy choices. (Dahl 1956, 131-132)

Power, according to Dahl, still resides in the voters, even though this power is not expressed as majority versus minority "will." Rather, each issue calls forth those voters interested enough in the issue to vote for the politician on the basis of that issue. Given that political demands are so diverse, some device is needed to translate these diverse demands into pluralities or majorities in elections for public officials, or produce a set of decisions most agreeable to or least disagreeable to the whole set of diverse individual or group demands. Political parties fulfill this function. The parties package political goods and offer the voters these packages; this produces a stable government which equilibrates demand and supply.

The resulting reformulation of utilitarianism for the modern industrial economy by Schumpeter, Dahl, and others is called pluralism.

Pluralism can be defined as a system of interest representation in which the constituent units are organized into an unspecified number of multiple, voluntary, competitive, nonhierarchically ordered and self-determined (as to type or scope of interest) categories which are not specifically licensed, recognized, subsidized, created or otherwise controlled in leadership selection or interest articulation by the state and which do not exercise a monopoly of representative activity within their respective categories. (Schmitter 1974, 96)

For pluralists, the State is neutral, an "empty slate," and still a servant of the citizenry—of the electorate—but the common good is defined as a set of empirical decisions that do not necessarily reflect the will of the majority. At the same time the State has some autonomy, and there is considerable disagreement among pluralists on to what degree the State itself makes decisions and to what degree the electorate controls those decisions. The debate parallels the economic discussion about the competitiveness of the market and the validity of the assumption of consumer sovereignty.

The more "optimistic" pluralists, agreeing that democracy depends on elites (i.e., that the very survival of democratic systems depends on maintaining the position of elites as the repository for democratic values), stress that what keeps this division of labor from evolving into a rigid oligarchy is the competition between groups of elites for decision-making power, and it is by competition that elites remain open and responsive to pressure from the mass of the public (Greenberg 1977, 41). "Ordinary citizens exert a high degree of control over leaders" (Dahl 1956, 3). For the optimists, the system fails to conform to the tenets of the classical democratic State, but is acceptable because it works. Since most citizens are uninformed and uninterested—even misinformed and irrational, with low tolerance for competing political views—the fact that many do not participate in the political process actually makes the system more efficient (functional apathy). That does not mean that the apathetic don't have power; it is just that—fortunately, for the system—they usually do not exercise it. They are basically satisfied with elite decisions. On the other hand, the system is relatively open to people who are interested and concerned. There are many points of access for participation and since people are free to express themselves, if they felt strong grievances, they *would* participate (Greenberg 1977, 38-40). All in all, according to Dahl, the American political system "does nonetheless provide a high probability that any active and legitimate group will make itself heard effectively at some stage in the process of decision. . . . it appears to be a relatively efficient system for reinforcing agreement, encouraging moderation, and maintaining social peace in a restless and immoderate people operating a gigantic, powerful, diversified, and incredibly complex society" (Dahl 1956, 150-151).

The "pessimists" like Schumpeter and Robert Michels (1966) argue that the consumer sovereignty that is fundamental to the democracy of the pluralistic model (as it is to the "democracy" of the neoclassical economic model) is questionable. In that view, elites not only control the decision-making process, they are *not* effectively responsive to the electorate. Schumpeter bases this argument on two grounds.

First, he contends that the competing elites not only formulate the issues, they attempt to manipulate opinions about those issues. "Since they can themselves be manufactured, effective political argument almost inevitably implies the attempt to twist existing volitional premises into a particular shape and not merely the attempt to implement them or to help the citizen to make up his mind. Thus, information and arguments that are really driven home are likely to be the servants of political intent" (Schumpeter 1942, 264). And he argues that citizens "neither raise nor decide issues but that issues that shape their fate are decided for them" (ibid.). So, the consumer and voter are not sovereign; the supplier (entrepreneur-politician) influences the consumer-preference function to such an extent that it is impossible to speak of an independent-voter demand curve.

Second, the bourgeoisie does not produce the types of politicians required by such a system. They lack independence from bourgeois economic interests. This, in turn, makes it impossible to settle social-structural questions. Politicians cannot separate themselves from a particular group in the social structure. The State is autonomous (elites make the decisions), but it is not neutral in its decision-making: "The democratic method never works at its best when nations are much divided on fundamental questions of social structure. . . . The bourgeoisie produced individuals who made a success at political leadership upon entering a political class of non-bourgeois origin, but it did not produce a successful political stratum of its own, although, so one should think, the third generations of the industrial families had all the opportunities to form one" (Schumpeter 1942, 298).

Corporatism

The perceived decline of liberal democracy and the observed rise of interest groups in the political arena led political thinkers to argue—as early as the late nineteenth and early twentieth centuries—that achieving class harmony and social unity required a "social and political order based on functional socioeconomic organizations in civil society, operating largely autonomously in their respective fields, but united with each other and the state in sectoral and national decision-making bodies and committed to maintaining the functional hierarchy of an organic society" (Panitch 1980, 160). In this *ideal type* called corporatism, the State is *defined* as representing the common good, and it is this final cause of the State that, in and of itself, gives the State moral authority and legitimacy (Stepan 1978). The State therefore embodies the morality, ethic, and ideology *for* the public rather than reflecting public values and norms. While the ideal-type corporatist State is not inherently antidemocratic, it is likely that the leadership will comprehend the common good without asking interest groups or the voters. But at the same time, the only possibility for functional socioeconomic organizations to influence the State is to obtain official recognition (Stepan 1978). It is the cooperation of groups having distinctly different economic positions vis-à-vis each other, and their relationship to the legitimate, independent, and powerful State that gives corporatism its particular features as a total system.

More recent arguments for corporatism as a logical replacement for liberal democracy have the same normative rationale as earlier ones: given the instability of liberal democracy, corporatism is preferable to a Marxist, one-party, authoritarian State, and, in fact, represents a humanistic alternative to authoritarian forms in general (Stepan 1978). Corporatism is seen as a noncoercive solution to conflict of interest in a system where there is supposed to be one overriding interest (Panitch 1980). It is also viewed as a logical replacement for liberal democracy in an economy where industry is highly concentrated and the free market is no longer the dominant form of economic relation. For example, John Kenneth Galbraith's earlier work (1967) had implicit in it a view that the complexity of the American economy, particularly the role of the large corporation and its sophisticated technology, plus the political unacceptability of economic inequality and boom-and-bust capitalist development, required State intervention in the economy and had increased political decision-making by experts. This increase was rationalized on the grounds that experts have the technological and economic information needed to make the society run efficiently and equitably.

The problem with this argument, as Panitch has pointed out, is that it assumes that the corporatist State is neutral and independent from any and all the interest groups sanctioned by the State, particularly the large capitalist firms whose expansion and profits the State's experts will allegedly control. But history makes quite clear that the State can only go so far in controlling and displacing private capital without a monumental political and social struggle with the bourgeoisie. The State's decisions are not autonomous from the power relations in capitalist society.[7] And the corporatist assumption that capital concentration and State intervention are incompatible with liberal democracy also ignores the fact that the extension of bourgeois democracy to the subordinate classes through suffrage and State recognition of trade unions coincided historically with that concentration and intervention. It was working-class struggle, not the purity of capitalist forms or social simplicity, that developed liberal democracy (Panitch 1980, 166).

Philippe Schmitter's (1974) approach to corporatism does not relate it to changes in the mode of production but rather confines it to a political subsystem—a polar opposite of pluralism—defined as a "system of interest intermediation" where a *limited* number of noncompetitive constituent groups are licensed (or created) by the State and given a monopoly within their respective categories in return for control of their leadership selection and their demands (Schmitter 1974, 93-94). Schmitter argues that there is an inevitable decay of pluralism and a replacement of it by corporatism. But although the origins of this decay lie in the "needs of capitalism to reproduce the conditions for its existence and continually to accumulate further resources" (Schmitter 1974, 107), Schmitter abandons his class analysis when it comes to describing and analyzing how societal corporatism functions (Panitch 1980, 171). Classes become submerged in their noncompetitive constituent groups—in interest-oriented organizations—and, Panitch argues, the only way that one can see corporatist structures as

---

[7] Galbraith recognizes this explicitly in later work (1973) and moves away from a corporatist to a democratic socialist position.

inherently stable (as Schmitter does) is to assume "that interest associations do not in fact represent their members' interests" (Panitch 1980, 172).

These views of corporatism as a *system* necessarily replacing pluralism, either as a result of changes in the mode of production or of the need of capitalism to reproduce itself under new political conditions, are fraught with theoretical difficulties. The most important of these is that the observed functioning of social democracies does not conform to ideal-type social (or inclusionary, in Stepan's terminology) corporatism as such: there is still class conflict, the membership of labor unions often does not go along with its leadership, and employers attempt to reduce unions' political power by electing pro-capitalist governments and implementing policies that increase profits. Stepan (1978) shows that no political system in Latin America approximates exclusive reliance on corporatist intermediation mechanisms—"corporatism as structure is always only a *partial* sectoral phenomenon of the overall political system. . . . [S]upplementary analytical frameworks must be used to study other aspects of the system" (Stepan 1978, 71).

But even with the problems of finding social corporatism as a system in the real world, we do observe important elements of noncoercive corporatism in almost every advanced capitalist society. Panitch suggests that corporatism develops *within* liberal democracy; that it should be seen as "a political structure within advanced capitalism which integrates organized socioeconomic producer groups through a system of representation and cooperative mutual interaction at the leadership level and mobilization and social control at the mass level" (Panitch 1980, 173).

Corporatism is therefore not an ideology but a way of organizing business-labor relations in industrial capitalist society. Panitch does not assume that the State is neutral or that the working and capitalist classes have equal power or influence on the State. Rather, he thinks that corporatism looked at in this way describes how corporatist structures mediate and modify the domination of capital and how they are themselves subject to the contradictions of capitalist society. Specifically, he argues that corporatist structures integrate the labor unions in economic policy-making in exchange for their incorporation of capitalist growth criteria in union wage policy and their administration of wage restraint to their members. State intervention in the economy is corporatist to the extent that it involves organized labor in State policy-making, so labor and capital interest groups interact at the level of the State (Panitch 1980, 174). Furthermore, the timing and the extent of the institutionalization of corporate structures in different societies is correlated with the economic strength of the union movement and its degree of centralization. In effect, corporatism in modern capitalist societies means integrating the organized working class in the capitalist

State, and—not just in its origins but in its functioning—fostering economic growth and securing class harmony in the face of class conflict. In Panitch's view, corporatism is specific only to those groups that *are* class-based and have contradictory relations with each other. Corporatist structures serve in part to maintain a limited, sectoral subordinate class identity for such groups, particularly for those that depend on the State-sanctioned organization for political power. Thus, trade unions serve to limit working-class identity to the extent that they restrict their "political" activity to collective bargaining at the firm or industry level. But for other, issue-oriented, groups, pluralist pressure politics and elected parliaments continue to play a central political function.

CONCLUSION

Such analyses and the intensity of debate about liberal democracy reflect the fact that capitalism and the role of the capitalist State have changed significantly since the days of Adam Smith and his followers, the utilitarians. The steady shift of the working population from self-employment—mainly in agriculture—to employment in increasingly large enterprises has transformed capitalist societies from nations of farmers and merchants to nations of employees whose work depends on the functioning of huge bureaucracies competing in international markets and often organizing their capital investment on an international scale. The State itself is one of those bureaucracies, employing directly (in the United States) approximately 16 percent of the labor force and commanding about one-third of the gross national product. The economic power of large private corporations and the State over investment policies and capitalist development seems to make Adam Smith's invisible hand of the free market of little use for analytical purposes.

The changing economy is associated with changing political structures. On the one hand, suffrage expanded in industrialized capitalist economies to include the working class, nonwhites, women, and young people. On the other, the working class organized itself into trade unions that were eventually legalized by the State as bargaining units. In the United States, this legalization defined the political limits within which unions could operate. In effect, the principal political unit to which many American workers belonged became largely depoliticized and undemocratic, maintaining a constrained relationship within civil society and an equally constrained relation to the State.

The concentration of economic power and the development of new kinds of political organizations in response to it have raised serious questions about the meaning of democracy in capitalist societies, both advanced and in the Third World. What is the relationship of the State apparatuses to the citizenry they allegedly represent?

The dominant approach in American political, economic, and social theory, as we have seen, uses the ideal type of the invisible hand and consumer sovereignty in analyzing political behavior and the nature of democracy in advanced capitalist societies. With the present crisis of the liberal State, there are those who attack the State itself as the greatest impediment to democracy and to the "perfection" of the invisible hand. There has been a renaissance in Smithian views of the "minimal" State and a return to the "free" market as the simplest and most "moral" means to social and material betterment. There are others who view liberal democracy as inherently unstable under modern industrial social conditions. Corporatists view the formation of new political structures as the basis for a different kind of State, one that represents the interests of group organizations and—with the cooperation of these groups—organizes economic and social development for the common good.

But there is a different approach to understanding the modern capitalist State. Schumpeter's critique of liberal democracy and Panitch's work on corporatism assume an underlying class conflict in capitalist democracy that the liberal State has difficulty solving and that prevents the extension of corporatist structures into a corporatist system. A class analysis of the State challenges the unity of purpose among the citizens of a capitalist society and the correspondence between majority interest and the public benefits of State action. It challenges the very notion of democracy in the context of capitalist development. It also rejects corporatism as an ideal type, on the grounds that corporatist system models assume away the underlying social-class nature of capitalist production, even in its new corporate forms.

It is to the class-perspective analysis of the State that we now turn.

CHAPTER TWO

Marx, Engels, Lenin, and the State

SINCE THE LATE 1950s, the State has become a central theme of Marxist research, both in Europe and the United States. It is not difficult to explain why. In addition to the arguments presented in the introduction to this work—the ever greater governmental social and economic involvement in modern, industrial economies, including Western capitalist democracies, an involvement that permeates social services, employment, the media, and even production itself—for Western Marxists, the late 1950s marked the end of Stalinism and the beginning of the end of the Cold War. That thaw saw the beginning of a period in which Western Communist parties opened up intellectually and could exhibit independence from the Soviet Union, and overt anti-Marxist repression loosened up in the United States. The decline in *both* controls over Marxist thought allowed for the flourishing of Western Marxist theory in an era of increased State involvement and increased electoral participation by Left political parties, a political participation that had been suspended by the rise of fascism and World War II.

This is not to say that such participation was part of a "new" policy, or that Marxist interest in the State began in the postwar period. German Social Democrats as far back as the 1890s, under the leadership of Karl Kautsky, reached significant levels of electoral strength, so much so that they thought they could take over State power by electoral means. Indeed, Engels was willing to afford the Social Democrats a "special" position within the overall body of revolutionary theory:

> We can count even today on two and a quarter million voters. If it continues in this fashion, by the end of the century we shall conquer the greater part of the middle strata of society, petty bourgeois and small peasants, and grow into the decisive power in the land, before which all other powers will have to bow, whether they like it or not. (Engels [1895] in Tucker 1978, 571)

However, with the success of the Russian Revolution, it was Leninist State and revolutionary theory that came to dominate Marxist thought, and Leninist interpretations of Marx's theory of politics remained—except for the notable exception of Antonio Gramsci—largely unquestioned or, if questioned, suppressed until the early 1960s. The theoretical base for earlier German Social Democratic strategies, strategies perhaps much more relevant for Left parties in advanced industrial economies, therefore never developed, although it sometimes manifested itself on the Western European political scene (in the Popular Front in France, for example). Even Gramsci's work was suppressed by the combination of fascism and Stalinism, so much so that although Gramsci himself was canonized by the Italian Communist Party (PCI) in the postwar period, his actual writings were manipulated or neglected. Twenty-five years after the end of the war, the PCI had not produced a serious critical edition of his works (Anderson 1976, 40).

It is important to stress that the uniqueness of the Russian Revolution (the first Communist victory) gave a dominant place to Lenin and Stalin in Marxist thought, to the exclusion of theoretical (and practical) work that deviated from the Russian line. Despite the tragic consequences this had for Western Socialist and Communist parties in the 1920s and 1930s, it was not until the late 50s that this influence began to weaken. As a result, many of the most serious questions about politics, from a Marxist perspective, were not discussed until the 1960s and 1970s: Why does the working class remain "unrevolutionary" in the face of economic crisis? What are the particular characteristics of the advanced bourgeois State? Why and how does the State develop those characteristics? What are appropriate strategies for radical change? Why have communist states developed in the way they have? What does this imply for the role of the State in the transition to socialism? How does the capitalist State differ in the periphery of the world system?

The debate in the last two decades has been conducted around those issues, and the rest of this study is devoted to following the development of that debate in Europe, the United States, and the Third World. But while we make the argument that Marx, Engels, and particularly Lenin's views of politics and the State were incomplete, the fact is that recent Marxist theories have their roots in these earlier works. It is therefore important to go back to them to understand both the fundamentals of the Marxist conception of the State (which remain, in one form or another) in today's research, and the disagreement among contemporary Marxist analysts.

Since Marx did not develop a single, coherent theory of politics and/or the State, Marxist conceptions of the State must be derived from Marx's critiques of Hegel, the development of Marx's theory of society (including his political economic theory), and his analyses of particular historical conjunctures, such as the 1848 Revolution in France and Louis Napoleon's dictatorship, or the 1871 Paris Commune. In addition, we have Engels's later work ([1884] 1968), and Lenin's *The State and Revolution* ([1917] 1965). The variety of interpretations possible based on these different sources has led to a considerable debate, ranging from a position that argues that the Leninist view is correct, to those who see a theory of the State clearly reflected in Marx's political and economic analysis, to those who view the autonomous State of the *Eighteenth Brumaire* (of Louis Napoleon) as the basis for analyzing the actual situation. Despite these differences, however, all Marxist writers, in one form or another, *do* derive their State "theories" from some Marxist "fundamentals," and it is these analytical fundamentals that frame the debate. What are they and why are they subject to so many different interpretations?

First, Marx viewed the material conditions of a society as the basis of its social structure and of human consciousness. The form of the State, therefore, emerges from the relations of production, not from the general development of the human mind or from the collective of men's wills. In Marx's conception, it is impossible to separate human interaction in one part of society from interaction in another: the human consciousness that guides and even determines these individual relations is the product of the material conditions—the *way* things are produced, distributed, and consumed.

> Legal relations as well as forms of the state are to be grasped neither from themselves nor from the so-called general development of the human mind, but rather have their roots in the material conditions of life, the sum total of which Hegel . . . combines under the name "civil society," that, however, the anatomy of civil society is to be sought in political economy. . . . In the social production of their life, men enter into definite relations that are indispensable and independent of their will, relations of production which correspond to a definite state of development of their material production forces. The sum total of these relations of production constitutes the economic structure of a society, the real foundation, on which rises a legal and political superstructure and to which corresponds definite forms of social consciousness. The mode of production of material life conditions the social, political, and intellectual life process in general. It is not the consciousness of men that determines their being, but, on the contrary, their social being that determines their consciousness. (Marx, in Tucker 1978, 4)

This formulation of the State directly contradicted Hegel's conception of the "rational" State, an ideal State involving a just, ethical relationship of harmony among elements of society. For Hegel, the State is eternal, not historical; it transcends society as an idealized collectivity. Thus it is more than simply political institutions. Marx, to the contrary, placed the

State in its historical context, and subjugated it to a materialist conception of history. It is not the State that shapes society, but society that shapes the State. Society, in turn, is shaped by the dominant mode of production and the relations of production inherent in that mode.

Secondly, Marx (again in contrast to Hegel) argued that the State, emerging from the relations in production, does not represent the common good, but it is the political expression of the class structure inherent in production. Hegel (and, as we have seen, Hobbes, Locke, Rousseau, and Smith) had a view of the State as charged with the representation of the "social collectivity," as standing above particular interests and classes and ensuring that competition among individuals and groups remains orderly while the collective interests of the social "whole" are preserved in the actions of the State itself. Marx eventually rejected this view that the State is the trustee of the society as a whole. Once he came to his formulation of capitalist society as a class society, dominated by the bourgeoisie, it necessarily followed that the State is the political expression of that dominance. Indeed, the State is an essential means of class domination in capitalist society. It is not above class struggles, but deeply engaged in them. Its intervention in the struggle is crucial, and that intervention is conditioned by the essential character of the State as a means of class domination.

> There may be occasions and matters where the interest of all classes happen to coincide. But for the most part and in essence, these interests are fundamentally and irrevocably at odds, so that the state cannot possibly be their common trustee; the idea that it can is part of the ideological veil which a dominant class draws upon the reality of class rule, so as to legitimate that rule in its own eyes as well as in the eyes of the subordinate classes. (Miliband 1977, 66)

Thus, because the bourgeoisie (the capitalist class) has a particular control over labor in the capitalist production process, this dominant class extends its power to the State and to other institutions.

Marx first expressed this complete formulation in *The German Ideology*, (1964) written with Engels in 1845-1846. Before turning to that in detail, it is worth noting that in an earlier work, still influenced by Hegel and actual German conditions in the early 1840s, Marx defined the State as a communal one, as representing communal interests (agreeing with Hegel) but, since *only a democratic State* could embody the communal interest, the Prussian State was *no State at all* (Draper 1977, 170). Furthermore, he saw the bourgeois era as one in which civil society was split from political society—the State separated from social power. Thus, he rejects Hegel's notion that the State bureaucracy is the "universal" element in

society, representing communal interests. To the contrary, the State is not
some *ideal*—it is people; the bureaucracy is a "particular" one that identifies its own particular interests with those of the State and vice versa
(Draper 1977, 81). For young Marx, then, the State had some life of its
own, separated from civil society, having its own particular interests. Given
conditions in Germany at the time, it is not unusual that Marx should see
the State in this way: there was a separation of the State on the one hand
and a rising civil society of the bourgeoisie on the other. The State was
not an instrument of the bourgeoisie. In absolutist Prussia, the State was
still in the hands of a precapitalist ruling class, with very different social
values from those of the increasingly powerful bourgeoisie. "This Prussian
State was indeed forced to exercise control over the aristocracy itself, it
was no longer the simple feudal state, but the *Beamtenstaat* of absolute
monarchy—the state of the functionaries, who had to keep a rein on all
classes in order to keep the growing antagonisms from pulling society
apart" (Draper 1977, 169).[1]

Marx himself did not abandon the concept completely in *The German
Ideology*. But now under Engels's influence and Marx's own visits to
Paris, the class struggle view of social dynamics enters into a theory of
the State as a *classbound* institution. According to Marx and Engels, the
State arises out of the contradiction between the interest of an individual
(or family) and the communal interest of all individuals. The community
becomes the State, apparently divorced from individual and community,
but in fact based on connections with particular groups—under capitalism,
with classes determined by the division of labor. All struggles within the
State are "merely the illusory forms in which the real struggles of the
different classes are fought out among one another" (Marx and Engels
1964, 45). The modern capitalist State is dominated by the bourgeoisie.
"Through the emancipation of private property from the community, the
State has become a separate entity, beside and outside civil society; but it
is nothing more than the form of organization which the bourgeoisie necessarily adopts both for internal and external purposes, for the mutual
guarantee of their property and interests" (Marx and Engels 1964, 78).
But it should not be inferred from this that the State is a class plot. Rather,
it evolves in order to mediate contradictions between individuals and community, and since the community is dominated by the bourgeoisie, so is
the mediation by the State. "Hence, the State does not exist owing to the
ruling will, but the state which arises from the material mode of life of

[1] The concept of the State as a bureaucracy with a "life of its own," acting in its own
interests and keeping a rein on all classes to hold society together, reappears in the writings
of Claus Offe, this time in the context of post-World War II German Social Democracy (see
the analysis of Offe in Chapter 5).

individuals has also the form of a ruling will" (Marx and Engels 1964, 358).

Yet it is unclear to what extent and in what way the State acts in the interests of the bourgeoisie "as a whole," while at the same time it is able to utilize its powers over private property in the course of those interests. The State *appears* to have power, but this power reflects relations in production—in civil society. The State is the political expression of the dominant class *without* arising out of a class plot. A *socially necessary* institution, needed to take care of certain social tasks necessary for community survival, becomes a *class* institution.

Later, in *The Origin of the Family, Private Property, and the State* ([1884], 1968), Engels developed his and Marx's fundamental concept of the relation between the material conditions of society, its social structure, and the State. There, he contended that the State has its origins in the need to control social struggles between different economic interests and that this control is carried out by the economically most powerful class in the society. The capitalist State is a response to the necessity of mediating class conflict and maintaining "order," and order that reproduces the bourgeoisie's economic dominance.

> The state is therefore by no means a power imposed on society from without; just as little is it "the reality of the moral idea," "the image of the reality of reason," as Hegel maintains. Rather, it is a product of society at a particular stage of development; it is the admission that this society has involved itself in insoluble self-contradiction and is cleft into irreconcilable antagonisms which it is powerless to exorcise. But in order that these antagonisms, classes with conflicting economic interests, shall not consume themselves and society in a fruitless struggle, a power, apparently standing above society, has become necessary to moderate the conflict and keep it within the bounds of "order"; and this power, arisen out of society, but placing itself above it and increasingly alienating itself from it, is the state. . . .
>
> As the state arose from the need to keep class antagonisms in check, but also arose in the thick of the fight between the classes, it is normally the state of the most powerful, economically ruling class, which by its means becomes also the politically ruling class, and so acquires new means of holding down and exploiting the oppressed class. The ancient state was, above all, the state of the slave owners for holding down the slaves, just as the feudal state was the organ of the nobility for holding down the peasant serfs and bondsmen, and *the modern representative state is the instrument for exploiting wage labor by capital*. (Engels 1968, 155, 156-157, italics added)

The third fundamental of Marx's State theory is that the State in bourgeoisie society is the repressive arm of the bourgeoisie. The rise of the State as a repressive force to keep class antagonisms in check not only describes the class nature of the State, but also its *repressive* function, which, in capitalism, serves the dominant class, the bourgeoisie. There are thus two issues here: the first concerns a primary function of community—enforcement of the laws—inherent in every society, and the second concerns the rise of the *State* and the *repression* inherent in that rise. According to Marx and Engels, the State appears as part of the division of labor, that is, part of the appearance of differences among groups in society and the lack of social consensus.

> The state, then, comes into existence insofar as the institutions needed to carry out the common functions of the society require, for their continued maintenance, the separation of the power of forcible coercion from the general body of society. (Draper 1977, 250)

> The second distinguishing characteristic is the institution of a *public force* which is no longer immediately identical with the people's own organization of themselves as an armed power. This special public force is needed because a self-acting armed organization of the people has become impossible since their cleavage into classes. . . . This public force exists in every state; it consists not only of armed, but also of material appendages, prisons and coercive institutions of all kinds. (Engels 1968, 156)

Thus, repression is part of the State—by historical definition, the separation of power from the community makes it possible for one group in society to use State power against other groups. If that were not true, why is it necessary to separate enforcement from the community itself?

Most analysts of the State, including the "common good" theorists we have already discussed, accept this concept. It is the notion of the State as the *repressive apparatus of the bourgeoisie* that is the distinctly Marxist characteristic of the State. As we move on to discuss Lenin's contributions to this analysis, we shall see that he perceived this as the primary function of the bourgeois State: the legitimation of power, of repression, to enforce the reproduction of the class structure and class relations. Even the juridical system is an instrument of repression and control, since it sets the rules of behavior and enforces them in line with bourgeois values and norms.

The degree to which the State in capitalist society is an agent of the dominant bourgeoisie is not altogether clear in Marx's work. On the one hand, we have the statement from the *Communist Manifesto* ([1848] 1955) that "the bourgeoisie has at last, since the establishment of Modern Industry and of the world market, conquered for itself, in the modern representative State, exclusive political sway. The executive of the modern State is but a committee for managing the common affairs of the whole bourgeoisie" (Marx and Engels 1955, 11-12). On the other hand, Marx (and Engels) consistently argued for the expansion of democracy to curb the power of the executive: "minimization of the executive power, the state bureaucracy—maximization of the weight in the governmental structure of the representative system. And not only in the period of revolution" (Draper 1977, 297).

Marx and Engels saw two sides of the whole issue of democracy, consistent with their concept of the class nature of the State, but it is in the two-sidedness of the issue that the ambiguity lies. As Draper notes, the two sides correspond to the two classes that struggle within the class political framework. One side consists of the dominant class "utilizing" the forms of democracy (elections, parliament) as a means of providing an illusion of mass participation in the State, while the economic power of the ruling class ensures reproduction of the relations between capital and labor in production. On the other side is the struggle to give the democratic forms a new social, or mass content by pushing them to the democratic extremes of popular control from below, including extending democratic forms from the political sphere to the whole society (Draper 1977, 310).

But if it is possible to extend democracy in a capitalist society through class struggle, democratic forms are both an instrument and a danger for the bourgeoisie. While they may be used to create illusions, they may also become the means for the masses to seize power. Marx and Engels suggested the notion of the democratic, popular State, even though the bourgeois State was antipopular. Put another way, the class character of society, for Marx and Engels, permeates every aspect of society, including democratic forms. Similarly, the needs of society cannot be met without passing through the political institutions of a class-conditioned society. The State acts in the interest of the dominant class, subordinating all other interests to those of that class. But it is not the *forms* that necessarily have class character, but the class antagonism inherent in society that infuses the forms. According to the nature of the class struggle, those same forms can be a threat to bourgeois rule.

Miliband (1977) poses the problem in terms of the Marxist notion of "ruling class." In that notion, the "ruling class" is designated as the group that owns and controls a predominant part of the means of material and mental production. *Because* of that ownership, it is assumed that the ruling class controls the State. But, as Miliband points out, this assumption hinges on the automatic translation of class power into State power. In fact there is no such automatic translation, and even where that relation can be shown to be close, questions of the form of the State and *why* it assumes different forms remain.

Since there is a lack of clarity in Marx on the degree to which the State is an agent of the dominant bourgeoisie, Marxists have given several different answers to why the State should be thought of as an instrument of the ruling class (see Miliband 1977, 68-74).

First, the personnel of the State system—the people who are located in the highest level positions of the executive, legislative, judicial, and repressive branches—tend to belong to the same class or classes that dominate civil society. Even where the people concerned are not directly (by social origin) members of the dominant bourgeois class, they are recruited into it by virtue of education and connections, and come to behave as if they were members of that class by birth. While a strong case can be made for such class correlation (e.g., see Domhoff 1967, 1979), Marx's earlier work analyzing the German State in the 1840s shows clearly that it was the German aristocracy, not bourgeoisie, that controlled the State. England at this time also represented a case where the aristocracy dominated the State while the bourgeoisie dominated civil society and shaped economic and social development. Finally, according to Miliband, the governments of most European countries have included a large number of leaders from the "lower classes," and even those governments led by dominant-class representatives have often pursued policies of which the ruling bourgeoisie disapproved, particularly during periods of economic and social crisis. Thus, insofar as the ruling class is not monolithic, it cannot simply use the State as its instrument, even where the personnel of the State is drawn from the "ruling class."

Second, the capitalist class dominates the State through its overall economic power. Through its control of the means of production, the ruling class is able to influence State policies in ways that no other group in capitalist society can develop, either financially or politically. The most powerful economic tool in the hands of the ruling class is the "investment strike," where capitalists bring the economy (and hence the State) to its knees by withholding capital. Nevertheless, Miliband argues that the pressure business is able to apply on the State is not in itself sufficient to explain the latter's actions and policies: sometimes that pressure is decisive and sometimes it is not.

Third, the State is an instrument of the ruling class because, given its insertion in the capitalist mode of production, it cannot be anything else. The nature of the State is determined by the nature and requirements of the mode of production (this, as we show below, is Marx's principal argument in analyzing the period of Louis Napoleon in France). There exist "structural constraints" that no government in capitalist society can ignore or evade. The weakness of the structuralist argument, according to Miliband, is that it tends toward a determinism ("hyperstructuralism") that turns the personnel of the State into direct instruments of the objective forces of class rule, rather than the bearers of orders from the ruling class, but still deprives them of any freedom of action. While the State may act, in Marxist terms, *on behalf* of the ruling class, it does not, Miliband contends, act *at its behest*. The State is a class State, but it must have a high degree of autonomy and independence if it is to act as a *class State*. The notion of the State as an instrument of the ruling class does not fit this requirement of relative autonomy and independence both from the ruling class *and* from civil society.

This leads us to Marx's discussion of State autonomy. We have already mentioned that in Marx's early writings, he proposed a conception of the State that had a life of its own, separated from civil society, with a bureaucracy that acted not in society's interest (Hegel), but in the private interests of the State itself. According to Draper, this conceptualization threads its way into the later class analysis of the State: that is, "Marx and Engels did not make the State out to be merely an extrusion of the ruling class, its tool, puppet, or reflection in some simplistic, passive sense. . . . Rather the State arises from and expresses a real overall need for the organization of society—a need which exists no matter what is the particular class structure. But as long as there is a ruling class in socioeconomic relations, it will utilize this need to shape and control the State along its own class lines" (Draper 1977, 319). The formulation allows the State even in "normal times" to have a certain amount of *autonomy*.

In "abnormal times," the possibilities for autonomy may increase: in his analysis of Louis Napoleon Bonaparte's empire (1852-1870), Marx returned to his original conceptualization, arguing that there are historical instances when *no* class has enough power to rule through the State. In those instances the State (executive) itself rules. What are the factors that enable this to happen? Marx wrote that the bourgeoisie, in this instance, "confesses that its own interests dictate that it should be delivered from the danger of its *own rule*; that in order to restore tranquility in the country, its bourgeois parliament must, first of all, be given its quietus; that in order to preserve its social power intact, its political power must be broken" (Marx and Engels 1979, 143). Engels emphasized, in turn, that Bonaparte was able to take power only after *all* the social classes showed their incapacity to rule, and exhausted themselves in the process of trying. By appealing to the most numerous class, the peasants, for votes, and using the power of the military (the sons of the peasantry) he gained undisputed control of the State and was able to advance his projects (Draper 1977,

406). He played off the different classes against each other and none of them had the forces to regain power.

Nevertheless, the Bonapartist State had to modernize the economy in order to achieve its own aggrandizement—economic capacity was necessary for imperial and military aspirations to be realized. Bonaparte did not change the relations of production; even while the bourgeoisie did not control the State, Bonaparte served their economic interests—*they* accumulated vast amounts of capital under his rule. But this arrangement contained the seeds of important contradictions; the bourgeoisie in France, growing wealthy, soon began to feel the fetters of the autonomous State and moved to regain control of the State apparatus. At the same time, the urban proletariat also expanded and strengthened. Ultimately, the emperor compromised with the bourgeoisie, and the end of his regime was marked by the most important worker revolt of the century, the Paris Commune.

For Marx and Engels, then, the Bonapartist State emerged in an *exceptional* period and was an exception to the "normal" form of the bourgeois State. Such periods are marked by balance between the warring classes, such that State power, as mediator between them, acquires a certain autonomy from either of them. Even in this case, however, the State serves the interests of the capitalist class, since—although it uses that class's accumulative capability for its own purposes—it also does not change the relations in production, thus leaving basic control over the economy in bourgeois hands. This also means that an autonomous State of this form must be short-lived, as the bourgeoisie *and* proletariat will regain strength to struggle even under favorable economic circumstances (i.e., a successful State development policy).

Therefore, two levels of State autonomy exist for Marx and Engels. In the first—the "normal" condition—the State bureaucracy has some autonomy from the bourgeoisie because of the bourgeoisie's inherent dislike of taking direct charge of the State apparatus and because of the conflicts among individual capitals (requiring an independent bureaucracy that can act as an executor for the capitalist class as a whole). Thus, in the normal status of the bourgeois State, the bourgeoisie assigns the task of managing the political affairs of the society to a bureaucracy (which is not the bourgeoisie or individual capitals), but that bureaucracy—in contradistinction to earlier social formations—is subordinated to bourgeois society and bourgeois production. Although bureaucracy, as the composite of individual bureaucrats, is autonomous from the bourgeoisie, it is, as an institution, reduced more and more to the status of a social stratum acting as the agent of the ruling class.

Nevertheless, this downgraded bureaucracy still strives for power, according to Marx (Draper 1977, 496). The second level of autonomy is achieved when the class struggle is "frozen" by the inability of any class to exhibit its power over the State. That "exceptional" historical situation allows the bureaucracy to gain autonomy from class control. It is not dominated by any ruling class of civil society. But even in this case, State power depends on political conditions in a class society.

> This power *rests* on the support of the peasantry, the support of toleration of sectors of the bourgeoisie, and above all, on the precarious equilibrium of the bourgeois-proletarian antagonism, the frozen class struggle. This highly autonomized state is not the "instrument" of any one of the propertied classes contending for political power; *but it is still the resultant of class society taken as a whole* in its current constellation of countervailing powers . . . even in this abnormal situation the class conception of the state is as central as ever. (Draper 1977, 499)

In this model of the autonomous State, the State is not the instrument of the bourgeoisie, but rather has its actions framed by the conditions of the class struggle and the *structure* of a class society. The Bonapartist State does not set itself against the ruling socioeconomic powers of civil society; to the contrary, it has to be accepted by them, or some bloc of them, in order to remain in power. Indeed, if the autonomous State does not change the configuration of economic power, it depends on the dominant bourgeoisie for capital accumulation, hence tax revenues and the State's own aggrandizement and military expansion. It is this version of the autonomous State that enters into Gramsci's work, and appears as the basis of Poulantzas's and Offe's theories of the State. We deal with these in later chapters.

However, there is yet another interpretation of Marx's theory of the State, this one derived from his political-economic analysis in *Capital*. Joachim Hirsch (1978) argues that the theory of the bourgeois State must be developed from the analysis of the basic structure of capitalist society in its entirety and that in so doing it is first of all necessary to define the bourgeois State as the "expression of a specific historical form of class rule and not simply as the bearer of particular social functions" (Hirsch 1978, 63). The State, he contends, is an apparatus removed from the process of competitive valorization of individual capitals and capable of creating for individual capitals the infrastructure that these capitals cannot establish of their own accord because of their limited profit interests. Hirsch goes on to claim that the capital accumulation process and the change in the technological basis of production embodied in it gives rise continuously to material barriers to realize profit. These manifest themselves through crisis, and the crisis itself becomes the necessary vehicle for the actual implementation of State interventions to safeguard production.

Thus, for Hirsch, Marx's theory of the State must be derived from the economic laws of capitalist development described and analyzed in *Capital*, particularly the law of the declining rate of profit. The form of the capitalist State emerges from the necessity of its intervention to offset this decline and thus reestablish capital accumulation. The State, therefore, develops as a function of the material barriers to realizing profit by individual capitals, or, in other words, to the extraction of surplus from workers. It is surplus extraction, not class struggle that is the fundamental variable in understanding the form of the State. "The logical and at the same time historical concretization of the movements of capital and the way in which they shape class struggles and competition must thus be the starting point for any investigation of political processes if it is not to relapse into the failing of mechanical economic determinism or abstract generalization" (Hirsch 1978, 81).

We shall examine this view in more detail in Chapter 6, as well as the whole German debate on the State, but for the moment, we simply are noting this view that Marx's theory of politics has to be "derived" from his theory of political economy; the logical connection between the investigation of capital in general, which Marx developed in his economic theories, and the investigation of politics—the conscious actions of social subjects—is to be found in the analysis of the law of the tendency of profit to fall. As we shall see, this derivation is precisely what Hirsch attempts to undertake.

Very briefly, these are the fundamentals of the Marxist conception of the bourgeois State. As we have shown, the relation between the "ruling class" and the State in Marx depends on the notion of State autonomy, and autonomy is a very much unsettled issue. Different concepts of autonomy are contained in different writings of Marx and Engels. Historically, autonomy and the development of class struggle are intertwined, and we could argue that although the State is defined as relatively autonomous from civil society, this "relativity" is a function of the relative power of the proletariat in the class struggle. Nevertheless, Marx and particularly Engels definitely viewed the nature of the *normal* bourgeois State as determined by the material conditions and their related social relations; the State represents the interests of a particular class even while it places itself *above* class antagonisms; and the State's primary means of expression is through institutionalized coercive power.[2]

It was on this basis that Lenin developed a much more detailed analysis

[2] Engels also discussed the territorial characteristic of the State, which Marxist (and non-Marxist) writers have come to deal with under the headings of "nation" and "nationalism." We will be discussing this issue later but not in any central way, since it forms only one (even though important) root of State power.

of the bourgeois State in terms of its role in the revolutionary process. For Lenin as well as Marx and Engels, interest in the State focused on revolutionary *strategy*, on a theory of change from capitalism to communism. Although this is not crucially different from "common good" theories, at least one of which—as we have seen—has also emerged from an interest in social change, Marxist writers place *primary* importance on discussing the nature of the capitalist State in terms of strategy for social transformation. In that sense, Marxist political theory is unambiguously a theory of action.

Lenin's views of the State—written in 1917—were developed in the particular context of the Russian Revolution and were written to support a particular strategy of political action at that moment of the revolution, in August, 1917. Much of *The State and Revolution* was also a response to what Lenin considered the treason of the German Social Democrats (led by Karl Kautsky) in supporting Germany's entry into World War I by voting for war credits. Lenin's strategy hinged on the Bolsheviks' overthrowing the existing State apparatus, physically seizing the State, and dismantling it. On this point, he was not only in conflict with other members of the soviet, but with some of those in his own party (Chamberlin 1965, 291-295).

Most important for Lenin was that the State is an organ of class rule and that although the State attempts to reconcile class conflict (in Engels's words [1968, 155], "a power seemingly standing above society became necessary for the purpose of moderating the conflict"), that conflict is *irreconcilable*. Although bourgeois democracy *seems* to allow participation and even control of political (and economic) institutions by the working class if they choose to exercise that political power, and thus *seems* to produce a State apparatus with the result of class reconciliation, Lenin argues that "according to Marx, the state could neither arise nor maintain itself if it were possible to reconcile classes. . . . According to Marx, the state is an organ of class *rule*, an organ for the *oppression* of one class by another; it is the creation of 'order' which legalizes and perpetuates this oppression by moderating the conflict between the classes" (Lenin 1965, 8). In Lenin's interpretation of Marx, the necessity for a State, since the State is the repressive apparatus of a dominant class, does not exist unless there is a class conflict. Without such conflict, there is no necessity for a State. The obverse of this interpretation should be obvious: "If the state is the product of the irreconcilability of class antagonisms, if it is a power standing *above* society and '*increasingly alienating* itself from it,' then . . . that the liberation of the oppressed class is impossible not only without a violent revolution, *but also without the destruction* of the apparatus of state power which was created by the ruling class and which is the embodiment of this 'alienation' '' (Lenin 1965, 9).

Thus, the destruction of the bourgeois State is essential to any revolutionary change, and this destruction has to take place through armed confrontation, since the State *is* the armed force of the bourgeoisie. The key here is that the State, for all its "democratic" institutions, is—in capitalist societies—controlled *directly* by the bourgeois class, and that its primary function is direct coercion. By meeting this coercive force head-on and defeating it by superior arms, the bourgeois State will be destroyed, the instrument of oppression will be removed, and the proletariat will take power, utilizing its own force of arms to protect that power.

It is fair to say that Lenin's principal objective in *The State and Revolution* was not to describe the nature of the bourgeois State per se, but to promote a particular strategy for socialist revolution. That strategy had two parts: first, the overthrow of the bourgeois State; and second, the transition to socialism. As we have argued, the overthrow of the State as defined by Lenin necessitated armed revolution, a direct confrontation of bourgeois armed force with proletarian armed force. But in the second part of his strategy, Lenin went much further: he argued that "the doctrine of class struggle was created *not* by Marx, *but* by the bourgeoisie *before* Marx, and generally speaking it is *acceptable* to the bourgeoisie. . . . Only he is a Marxist who *extends* the recognition of the class struggle to the recognition of the dictatorship of the proletariat" (Lenin 1965, 40). This means, in its simplest terms, that for Lenin the class struggle goes on in the transition from capitalism to communism, and requires a State that *eliminates* the bourgeoisie: thus, the *dictatorship* of the proletariat. What Lenin foresaw was the reaction of the bourgeoisie to a revolutionary regime: since, from the standpoint of the working class, capitalists are not essential to the proletarian economy, the revolution for the bourgeoisie means the end of their favored position (their alternative is to become ordinary workers), and so they are likely to fight against the new regime with everything at their disposal. Lenin argued that the abolition of the bourgeoisie as a class required an all-powerful worker State ready to eliminate that group coercively.

> In reality, this period inevitably is a period of unprecedentedly violent class struggle in unprecedentedly acute forms and, consequently, during this period the state must inevitably be a state that is democratic *in a new way* (for the proletariat and the propertyless in general) and dictatorial *in a new way* (against the bourgeoisie). . . .
>
> To proceed, the essence of Marx's teaching on the state has been mastered only by those who understand that the dictatorship of a *single*

class is necessary not only for every class society in general, not only for the *proletariat* which has overthrown the bourgeoisie, but also for the entire *historical period* which separates capitalism from the "classless society," from Communism. (Lenin 1965, 41)

So for Lenin, the dictatorship of the bourgeoisie is replaced by the dictatorship of the proletariat during the transition from capitalism to communism. What of the famous Engels argument that under socialism the State will "wither away"?[3] Lenin discusses this issue in great detail (1965, 17-25), but for our purposes his most important point is that when Engels speaks of the State withering away, he "refers quite clearly and definitely to the period *after* the state has 'taken possession of the means of production in the name of the whole society,' that is, *after* the socialist revolution. At that time, there is no need for a state because there is no need to repress one group for the purposes of another; everyone is working together, they own the means of production together, and the political form of the state is a 'complete democracy' " (Lenin 1965, 21). The rationale for a State under these circumstances—even a completely democratic State—ceases to exist if, as do Engels and Lenin, one considers the State's functions as primarily coercive.

Yet, in discussing democracy and a democratic State, Lenin distinguishes quite clearly between a bourgeois democracy and a worker democracy (which can wither away once it has crushed bourgeois opposition). Lenin— in accordance with Marx and Engels—considered the State apparatus as a "product and manifestation of the irreconcilability of class antagonisms." Bourgeois democracy, he contended, is a "democracy for an insignificant minority, democracy for the rich" (Lenin 1965, 104) where capitalists not only control the political institutions of capitalist society, but structure the institutions in ways that guarantee that control (see Wright 1974-75, 81). This argument is critical to Lenin's view that the State apparatus in a capitalist society is a distinctly *capitalist* apparatus, organized structurally—in form and content—to serve the capitalist class, and cannot possibly be taken over by the working class to serve its ends. It has to be destroyed and replaced by a radically different form of the State, by a different set of institutions organized by the proletariat to serve the proletariat and abolish the bourgeoisie.

---

[3] In Engels's words, "The first act in which the state really comes forward as the representative of society as a whole—the taking possession of the means of production in the name of society—is at the same time its last independent act as a state. The interference of state power in social relations becomes superfluous in one sphere after another, and then ceases of itself. The government of persons is replaced by the administration of things and the direction of the process of production. The state is not 'abolished,' it withers away" (in Lenin 1965, 19).

Wright (1974-75) breaks down this Leninist view of the domination of capitalist democracy by the bourgeoisie into two categories: (1) the use of parliament—ostensibly the institution of democratic representation—as a means of mystifying the masses and legitimizing the bourgeois-controlled social order; and (2) the bourgeois control of parliament. Parliament mystified by appearing as the basic organ of power in the society, seeming to run the State through elected representatives, when, in fact, all important decisions are made behind the scenes by the "departments, chancelleries and General Staffs. Parliament is given up to talk for the special purpose of fooling the 'common people' " (Lenin 1965, 55). Furthermore, parliament is not—in practice—even a representative body. "If we look more closely into the machinery of capitalist democracy, we shall see everywhere in the 'petty'—supposedly petty—details of the suffrage (residential qualifications, exclusion of women, etc.), in the technique of the representative institutions, in the actual obstacles to the rights of assembly . . . in the purely capitalist organization of the daily press, etc., etc.—we shall see restriction after restriction upon democracy" (Lenin 1965, 104). These restrictions in addition to the capitalist exploitation of the modern wage slaves (which leaves them so crushed that they cannot be bothered by democracy or politics) bar the majority of the population from participation in public and political life.

Lenin adopts a clear "democratic swindle" view of bourgeois democracy. There is considerable evidence in his works of this period that the mystification of bourgeois democracy would be replaced by revolutionary democracy extended to the mass of working people. In *The State and Revolution*, for example, he discusses the experience of the Paris Commune of 1871 in terms of the error that the Communards made in laying hold of the bourgeois State but not *smashing* it: "As a matter of fact, *exactly the opposite is the case*. Marx's idea is that the working class *must break up, smash* the 'ready-made state machinery,' and not confine itself merely to laying hold of it" (Lenin 1965, 44). Yet, he agrees that the Commune acted correctly to decree a fuller democracy in the abolition of the standing army and making all officials elected and subject to recall.

> But as a matter of fact this "only" signifies a gigantic replacement of other certain institutions by other institutions of a fundamentally different order. This is exactly a case of "quantity being transformed into quality": democracy, introduced as fully and consistently as is at all conceivable, is transformed from bourgeois democracy into proletarian democracy; from the state (= a special force for the suppression of a particular class) into something which is no longer really the state.
> It is still necessary to suppress the bourgeoisie and crash its resistance.

. . . But the organ of suppression is now the majority of the population, and not a minority, as was always the case under slavery, serfdom, and wage slavery. (Lenin 1965, 50)

Lenin appears to sanction a revolutionary State that is based on the concept of a "worker democracy," a democracy *extended* beyond the mystification of bourgeois parliamentarianism to mass participation in all social institutions. Yet, in practice, he led the Bolsheviks to abolish all democratic forms, including gradually taking power from the soviets and putting it into the hands of the Central Committee of the Bolshevik Party, backed by the Red Guards. This strategy was squarely consistent with Lenin's idea of smashing the bourgeois State and crushing opposition to the revolution, but it resulted in the destruction of all attempts to build the democratic workers' State envisaged by Marx in his writings on the Paris Commune. Lenin, in fact, saw the transition to socialism being carried out by a vanguard Communist Party Central Committee that would *lead* the workers toward communism, rather than relying on them to provide the dynamic for social change.

It was Rosa Luxemburg, a Polish Marxist, who criticized Lenin and Trotsky for their centrism and for their turn away from worker democracy after October 1917 (Luxemburg 1961). She argued against both the position—represented by Kautsky and the Social Democrats in Germany at the time—that bourgeois democracy had to be preserved *and* the Leninist position, which interprets the dictatorship of the proletariat as the dictatorship of a handful of persons, a dictatorship—as Luxemburg saw it—on the bourgeois model. In other words, she accused Lenin and Trotsky of abandoning the Marxist concept of the dictatorship of the proletariat, the concept that Lenin himself described in *The State and Revolution* as a worker democracy, with full worker participation in a "working parliament." It could never become clear what Luxemburg herself proposed institutionally as an alternative to early Leninism (she was killed in 1919), but we do know that, in Luxemburg's terms, the proletariat, when it seizes power, should undertake socialist measures. It should exercise dictatorship, but a dictatorship of *class*, not of party or clique, which means a dictatorship on the basis of the "most active, unlimited participation of the mass of the people, of unlimited democracy" (Luxemburg 1961, 76-77).

We have always distinguished the social kernel from the political form of *bourgeois* democracy: we have always revealed the hard kernel of social inequality and lack of freedom hidden under the sweet shell of formal equality and freedom—not in order to reject the latter but to spur the working class into not being satisfied with the shell, but rather by conquering political power, to create a socialist democracy to replace bourgeois democracy—not to eliminate democracy altogether.

But socialist democracy is not something which begins only in the promised land after the foundations of socialist economy are created; it does not come as some sort of Christmas present for the worthy people who, in the interim, have loyally supported a handful of socialist dictators. Social democracy begins simultaneously with the beginnings of the destruction of class rule and of the construction of socialism. It begins with the very moment of the seizure of power by the socialist party. It is the same thing as the dictatorship of the proletariat.

Yes, dictatorship! But this dictatorship consists in the *manner* of applying democracy, not in its *elimination,* in energetic, resolute attacks upon the well-entrenched rights and economic relationships of bourgeois society, without which a socialist transformation cannot be accomplished. But this dictatorship must be the work of the *class* and not of a little leading minority in the name of class—that is, it must proceed step by step out of the active participation of the masses; it must be under their direct influence, subjected to the control of complete public activity; it must arise out of the growing political training of the mass of people. (Luxemburg 1961, 77-78)

It should be clear from this long quote that the usual criticism of Marx's theory of the State—that it leads *inherently* to lack of political participation, to the development of a centralized powerful State (e.g., see Popper 1945, vol. 2)—is really a criticism of socialism as it developed in the Soviet Union under Lenin, Trotsky, and then Stalin. Even more important, the economic and military power of the Soviet Union in the socialist world has imposed the Leninist view of the "dictatorship of the proletariat" on "socialist" countries rather than allowing Rosa Luxemburg's defense of democratic guarantees to prevail: "It is a well-known and indisputable fact that without a free and untrammeled press, without the unlimited right of association and assemblage, the rule of the broad mass of the people is entirely unthinkable" (Luxemburg 1961, 66-67).

Whether it is possible to have the kind of socialist democracy envisaged by Luxemburg, given the continued power of the bourgeoisie in the values and norms held in most societies even by much of the working class, is a controversial question. Certainly, Chile during Allende's presidency contained elements to support both her and Lenin's position. Had it been allowed to happen, Czechoslovakia after 1968 might have served as an important model of democratic socialism, a rapid move away from bureaucratically run communism to Luxemburg's vision of mass participation of workers in the building of socialism. Poland may have become a democratic socialist State if the workers' movement there had not been suppressed by the Soviet-backed Polish bureaucracy and military. However, in our view it is a mistake to attribute the abandonment of democracy to Marx, either through Marx's vision of the dictatorship of the proletariat, or through his alleged downplaying of the State's role in the revolutionary and political process. No Marxist has considered politics—in the revolutionary sense—below the top of the list even though the issue of democratic participation—after Lenin—definitely became a topic absent from the Soviet agenda. Yet, that absence prevailed after Lenin and Trotsky made a particular choice to dissolve the Constituent Assembly in January 1918 in favor of the soviets, as the only true representatives of the laboring masses, and then to abandon the soviets in favor of the Central Committee of the Communist Party. Other Marxists like Luxemburg correctly foresaw that "with the repression of political life in the land as a whole, life in the soviets must also become more and more crippled. Without general elections, without unrestricted freedom of the press and assembly, without a free struggle of opinion, life dies out in every public institution, and becomes a mere semblance of life, in which only the bureaucracy remains as the active element," as Luxemburg (1961, 71) wrote in 1918. At the same time, she insisted that—totally in keeping with Marx's theory of the State—full democracy was impossible as long as the bourgeoisie had power. While both she and bourgeois critics of Marx defend democratic ideas, they have different theories of the capitalist State, the bourgeois critics believing that it can be reformed—that political power is independent from, and dominates economic power—and Luxemburg agreeing with Marx that the two are totally intertwined and inseparable.

Ultimately, the disagreement between Lenin and Luxemburg hinged on their very different views of the role of the vanguard party in relationship to the working class. Lenin believed that consciousness had to be brought to the working class from outside, and the agency he saw carrying this out was not the traditional intelligentsia but the revolutionary party itself, a party in which former workers, and former professional intellectuals of bourgeois origin were fused into a cohesive unit. Left to its own devices, Lenin wrote, the working class is incapable of developing any conception of the historic mission that Marx assigned to it. "The *spontaneous* development of the workers' movement leads precisely to its subordination of bourgeois ideology . . . [and to] the ideological enslavement of the workers to the bourgeoisie" (Lenin, in Luxemburg 1961, 13). Lenin argued that such a "party of a new type" needed an organization of a new type. It was to be organized like an army and centralized like an army, with all the power and authority residing in its Central Committee (Luxemburg 1961, 13-14).

In an earlier pamphlet, "Leninism or Marxism," written in 1904, Luxemburg predicted that Lenin's future party and its Central Committee would perpetuate itself, dictate to the party, and have the party dictate to the masses. She believed in the creativity of the masses and their autonomy, respected their spontaneity and also their right to make their own mistakes and be helped by them: "Let us speak plainly," she said, "historically, the errors committed by a truly revolutionary movement are infinitely more fruitful than the infallibility of the cleverest Central Committee" (Luxemburg 1961, 15).

CHAPTER THREE

Gramsci and the State

MARX DID NOT develop a comprehensive theory of politics comparable to his analysis of political economy, largely because he believed that political economy was central to understanding civil society, and that the State was rooted in the material conditions of life. Yet, as we have seen, since politics was absolutely crucial to Marx's praxis, a theory of politics was implicit in his writings.

Antonio Gramsci's major contribution to Marxism is that he systematized, from what is implicit in Marx, a Marxist science of political action. But Gramsci did more than simply recognize that politics is an autonomous activity within the context of historically developing material forces. For him, "politics is the central human activity, the means by which the single consciousness is brought into contact with the social and natural world in all its forms" (Hobsbawm 1982, 23).

Gramsci's emphasis on politics came out of the historical situation in which he lived and participated as an intellectual leader involved with a mass proletarian movement—that of Turin—during World War I and the years immediately following. Italy at the end of the war was the scene of an important struggle between political parties of the Left and Right, a struggle that rapidly turned into a victory for fascism in 1922 and the suppression of political rights. As a key member of the Italian Socialist and then Communist Party (PCI), Gramsci saw the failure of a revolutionary mass workers' movement and the rise of a reactionary fascism supported by much of the working class.[1] Out of this experience, he developed an alternative Marxist view of the State—"the entire complex of practical and theoretical activities with which the ruling class not only justifies and maintains its dominance, but manages to win the active consent of those over whom it rules" (Gramsci 1971, 244)—and a Marxist theory of politics—an alternative strategy for overthrowing the bourgeois State and for building socialism.

THE CONCEPT OF CIVIL SOCIETY

Gramsci's thinking was, of course, rooted in Marx and Lenin. He made all the Marxist assumptions about the material origins of class and the role

[1] See Fiori (1970) and Joll (1978) for biographies of Gramsci.

of class struggle and consciousness in social change. He also took Marx's notion of bourgeois "hegemony" in civil society as expressed by Marx and Engels in *The German Ideology* ([1845-46], in Tucker 1978, 172-174), and made it a central theme of his own version of the functioning of the capitalist system. This hegemony, in Gramscian terms, meant the ideological predominance of bourgeois values and norms over the subordinate classes: it is, in the words of one analyst, "an order in which a certain way of life and thought is dominant, in which one concept of reality is diffused throughout society in all its institutional and private manifestations, informing with its spirit all taste, morality, customs, religious and political principles, and all social relations, particularly in their intellectual and moral connotations" (Williams, in Miliband 1973, 162).

It was in his concept of civil society and his elevations of bourgeois hegemony to a predominant place in the science of politics that Gramsci went beyond Marx, Engels, Lenin, and Trotsky. In so doing, he emphasized much more than earlier writers the role of the superstructure in perpetuating classes and preventing the development of class consciousness (Texier, in Mouffe 1979). He assigned to the State part of this function of promoting a single (bourgeois) concept of reality, and, therefore, gave the State a more extensive (enlarged) role in perpetuating class. Gramsci gave the mass of workers much more credit than Lenin for being able to develop class consciousness themselves, but he also saw the obstacles to consciousness as more formidable in Western society than Lenin had imagined: it was not merely lack of understanding of their position in the economic process that kept workers from comprehending their class role, nor was it only the "private" institutions of society, such as religion, that were responsible for keeping the working class from self-realization, but it was the *State itself* that was involved in reproducing the relations of production. In other words, the State was much more than the coercive apparatus of the bourgeoisie; the State included the hegemony of the bourgeoisie in the superstructure.

These notions emerge more clearly when we understand the differences between the concepts of civil society and the State as used by "naturalists" like Locke and Rousseau, and those of Hegel, and Marx and Engels. The naturalist view saw civil society as the reign of order over a state of nature in which men found themselves in some pre-Statal society. Civil society meant an organization of individuals beyond the family, production, etc., into a collective entity governed by laws. Men voluntarily entered this collective, giving up freedom to protect their freedom. Civil society, then, was the state of nature organized and ordered by the collective will—by the *State*. And under some interpretations civil society could even be regarded as the State itself.

Hegel, on the other hand, called civil society the *pre*-political society, that which the naturalists had named the state of nature. For Hegel, the civil society was the reign of "dissoluteness, misery, and physical and ethical corruption" (Hegel, in Mouffe 1979, 28), just the opposite of the naturalist conception. Hegel's civil society had to be regulated and dominated by the superior intellectual capacity of the State, which was the highest form of man's ethical and moral order. According to Mouffe, it is in this sense and only in this sense that the Hegelian concept of the civil society is pre-Marxist (Mouffe 1979, 28). It includes the relations of production and class formation, as well as the administrative and corporate rules that regulate these relations.

Marx and Engels went on to change the Hegelian view. Hegel had defined civil society as all pre-Statal life; as the development of economic relations that precedes and determines political structures and organization. Civil society and the State are antitheses for Marx and Engels. Engels argued that the State—political order—is the subordinate element, whereas civil society—the realm of economic relations—is the decisive element (Bobbio 1979). Thus, structure and superstructure—civil society and the State—form a fundamental dialectical antithesis in the Marxist system. Civil society dominates the State; the structure dominates the superstructure: "The sum total of these relations of production constitutes the economic structure of society; the real foundation on which rises a juridical and political superstructure and to which correspond definite forms of social consciousness" (Marx, in Tucker 1978, 4). And, "civil society embraces the whole material intercourse of individuals within a definite stage of development of productive forces. It embraces the whole commercial and industrial life of a given stage of development and therefore transcends the state and the nation, although, on the other hand, it must assert itself again in the foreign relations as nationalist and organize itself inwardly as the State" (Marx, in Tucker 1978, 163). Marx therefore clearly subsumes the State under civil society, and it is civil society that defines the State and sets the organization and goals of the State in conformity with the material relations of production at a particular stage of capitalist development. It is only to the outside world that the nation-State appears to be directing the process of development, since it is the State that carries on relations with other countries, including wars and the definition of national boundaries.

The Marxian concept of civil society as the structural moment can be considered as the point of departure of Gramsci's analysis. But Gramsci's theory, according to Bobbio (1979), introduced a profound innovation in the Marxist tradition: civil society in Gramsci does not belong to the structural moment, but to the *superstructural* one.

What we can do, for the moment, is to fix two major superstructural "levels": the one that can be called "civil society," that is, the ensemble of organisms commonly called "private," and that of "political society" or "the State." These two levels correspond on the one hand to the function of "hegemony" which the dominant group exercises throughout society and on the other hand to that of "direct domination" or command that is exercised through the State and juridical government. (Gramsci 1971, 12)

For both Marx and Gramsci, civil society is the key factor in understanding capitalist development, but for Marx civil society is structure (relations in production). For Gramsci, on the other hand, it is *superstructure* that represents the active and positive factor in historical development; it is the complex of ideological and cultural relations, the spiritual and intellectual life, and the political expression of those relations that become the focus of analysis rather than structure.

HEGEMONY AND THE STATE

This is the reason that *hegemony* becomes such a crucial concept in the Gramscian system. But its importance also derives from the historical situation of Italy in the 1920s. Despite a significant degree of working-class consciousness and revolutionary activity in Turin (where Gramsci was studying and writing), the Turin movement of 1919-1920 had relatively little support in the rest of Italy. Instead, bourgeois reaction in the form of Mussolini's fascist movement drew in much of the peasant and working class. Under conditions of relative political freedom after World War I, the parties of the working classes, explicitly pledged to the defense and liberation of the subordinate classes, generally did much less well politically than their conservative rivals, whose purpose was to preserve and promote the advances of capitalism. It was through the concept of hegemony that Gramsci attempted to explain why this was so: as we discussed above, hegemony means the ideological predominance of the dominant classes in civil society over the subordinate.

Gramsci's originality as a Marxist lay partly in his conception of the nature of bourgeois rule (and indeed of any previous established social order), in his argument that the system's real strength does not lie in the violence of the ruling class or the coercive power of its state apparatus, but in the acceptance by the ruled of a "conception of the world" which belongs to the rulers. The philosophy of the ruling class passes through a whole tissue of complex vulgarizations to emerge as "common sense": that is, the philosophy of the masses, who accept the morality, the customs, the institutionalized behavior of the society they live in. The problem for Gramsci then is to understand *how* the ruling class has managed to win the consent of the subordinate classes in this way; and then, to see how the latter will manage to overthrow the old order and bring about a new one of universal freedom. (Fiori 1970, 238)

Bobbio (1979) argues that Gramsci inverts traditional Marxist theory in two ways: first, Gramsci emphasizes the primacy of the ideological superstructures over the economic structure; second, he emphasizes the primacy of civil society (consensus) over political society (force). Although for both Marx and Gramsci, civil society is fundamental to understanding capitalist relations and their reproduction, Bobbio suggests that for Gramsci, it is superstructure that represents the active and positive factor in historical development; rather than economic structure, it is the complex of ideological and cultural relations, spiritual and intellectual life, and the political expression of those relations that become the focus of analysis.[2]

Marx and Engels wrote in *The German Ideology* that the ideas of the ruling class in every historical period are the ruling ideas, and that "the class which is the ruling *material* force in society, is at the same time its ruling *intellectual* force. The class which has the means of material production at its disposal, has control at the same time over the means of mental production, so that thereby, generally speaking, the ideas of those who lack the means of mental production are subject to it" (Marx and Engels, in Tucker 1978, 172).

What Gramsci added to this idea—at the same time transforming it— was the concept of hegemony. For him neither force nor the logic of capitalist production could explain the consent that production enjoyed among the subordinate classes. Rather, the explanation for this consent lay in the power of consciousness and ideology. But, at the same time, in that very consciousness that could consent to the relations of capitalist society lay the foundations of a strategy for gaining the active consent of the masses through their self-organization, starting from civil society, and in all the hegemonic apparatuses—from the factory to the school and the family (Buci-Glucksmann 1982, 119).

Gramsci's concept of hegemony has two principal meanings: first, it is

[2] Yet, as a number of other writers have pointed out, there is no divergence between Marx's problematic and Gramsci's since it is the economy that is determinant for both in the last instance (Texier 1979). Furthermore, Bobbio's interpretation separates Gramsci's writings from his political praxis, in which Gramsci allied himself with the Italian revolutionary working-class movement, Leninism, and the Third International (Mouffe, 1979, 3-4).

a process in civil society whereby a fraction of the dominant class exercises control through its moral and intellectual leadership over other allied fractions of the dominant class. The leading fraction has the power and ability to articulate the interest of the other fractions. The dominant fraction does not impose its own ideology upon the allied group; rather, it "represents a pedagogic and politically transformative process whereby the dominant class [fraction] articulates a hegemonic principle that brings together common elements drawn from the world views and interests of allied groups" (Giroux 1981, 418).

Second, it is a relationship between the dominant and dominated classes. Hegemony involves the successful attempts of the dominant class to use its political, moral, and intellectual leadership to establish its view of the world as all-inclusive and universal, and to shape the interests and needs of subordinate groups. As Buci-Glucksmann (1974), Mouffe (1979), and Giroux (1981) all point out, this consent relationship is not at all static. It moves on a terrain that is constantly shifting in order to "accommodate the changing nature of historical circumstances and the demands and reflexive actions of human beings" (Giroux 1981, 419). Neither is hegemony a cohesive force. It is rife with contradictions and subject to struggle.

Buci-Glucksmann (1974) argues further that Gramsci's hegemony is expressed in society as the complex of institutions, ideologies, practices, and agents (hence the intellectuals whom Gramsci discusses at length in the *Prison Notebooks*) that comprise the dominant culture of values. In Buci-Glucksmann's view, this "apparatus" of hegemony only finds its unification in the expansion of a class. Hegemony unifies itself as an apparatus by reference to the class in which it is constituted and by which the mediation of the multiple subsystems takes place: "the school apparatus (lower and higher education), the cultural apparatus (the museums and the libraries), the organization of information, the framework of life, urbanism, without forgetting the specific weight of apparati possibly inherited from a previous mode of production (i.e., the church and its intellectuals)" (Buci-Glucksmann 1974, 64). According to Buci-Glucksmann, Gramsci avoided the institutionalism and institutional determinism of Weber, because the apparatus of hegemony is spanned by the class struggle: the institutions that form the hegemonic apparatus only have meaning in the Gramscian analysis when set in the context of the class struggle and the dominant class that expands its power and control in the civil society through these same institutions. They are not "purely" administrative and technological institutions; rather, like the production system, they are infused with political content. Political content is the attempt of the dominant classes to expand their capacity to reproduce their control over societal development. For Gramsci, it is the superstructure that evokes the extent and nature of this capacity.

Seen another way, a principal difference between the Marxist-Leninist analysis of bourgeois society and Gramsci's was the latter's concern with the *ethical-political* element in historical development. Gramsci took from Benedetto Croce the idea that man was the unique protagonist in history: his thought stimulates action—concrete ethical-political action—which is the creation of new history. "Croce's philosophy reinstated man's active role in the unfolding of reality, as against the determinism in vogue [in Croce's and Gramsci's time]. It should consequently be seen as one of the models for the renovation of Marxist thought, as the latter struggles to free itself from the confusions of economism and fatalistic determinism'' (Fiori 1970, 239). Yet, Croce not only situated man in a unique historical position; according to Gramsci, he made him ahistorical. Croce's man is a meta-physical entity, rather than a social creature whose personality and way of thought are determined by his relationship to himself, to other men in society, and nature (ibid.). Gramsci took Croce's view of man as an innovator in history and situated it in the Marxist dialectical framework, in the set of choices that are conditioned by the historical context in which men and women find themselves at a particular moment. Croce, like Popper (1945) wanted to dictate a priori the rules of the dialectical process. The two philosophers wanted to establish beforehand what was valuable in the past and what had to be retained from it in the process of innovation and social change. Principally, they define the notions of freedom and de-mocracy in a particular way (in the context of the liberal State) and then argue for their universality and immutability. For Croce and Popper, the liberal, juridical State must be preserved along with its definition of freedom (including the rules of property and economic interaction), which is based on particular relations in production and particular rights of individuals. Political action thus has to be reformism—indeed is strictly limited to reformism once the limitation of a particular set of juridical norms is imposed.

According to his principal biographer, Giuseppe Fiori, Gramsci reasoned that this type of historicism (interestingly enough, Popper claims that his own philosophy and method is antihistorical, whereas Gramsci argues that Croce's analysis—so close to Popper's later interpretations—is a *type* of historicism, not its negation at all) for moderates and reformists is "no scientific theory, it is not identical with 'true' reformism—it is only the intellectual reflection of a form of political practice, an 'ideology' in the most destructive sense'' (Fiori 1970, 240). In Fiori's interpretation of Gramsci's views, he suggests that Gramsci saw no particular reason for the liberal State and its rules to be preserved in a process of change; to the contrary, in "true" dialectical change, thesis gives rise to an antag-onistic (contradictory) antithesis that together in their conflicted interaction produce the synthesis. "The past is complex, an interwoven tapestry of the live and the dead, and the choice cannot be made arbitrarily or in an *a priori* fashion, by an individual or a political movement. . . . The syn-thesis is indeed the overcoming, the resolution of this conflict; but no one can say, *a priori* what of the original thesis will be conserved in this synthesis" (Fiori 1970, 240)

With these concepts of hegemony and the inclusion of the historical man in the innovative process of dialectical change, we can begin to understand Gramsci's analysis of the State, the role of intellectuals (and education) in the superstructure (and therefore in the process of historical change), and his view of the strategy necessary to replace the bourgeois State (and civil society) in Western Europe with a proletarian hegemony.

Gramsci did not seem to settle on a single, wholly satisfactory theory of the State, but he clearly saw it differently from Marx or Lenin. For Gramsci, the State as superstructure becomes a primary rather than a secondary variable in understanding capitalist society. Furthermore, he incorporated the apparatus of hegemony in the State as well as civil society, thereby expanding it beyond the Marxist-Leninist conception of the State as a coercive instrument of the bourgeoisie. Thus, the State is, at one and the same time, a primary instrument for the expansion of dominant-class power, and a coercive force (political society) that keeps subordinate groups weak and disorganized.

> We are still on the terrain of the identification of State and government—an identification which is precisely a representation of the economic-corporate form, in other words of the confusion between civil society and political society. For it should be remarked that the general notion of State includes elements which need to be referred back to the notion of civil society (in the sense that one might say that State = political society + civil society, in other words hegemony protected by the amour of coercion). (Gramsci 1971, 263)

This is *one* view of what Gramsci meant by the State and its role in dominant-class hegemony. However, as Anderson (1977) has shown, there are several definitions of hegemony and the State's place in it appearing in the *Prison Notebooks*. In the first "oscillation," the opposition is *be-tween* the State and civil society; hegemony (direction) pertains to civil society and coercion (domination) to the State. There is a contrast between civil society and the State—the dominant group exercises hegemony through society and direct domination through the State and its juridical govern-ment. The dominant class gains *consent* to its social domination through hegemony in the society as a whole, but exercises domination through the control of the State's coercive apparatuses. "The State is the entire complex of practical and theoretical activities with which the ruling class not only justifies and maintains the domination, but manages to win the active consent of those over whom it rules" (Gramsci 1971, 244).

In the second definition, the State includes civil society; it *encompasses* civil society. "The general notion of the State includes elements which need to be referred back to the notion of civil society (in the sense that one might say that the State = political society + civil society, in other words hegemony armoured with coercion)" (Anderson 1977, 12-13). In that case, hegemony is not a pole of consent in contrast to another of coercion, but as a *synthesis* of consent and coercion. Hegemony is no longer confined to civil society but is also located in the State as "political hegemony," contrasted with "civil hegemony." Thus, hegemony is everywhere, but in different forms; the State becomes an apparatus of hegemony, encompassing civil society and only distinguished from it by the coercive apparatuses pertaining only to the State.

In the third definition, the State and civil society are identical; thus, consent and coercion become co-extensive with the State, and hegemony is inseparable from the State apparatuses themselves. No longer is there a distribution of hegemony between civil society and political society. State and civil society are merged into a larger unity; the State is the same as the social formation itself, including governmental and private apparatuses. As we will see, it is this last definition that Althusser uses in his "ideological State apparatuses": all ideological and political superstructures—including the family, trade unions, reformist political parties, and private media—are by definition State apparatuses, or—to put it another way—are hegemonic apparatuses.

It is the second definition that seems most useful to analyze advanced capitalist societies. Hegemony is expressed both in the civil society and the State, yet there is considerable autonomy of private hegemonic apparatuses from the State. (There is often tension between the two, particularly when the fraction of the dominant class with political power is not the hegemonic class.) We could even argue that the function of hegemony in the civil society, where the ideological apparatuses are much less obvious, and therefore much more effective in mystifying the dominance of class rule, differs from the State's hegemonic apparatuses, which are much more apparent in their reproductive role, especially since they carry coercion's armor (the juridical system and the school, for example). Below, when we discuss Gramsci's strategies for change based on his concept(s) of hegemony, we will see how he focuses primarily on developing a counterhegemony in the civil society and surrounding the State. But in the very creation and growth of counterhegemony, the hegemonic State apparatuses are confronted, or put in crisis. Similarly, as Poulantzas's later work argues, electoral victories by the Left constitute a counterhegemony in the State apparatuses, hence posing important counterbalances to the dominant-class hegemony in the civil society.

If we use that second conception of the State, we see that it is part of dominant-class hegemony. In this definition, Gramsci viewed the State as an extension of the hegemonic apparatus—as part of the system developed by the bourgeoisie to perpetuate and expand their control of society in the context of class struggle. The incorporation of the State into dominant-class hegemony emerged, according to him, from the *nature of the bourgeois class itself*—from the fact that the class had constituted itself as an organism of continuous movement, capable of absorbing and culturally transforming the entire society:

> The revolution which the bourgeois class has brought into the conception of law, and *hence into the function of the State*, consists especially in the will to conform (hence ethicity of the law and of the State). The previous ruling classes were essentially conservative in the sense that they did not tend to construct an organic passage from the other classes into their own, i.e., to enlarge their class sphere "technically" and ideologically: their conception was that of a closed caste. The bourgeois class poses itself as an organism in continuous movement, capable of absorbing the entire society, assimilating to its own cultural and economic level. The entire function of the State has been transformed; the State has become an "educator," etc. (Gramsci 1971, 260; italics added)

However, in practice, the bourgeoisie is not able to carry out this conception, or never intends to do it; rather, the dominant class is saturated—not only does it not expand, it starts to disintegrate. Yet the State continues to behave as if the bourgeoisie can and will exercise its function of continuous expansionary movement; indeed, it enforces bourgeois laws as if there is only *one* class and *one* society.

All of this suggests that Gramsci's view of the State was principally ideological, that it was a hegemonic apparatus that arose from the conception of the bourgeois class as a potentially totally inclusive group, and hence to a system of laws and norms that treated individuals as if they were going to be incorporated into the bourgeoisie. In Buci-Glucksmann's analysis:

> In effect, in the case of *successful hegemony*, a class tries to advance the whole of society (national function). Its "attraction" to the allied classes (and also to the enemies) isn't *passive*, but *active*. Not only

doesn't it simply ease administrative coercive mechanisms of *constraint*, but it also doesn't exhaust itself in "the strictly ideological mechanisms of ideological imposition" (Althusser) or of legitimation by symbolic violence (Bourdieu). (Buci-Glucksmann 1974, 81)

The bourgeoisie utilizes all these elements *and* its illusory expansion to incorporate the working class *as a working class*, without consciousness of its class position, into overall bourgeois development. By acceding to bourgeois power and control, workers remain an exploited class, essentially contributing to the enrichment of a minority (which remains a minority) at the workers' expense.

Nevertheless, the importance of the State as an apparatus of hegemony is for Gramsci still *rooted in the class structure*, a class structure defined by and tied to the relations in production. This is the key to understanding Gramsci: he provides an analysis of historical development that rejects the narrower Marxist version of civil society as incomplete and not relevant to the Western (Italian) situation. But at the same time, he does not deny that the superstructure—hegemony and its extension into and through the State apparatus—is intimately connected to relations in production: "for though hegemony is ethical-political, it must also be economic, must necessarily be based on the decisive function exercised by the leading group in the decisive nucleus of economic activity" (Gramsci 1970, 161). It is not the *separation* of superstructure from structure that Gramsci stresses, but rather the dialectical relation between them.[3] Hegemony and the hegemonic function of the State emanate from both the nature of the bourgeoisie as an ideologically all-encompassing class *and* its particular position of economic power in capitalist society. It is Gramsci's treatment of hegemony and ideology that explains the development (or lack of development) of working-class consciousness, so important to any Marxist political analysis. "In this connection Engels' statement too should be recalled, that the economy is only the mainspring of history 'in the last analysis' (to be found in his two letters on the philosophy of praxis also published in Italian); this statement is to be related directly to the passage in the preface to the *Critique of Political Economy* which says that it is on the level of ideologies that men become conscious of conflicts in the world of the economy" (Gramsci 1971, 162).

Gramsci raises man's thought (consciousness) to a newly prominent place in the "philosophy of praxis" (as he calls Marxism). Control of consciousness is as much or more an area of political struggle as control of the forces of production: "Furthermore, another proposition of the

[3] See the exchange between Norberto Bobbio and Jacques Texier in Mouffe (1979), for a further discussion of this point.

philosophy of praxis is also forgotten: that 'popular beliefs' and similar ideas are themselves material forces" (1971, 165). The State, as an instrument of bourgeois domination (as part of the civil society), must be an intimate participant in the struggle for consciousness. Bourgeois development is not only carried out through the development of the forces of production but through hegemony in the arena of consciousness. The State is involved in this extension, not only in the coercive *enforcement* of bourgeois economic power. Without power (control) in the arena of struggle over consciousness, Gramsci argues, the bourgeoisie will try to fall back on the coercive power of the State as its *primary* instrument of domination. Otherwise, coercive forces remain in the background, acting as a system of enforcement and threat but not overt coercion.

In reality, the State must be conceived of as an "educator," in that it tends precisely to create a new type or level of civilization. Because one is acting essentially on economic forces, reorganizing and developing the apparatus of economic production, creating a new structure, the conclusion must not be drawn that superstructural factors should be left to themselves, to develop spontaneously to a haphazard and sporadic germination. The State in this field, too, is an instrument of "rationalization," of acceleration and Taylorization. It operates according to a plan, urges, incites, solicits, and "punishes"—for, once the conditions are created in which a certain way of life is "possible," then "criminal action or omission" must have a punitive sanction, with moral implications, and not merely be judged generically as "dangerous." The law is the repressive and negative aspect of the entire positive, civilizing activity undertaken by the State (Gramsci 1971, 247).

This brings us to Gramsci's concept of "passive revolution," which relates changes in politics, ideology, and social relations to changes in the economy (Buci-Glucksmann 1979; Showstack Sassoon 1980, 1982c). Gramsci uses the term passive revolution to indicate the *constant reorganization of State power* and its relationship to the dominated classes to preserve dominant-class hegemony and to exclude the masses from exerting influence over political and economic institutions. Implicit in the concept is a State that, as we have already mentioned, is *extended*, and extension is itself the product of a modern age in which the masses have organized themselves and have—for the first time in history—a potential for self-government. The presence of the masses in politics is a precondition for their autonomy, but also results in an extended State that can respond to the threat of mass movement (Showstack Sassoon 1982b, 102-103).

Faced by potential active masses, then, the State institutes passive revolution as a technique that the bourgeoisie attempts to adopt when its hegemony is weakened in any way. The "passive" aspect consists in "preventing the development of a revolutionary adversary by 'decapitating' its revolutionary potential'' (Showstack Sassoon 1982c, 133). Gramsci developed this concept in order to explain how the bourgeoisie survives despite political and economic crises. "The acceptance of certain demands from below, while at the same time encouraging the working class to restrict its struggle to the economic-corporative terrain, is part of this attempt to prevent the hegemony of the dominant class from being challenged while changes in the world of production are accommodated within the current social formation'' (Showstack Sassoon 1982c, 133).

So the bourgeoisie—through the State—attempts a strategy of passive revolution whenever its hegemony is threatened or whenever its political superstructure (force plus hegemony) cannot cope with the need to expand the forces of production. In the 1930s, for example, the State's intervention in the society increased dramatically in Europe and the United States, and the relatively weak hegemony of the dominant class was expanded to include new popular elements. For Gramsci, as we shall show below, the lesson of passive revolution was to make explicit the difference between reformist and revolutionary politics, where reformism is a version of the passive revolution. The necessity of counteracting passive revolution is based on the fundamental asymmetry between the revolution made by the working class and that of the bourgeoisie, and between the modern bourgeois State (which is organized for passive revolution) and a working-class, revolutionary State in which the very concept of politics is transformed.

THE PROCESS OF RADICAL CHANGE

If the arena of consciousness for Gramsci is the primary struggle between the dominant and subordinate classes, then how do things change? How do the subordinate classes overcome the hegemony of the dominant classes? Gramsci's interest in analyzing the development of capitalism in Western countries was to understand the failure of Italian "revolutionary" activity of 1919-1920, and to seek out a more relevant strategy in the face of capitalist hegemony. There are three parts to the answer Gramsci gives to these questions: (1) the concept of crisis of hegemony, derived in part from Marx's analysis of the *Eighteenth Brumaire*; (2) the concept of the "war of position" versus the "war of maneuver"; and (3) the role of intellectuals. All three emerge directly from Gramsci's notion of the superstructure playing the primary role in the expansion of and domination by the ruling bourgeoisie.

The Crisis of Hegemony

Regarding the crisis of hegemony, Buci-Glucksmann writes:

> Gramsci's revolutionary dialectic escapes from all structural-function-
> alist models, where the manner of integration into a structure (function)
> consolidates the manner of institutionalizing controls. . . . which makes
> it seem that whenever he uses an integration model, this calls forth a
> model of *disintegration*, the theoretical and methodological couples of
> Gramsci being *bipolar*. In sum, no theory of hegemony without a theory
> of the crisis of hegemony (the organic crisis); no analysis of integration
> of the subordinate classes to a dominant class without a theory of the
> atomization and constitution of classes which permits a formerly sub-
> ordinate class to become hegemonic; no enlargement of the State without
> the redefinition of a new strategic perspective: "the war of position,"
> which permits the working class to fight for a new State. (Buci-Glucks-
> mann 1974, 75)

In this bipolar theory, Gramsci contends (as did Engels and Marx before
him) that there are periods of history in which social classes become
detached from their political parties; the class no longer recognizes the
men who lead the parties as its expression. When this happens, the situation
becomes dangerous because violent solutions can occur, and the traditional
means of using the State to maintain dominant-class hegemony deteriorates.
In this moment, those elements of the society-bureaucracy, Church, high
finance, and other institutions—that are independent of public opinion
increase their power and autonomy. How do these crises occur? They are
the result of unpopular actions of the ruling classes (through the State), or
the increased political activism by previously passive masses. In either
case they add up to a "crisis of authority." This is what Gramsci calls
the "crisis of hegemony, or general crisis of the State" (1971, 210). "If
the ruling class has lost its consensus, i.e. is no longer 'leading' but only
'dominant,' exercising coercive force alone, this means precisely that the
great masses have become detached from their traditional ideologies, and
no longer believe what they used to believe previously, etc. The crisis
consists that the old is dying and the new cannot be born" (1971, 25-26).

Gramsci did not believe that this crisis of hegemony was the *result* of
economic crisis. Rather, economic crisis could create the conditions for a
crisis of hegemony by putting the bourgeoisie (through the State) in the
position of making serious mistakes in handling its response to economic
problems, and in carrying out reforms (passive revolution). The bourgeoisie
would respond in various ways to these problems, attempting at the same
time to keep control through the apparatus of hegemony. It would be the

failure to do this successfully that could lead to widespread revolutionary activity. Nonetheless, there are also other possible reasons for a crisis of hegemony:

It may be ruled out that immediate economic crises of themselves produce fundamental historical events; they can simply create a terrain more favorable to the dissemination of certain modes of thought, and certain ways of posing and resolving questions involving the entire subsequent development of national life. . . . Changes can come about either because a situation of well-being is threatened by the narrow self-interest of a rival class, or because hardship has become intolerable and no force is visible in the old society capable of mitigating it and of re-establishing normality by legal means. (Gramsci 1971, 184-185)

Ultimately, for Gramsci, crisis could only lead to action if mass consciousness was there, and ready to go into action—so it was the development of this consciousness that would produce revolutionary change, not the declining rate of profit. "A crisis cannot give the attacking forces the ability to organize with lightning speed in time and space; still less can it endow them with fighting spirit. Similarly the defenders are not demoralized, nor do they abandon their positions, even among the ruins, nor do they lose faith in their own strength or their own future" (Gramsci 1971, 235).

Since the superstructure (bourgeois hegemony) plays such a key role in Gramsci's analysis of capitalist development, it is logical that his analysis of the disintegration of capitalism also hinges on hegemony, this time on its crisis. And with the crisis of hegemony in the forefront of his analysis of radical change, the State comes to the forefront of revolutionary strategy. Although for Marx and Lenin, the bourgeois State is the coercive arm of bourgeois power, part and parcel of the bourgeois project, for Gramsci, the State is also an instrument of bourgeois *ideology*, of the legitimization of the bourgeois social needs. For Marx, economic impoverishment through the increased exploitation of labor is a key factor in the ability of a revolutionary party to raise working-class consciousness to the point of bringing that class to a confrontation with the power of the State. For Gramsci, increased impoverishment is only *one* element in the possibilities for raising this consciousness. More important for him is the disintegration of the capability of the State to extend and maintain bourgeois hegemony—that is, a crisis in the belief system developed by the bourgeoisie to serve its own ends. Nevertheless, as Gramsci makes clear, the crisis of the State— the crisis of the bourgeois capability to rule indirectly through the ideological State apparatus—is only *part* of the apparatus of hegemony:

The same reduction must take place in the art and science of politics, at least in the case of the most advanced States, where "civil society" has become a very complex structure and one which is resistant to the catastrophic "incursions" of the immediate economic element (crisis, depressions, etc.). The superstructures of civil society are like the trench-systems of modern warfare. In war it would sometimes happen that a fierce artillery attack seemed to have destroyed the enemy's entire defensive system, whereas in fact it had only destroyed the outer perimeter; and at the moment of their advance and attack the assailants would find themselves confronted by a line of defense which was still effective. The same thing happens in politics, during the great economic crises. A crisis cannot give the attacking forces the ability to organize with lightning speed in time and space; still less can it endow them with fighting spirit. (1971, 235)

In other words, bourgeois hegemony is not just the State, and for Gramsci control of the State is definitely not enough to ensure power passing to a contending group (such as the proletariat).

The War of Position

This reasoning led him to develop an alternative strategy, the "war of position," to what he termed the "war of maneuver," or the "frontal" attack of the State. He argued that:

In Russia the State was everything, civil society was primordial and gelatinous; in the West, there was a proper relation between State and civil society, and when the State trembled a sturdy structure of civil society was at once revealed. The State was only an outer ditch, behind which there stood a powerful system of fortresses and earthworks: more or less numerous from one State to the next, it goes without saying— but this precisely necessitated an accurate reconnaissance of each individual country. (1971, 238)

Thus, capturing the State—overthrow and control of the State—per se did not mean control of society; it did *not* mean establishing an alternative proletarian hegemony. At the same time, he thought it unlikely that the proletariat could get control of the State by direct attack, as in Russia. Since the State was so much more than the coercive forces of the bourgeoisie, since it was part of the ideological (hegemonic) superstructure of bourgeois-dominated civil society, it had to be approached as a *piece* of the system of power, not necessarily even *the* crucial element of power. Gramsci, after all, had witnessed the defeat of the Left in Central and

Southern Europe in 1918-1920, in some cases where it had held State power for short periods of time (Austria, Hungary, Bavaria). He attributed this defeat to a capitalism much more developed than in Russia, developed not only in the forces of production but in its ideological superstructure, and to the correspondingly less-militant working class.

Faced with this paradox of a more *extensive* industrial proletariat in the more advanced capitalist countries, but one that was *less militant* than in Russia and less willing to overthrow capitalism, Gramsci developed a strategy that was consistent with his analysis explaining the paradox—a strategy that confronted bourgeois hegemony. He called this strategy the "war of position." The "war of position" has four important elements.

First, it stresses that each individual country would require an "accurate reconnaissance." This was an argument against the "internationalist" position first developed by Marx and Engels and then pushed by Trotsky as "permanent revolution," a revolution by all the workers of the world (the industrial world) simultaneously using the same strategy (a frontal attack on the State—armed revolution against the coercive arm of the bourgeoisie). Gramsci believed that each country's Communist Party had to develop its own plan of how to create socialism in that particular political context before any world socialistic order could be developed; indeed, the Bolshevik strategy itself, he argued, had been one of "purging internationalism of every vague and purely ideological (in a pejorative sense) element, to give it a realistic political content" (1971, 241). The inherently national character of socialist movements and strategy in the first phases of world socialism is rooted in the hegemony of the dominant class: "It is in the concept of hegemony that those exigencies which are national in character are knotted together" (ibid.). And the concept of permanent revolution does not take account of the enormous changes that took place in the capitalist world between 1870 and World War I:

> The formula belongs to a historical period [before 1848] in which the great mass political parties and the great economic trade unions did not yet exist, and society was still, so to speak, in a state of fluidity from many points of view: greater backwardness of the countryside, and almost complete monopoly of political and State power by a few cities or even a single one (Paris in the case of France); a relatively rudimentary State apparatus, and a greater autonomy of civil society from State activity. . . . In the period after 1870, with the colonial expansion of Europe, all these elements change: the internal and international organizational relations of the State become more complex and massive, and the Forty-Eightist formula of the "Permanent Revolution" is expanded

and transcended in political science by the formula of "civil hegemony." (Gramsci 1971, 242-243)

Secondly, the "war of position" is based on the idea of *surrounding* the State apparatus with a counterhegemony, created by mass organization of the working class and by developing working-class institutions and culture. "A social group can, and indeed must, already exercise leadership (i.e. be hegemonic) before winning governmental power (this indeed is one of the principal conditions for the winning of such power)" (Gramsci, 1971, 207). The basis of Gramsci's strategy, then, was not to organize workers and peasants in order to wage a frontal attack on the State, but to establish working-class organizations as the foundations of a new culture—the norms and values of a new, proletarian society. This proletarian hegemony would confront bourgeois hegemony in a war of position—of trenches moving back and forth in an ideological struggle over the consciousness of the working class—until the new superstructure had surrounded the old, including the State apparatus. Only at that time would it make sense to take over State power, since only then would the working class in fact control social values and norms to the point of being able to build a new society using the State apparatus (Showstack Sassoon 1982c, 141). "That is, the proletarian army must be ideologically equipped, it must be armed with a new *Weltanschauung*, new ways of living and thinking, a new morality, new ideas, to oppose the bourgeois vision of existence. Only thus will the emplacements fall, will the liberal consensus be weakened, and a new proletarian State sustained by the active consent of its future subjects be born" (Fiori 1970, 243).

Once the proletariat took power, Gramsci's war of position became the natural basis for the new State, which could not be the case without first establishing proletarian hegemony. As we have discussed above, Gramsci developed the theory of hegemony and the role of the State in dominant-class hegemony as a complement to a theory of the "coercive State," the Marxist-Leninist doctrine up to that time. Coercion, he argued, was *one* form of power, and historically necessary for the new proletarian State at a given moment, the moment in which the bourgeoisie attempted to overthrow the new society by force. But

rule by intellectual and moral hegemony is the form of power which guarantees stability, and founds power upon wide-ranging consent and acquiescence. "From the moment in which a subordinate social group becomes really autonomous and hegemonic, and calls forth a new type of State, there arises the concrete need for a new intellectual and moral order, that is, a new type of society, and hence *a need for the most*

universal concepts, the most refined and decisive ideological weapons.''
(Fiori 1970, 243, italics added by Fiori)

Thus Gramsci not only calls for the building of proletarian hegemony as
the means for surrounding the bourgeois State, but as the basis for the
new proletarian State: the institutions and organizations that form part of
the proletarian hegemony in the process of the carrying out the war of
position *become* the foundation of the new moral and intellectual order.
He sees the war of maneuver (frontal assault) not only as incorrect from
the standpoint of strategy, but also as leaving a void in the development
of a new society once the State is taken over (for example, in the Russian
case). This is much the same point made by Rosa Luxemburg, but with
the added conception of an alternative process that would lead to the type
of democratic, mass-based proletarian society (hegemony) and State envisaged by both theoreticians. "In this sense, hegemony as anti-passive
revolution, far from being a totalitarian concept opposed to pluralism, is
the very condition of pluralism. . . . Gramsci designates a point of no
return for political reflection: no democratic transition to socialism without
an anti-passive revolution" (Buci-Glucksmann 1982, 125-126).

This brings us to the third element in the war of position: Gramsci's
focus on consciousness as the key ingredient in the process of change. The
war of position is a struggle for working-class consciousness, and the
relation of political forces in a society depends on the various "moments"
or "levels" of collective political consciousness. The first level of consciousness is professional identification: members of a professional group
are conscious of its unity and homogeneity, and of the need to organize
it. The second level is attained when there is a consciousness of the
solidarity of interests among all the members of a social class—but only
in the economic field, in production. At this level of consciousness, the
working class demands political-juridical equality with the ruling groups;
it demands the right to vote—to participate in the State apparatus (legislative and administrative) and even to reform it, but within the existing
fundamental structures, within the norms and values set by the dominant
groups. At the third level of consciousness, the individual becomes aware
that his or her own corporate interests transcend the corporate limits of an
economic class and extend to all subordinate groups, who all share the
culture of subordination and can come together to form a counter-ideology
that frees them from the subordinated position.

The fourth element translates this topology of ideological development
into action. Gramsci, like Lenin, saw the political party as the instrument
of consciousness-raising and education among the working class and developing the institutions of proletarian hegemony. But unlike Lenin, he

did not see the revolutionary party as a "vanguard," bringing socialist consciousness from the outside. Lenin's party fuses former workers and former professional intellectuals of bourgeois origin into a single cohesive unit of organizer-intellectuals who develop policy and strategy *for* the working class. Gramsci, to the contrary, relates the revolutionary party to the working class as a whole. He writes that the working class, like the bourgeoisie before it, "is capable of developing from within its ranks its own organic intellectuals, and the function of the political party, whether mass or vanguard, is that of channeling the activity of these organic intellectuals and providing a link between the (working) class and certain sections of the traditional intelligentsia" (1971, 4).

Gramsci also views the revolutionary political party as having its own "hegemonic" conditions for permanence (a party that cannot be destroyed by normal means). Any political party has three fundamental elements— (1) the mass element, composed of "ordinary, average men, whose participation takes the form of discipline and loyalty, rather than any creative spirit or organizational ability"; (2) the principal cohesive element, which "centralizes nationally and renders effective and powerful a complex of forces which left to themselves would count for little or nothing"; and (3) an intermediate element, which "articulates the first element with the second and maintains contact between them, but also morally and intellectually." The moment when a party cannot be destroyed by normal means is reached when the necessary second element is present *and* the other two elements cannot help being formed, that is, only when there is a ferment formed by the second element in the first that helps re-create the second element out of the first and the third should the second element be destroyed (Gramsci 1971, 152-154).

Thus, Gramsci responded to the World War I and postwar experience of decimated Leftist parties by arguing for a leadership that generated the kind of activity in the mass base that would make every worker an "intellectual," a potential party leader and organizer. This definition of a mass-based party was totally opposed to the Leninist concept, just as his war of position was a completely different strategy than the frontal attack on the State described by Lenin in *The State and Revolution*. Both differences emerged from Gramsci's fundamental premise about the role of ideology and his concept of hegemony. Just as the proletariat in the West could not effectively seize State power without developing a counterhegemony that competed with and replaced the dominant bourgeois values and norms, so the revolutionary party could not survive—could not act as the builder and educator of the counterhegemony—without creating an ideological base within the party itself that would produce a steady stream of workers with "great cohesive, centralizing and disciplinary powers; also with the power of innovation" (Gramsci 1971, 152).

The Role of Intellectuals

This brings us to the third part of Gramsci's theory of the process of radical change, his analysis of intellectuals. Gramsci built on Lenin's critique of Karl Kautsky, who tended to see the relationship between workers and intellectuals in the socialist movement as one of the led and the leaders, a hierarchical division based on the superior capacity for theoretical and ideological leadership by the intellectuals, which put them above the mass base of nonintellectual workers. Lenin argued that this division had to be obliterated; the vanguard party, which would raise the consciousness of the masses of workers, would be composed of former workers and former bourgeois intellectuals fused into a cohesive unit. Yet Lenin's party still put this new group of leaders, intellectuals, and workers *above* the mass of workers, who Lenin saw as not being capable of generating theory and conscious political leadership by themselves.

Gramsci rejected this notion. In its place, he criticized Kautsky by contending that the concept of "the intellectuals" as a distinct social category independent of class is a myth: "Every social group, coming into existence on the original terrain of an essential function in the world of economic production, creates together with itself, organically, one or more strata of intellectuals which give it homogeneity and an awareness of its own function not only in the economic but also in the social and political fields" (1971, 5).

Normally, when we think of intellectuals, we identify the particular social role of the professional category of the intellectuals. Gramsci characterizes this definition of intellectuals as "traditional" professional intellectuals, literary, scientific, etc., whose position in the "interstices" of society has a certain interclass aura about it, but derives ultimately from past and present class relations and conceals an attachment to various historical class formations. For example, each class produces such intellectuals "organically"—that is, intellectuals from their own class who function to build the hegemony of that class. On the other hand, the dominant classes also reach into the subordinate classes for additional intellectuals to give homogeneity and self-awareness to the dominant group. These traditional intellectuals who come from the subordinate groups, while they are not distinguished professionally from their organic counterparts, are—for Gramsci—different: they cease to be organically linked to their class of origin.

But Gramsci contended that there was a second, and for his purposes, more important definition (or category) of intellectual. This is any person who is the possessor of a particular technical capacity—the thinking and organizing element of every social class. These "organic" intellectuals are distinguished "less by their profession, which may be any job characteristic of their class, than by their function in directing the ideas and aspirations of the class to which they organically belong" (1971, 3).

> Each man, finally, outside his professional activity, carries on some form of intellectual activity, that is, he is a "philosopher," an artist, a man of taste, he participates in some conception of the world, has a conscious line of moral conduct, and therefore contributes to sustain a conception of the world or to modify it, that is, to bring it into being new modes of thought.
>
> The problem of creating a new stratum of intellectuals consists therefore in the critical elaboration of the intellectual activity that exists in everyone at a certain degree of development, modifying its relationship with the muscular-nervous effort towards a new equilibrium, and ensuring that the muscular-nervous effort itself, in so far as it is an element of a general practical activity, which is perpetually innovating the physical and social world, becomes the foundation of a new and integral conception of the world. (1971, 9)

The dominant class attempts in its political parties to weld together the traditional intellectuals with the organic intellectuals of the dominant group, where traditional intellectuals include professional intellectuals both from the dominant and subordinate groups. At the same time, the revolutionary party should try to do the same thing, only in its case, it would weld together disaffected bourgeois professional intellectuals, professional (traditional) intellectuals from the proletariat, and organic proletarian intellectuals, the thinker-organizers with a conscious conception of the world that transcends their class interests. These latter intellectuals are the first element of a nondestroyable party discussed above. It is these intellectuals whom the party must stimulate and mobilize into being by awakening workers to their intellectual possibilities through the educational functions of the party. This, then, is the crucial political difference between Gramsci and Lenin: Gramsci believed in a party and a strategy that was based on the idea that "all men are philosophers."

Conclusion

In summary, Gramsci's theory of the State, although not presented systematically in any of his writings, emerges from the Marxist notion of a superstructure rooted in class and a juridical-political system rooted in the social class struggle. At the same time, Gramsci's theory makes a clear break with (or advance of) the Marxist-Leninist coercive State apparatus that we discussed above: "Gramsci rejected the crude dialectical materialism which he thought was represented by the Bolshevik theorist Nikolai Bukharin, and he attempted to reformulate doctrine of historical materialism in such a way as to allow room both for the influence of ideas on history and for the impact of the individual will" (Joll 1978, 16). The emphasis on the influence of superstructure—on the intellectual and cultural influences rather than the economic—enabled Gramsci to explain how capitalism in the more advanced industrial societies of the West was able, despite the activity of revolutionary movements, to retain its hold on and support among such a sizable proportion of the working class. In his doctrine of "hegemony," Gramsci saw that the dominant class did not have to rely solely on the coercive power of the State or even its direct economic power to rule; rather, through its hegemony, expressed in the civil society *and* the State, the ruled could be persuaded to accept the system of beliefs of the ruling class and to share its social, cultural, and moral values.

But Gramsci did more than introduce a concept—hegemony—that would explain the lack of successful revolution in the West in the post-World War I period or the rise of fascism. This same concept became the central focus of Gramsci's ideas on revolution itself: hegemony meant counter-hegemony; bourgeois dominance through the superstructure meant the necessity of struggling for fundamental structural change by developing new superstructural institutions—by creating a new concept of society that was not bourgeois but proletarian. Political leadership came through a war of position—cultural and moral ascendancy as well as economic predominance.

Gramsci regarded intellectuals as playing an important role as "the dominant group's 'deputies' exercising the subaltern functions of social hegemony and political government" (1971, 12) and, at the same time, a central role in the revolutionary process. Such "organic" intellectuals, coming out of the working class and keeping their ties to it by creating political change through a revolutionary party, provided the basis for Gramsci's political strategy—the establishment of the proletariat's cultural and moral superiority independent of its direct political power.

Gramsci, in the last analysis, was, like Marx and Lenin, an *educator*. Yet, unlike Lenin, he believed in the intellectual qualities of the masses and their capability to create themselves the hegemony of their class rather than having it done for them by an elite vanguard party or an elite bureaucracy responsible for revolutionary theory and tactics. The development of working-class consciousness, such a crucial element in Marxist theory, is for Gramsci the principal moment in explaining both capitalist domination *and* its overthrow. This consciousness comes from within the masses in the form of a mass party.[4] *Consciousness itself* becomes the source of power for the proletariat in laying siege to the State and the means of production, just as lack of proletarian consciousness is the principal reason that the bourgeoisie remains in its dominant position.

[4] This party would not only have mass character but its leadership would be united to the movement and the base by a democratic centralism (Buci-Glucksmann 1979, 232).

CHAPTER FOUR

Structuralism and the State: Althusser and Poulantzas

THE STRUCTURAL version of Marxism that arose in France in the mid-1960s sought to harmonize Marxist thought with the seemingly organized and "automatic" nature of advanced capitalist society, a society where the working class and bourgeoisie both carry out "prescribed" roles. For thinkers like Saussure and Jacobson, who researched the underlying structure of language, Lévi-Strauss, who applied structuralism to primitive rituals, Lacan, who did the same in psychology, and Foucault in social relations and knowledge, the crucial element in understanding human society is "not the conscious activities of the human subject, but the unconscious structure which these activities presupposed" (McLellan 1979, 298). Louis Althusser brought this structuralist perspective to Marx's writings as part of a critique of Lefebvre's and Sartre's Marxist humanism (Althusser 1969; Althusser and Balibar 1970). Like Lévi-Strauss, Foucault, and other structuralists, Althusser wanted to combat the subjectivism that placed "man" the subject at the center of metaphysical systems. Sartre's emphasis on the individual and individual action is confronted by Althusser's views of conditioned acts and the individual subjugated by ideological apparatuses.

The debate over structuralism as epistemology (and as a philosophy of science and knowledge) has been long and involved; to do it justice in a few pages is difficult and not really necessary for our discussions of the structuralist view of the State.[1] This view hinges on two key points in Althusser's work, and we will concentrate on these.

First, as a structuralist, Althusser claims that the social structure has no creative subject at its core. Rather, the social formation is a system of objective processes without subjects. Thus, Althusser rejects the notion of man as the subject or agent of history, arguing instead that individuals are the "supports" or "bearers" of the structural relations in which they are situated. It is the *relations of production* (social classes) that are the subject

[1] For summaries of Althusser's philosophical contributions, see Burris (1979), McLellan (1979), and Hirsch (1981). The most detailed attack on Althusser is by E. P. Thompson (1978), and the most detailed defense of Althusser (in response to Thompson) is by Perry Anderson (1980).

of history, not individual actors as free agents. Only classes, rather than individuals, have a history as they develop and come into conflict in a specific mode of production. Second, although Althusser's structural determinism has led his critics to brand him as neo-Stalinist (e.g. Thompson 1978), Althusser's theories, very much unlike Stalinism, reject economic determinism and argue instead for the *relative autonomy* of politics and ideology from the economic base. He proposes that Marx's concept of the mode of production involved three distinctly articulated structures or levels (the economic, the political, and the ideological) that "were intimately and internally combined to form the matrix of the mode of production" (Hirsh 1981, 173). Although the economic structure is always "determinate in the last instance," any one of the three structures can be the "structure in dominance" in a particular mode of production (capitalism or feudalism, for example). Therefore, in a given social formation, the economic, political, or the ideological could be the dominant structure, but the economic structure would always determine which of the three would be dominant (Althusser and Balibar 1970, 216-218).

Nicos Poulantzas used these structuralist elements to develop a theory of the State (Poulantzas [1968] 1974) and Althusser himself also applied his ideas on economic, political, and ideological structures to the State (Althusser 1971). Before going on to Poulantzas's work, which is the major structuralist effort regarding the State (and which—as we shall show— he gradually changed by integrating the insights of structuralism into the broader framework of a class struggle perspective), an analysis of Althusser's major essay "Ideology and Ideological State Apparatuses" (1971) will both exemplify the elements of his position, and show specific connections between Althusser's work and Gramsci's views of base and superstructure.

ALTHUSSER: IDEOLOGY AND THE STATE

For Althusser (and for Marx) the issue of ideology is crucial to the *reproduction of the relations of production*, because if the reproduction of the relations of production is to be assured, "individual-subjects" occupying the posts that the sociotechnical division of labor assigns to them in production, exploitation, repression, ideologization, scientific practice, etc., must be "inserted into practices" governed by rituals of ideology (Althusser 1971, 169-170). "Their concrete material behavior is simply the inscription of life of the admirable words of the prayer: 'Amen—so be it' " (1971, 181).

What is a theory of such an ideology? Althusser argues that *ideology has no history*. Ideology exists as a construct that transcends any history of social formations; it does not depend on a particular social formation but rather exists independent of any moment in time.

The peculiarity of ideology is that it is endowed with a structure and a functioning such as to make it a non-historical reality, i.e., an *omni-historical* reality, in the sense in which that structure and functioning are immutable, present in the same form throughout what we call history, in the sense in which the *Communist Manifesto* defines history as the history of class struggles, i.e., the history of class societies. (1971, 151-152)

Althusser uses the plain term "ideology" to designate ideology in general, a theoretical construct that is not rooted in any particular empirical context. However, he notes that a theory of *particular* ideologies, whatever their form (religious, ethical, legal, or political), *does* depend in the last resort ("in the last instance") on the history of social formations, and thus on the modes of production combined in social formations, and on the class struggles that develop in them. This theoretical construct of ideology in general defines ideology as representing "the imaginary relationship of individuals to their real conditions of existence" (1971, 153). He then goes on to argue that ideology has a material existence: an ideology always exists in an apparatus and its practices. This existence is material; this imaginary relation to real relations (ideology) is itself endowed with a material existence, and material existence is the practice of ideology within particular apparatuses of society. Thus, Althusser expresses the structuralist notion that knowledge of the internal functioning of a structure has to *precede* the study of its genesis and evolution. The internal functioning is studied by defining the *existence* of ideology in terms of the way it is inscribed in the "actions of practices governed by rituals defined in the last instance by an ideological apparatus" (1971, 170). An individual's beliefs are his "material actions inserted into material practices governed by material rituals which are themselves defined by the material ideological apparatus from which derive the ideas of that subject" (1971, 169). It is this notion that precedes the study of particular ideological apparatuses which are tied to the development of particular social formations.

The notion goes further: individuals and their ideas are no longer the source of the dynamic of this dialectic. As we have noted, Althusser sees human individuals as the "supports" or "bearers" of the structural relations in which they are situated. In the case of ideology, Althusser's subject "acts insofar as he is acted upon by a system in which ideology existing in a material ideological apparatus, prescribing material practices governed by a material ritual, which practices exist in the material actions of a subject acting in all consciousness according to his belief" (1971,

159). He contends that ideology recognizes individuals as subjects, subjects them to the "subject" of the ideology itself (for example, God, capital, the State), guarantees that everything really is so, and that on the condition that the subjects recognize what they are and behave accordingly, everything will be all right. Therefore, the vast majority of "good" individuals internalize the ideology and are inserted into practices governed by the rituals of the ideological apparatuses. The individual is therefore "free," author of and responsible for his actions, but is at the same time subjected to an ideology that acts as a higher authority. The individual is stripped of all freedom except that of accepting his submission. "The individual is interpolated as a (free) subject in order that he shall submit freely to the commandments of the Subject, i.e., in order that he shall (freely) accept his subjugation. . . . There are no subjects except by and for their subjugation" (1971, 169).

With this theory of ideology, Althusser constructs a mechanism by which individuals willingly subject themselves to an ideology (Gramsci's hegemonic "consensus"), and it is this subjugation that defines them in the society itself. Inherent in the ideology is the necessary ignorance of the reality that the ideology represents, and this reality is, in the last resort, the reproduction of the relations of production and of the relations deriving from them (1971, 170).

This position could not be more anti-existentialist. Rather than an individual who defines himself or herself through individual acts and the assumption of responsibility for those acts, Althusser's subject is *defined* by subjugation to the ruling ideology, by placing himself willingly into the context of the ideological apparatuses and having his freedom defined by those apparatuses. Sartre's existential freedom is, according to Althusser, a totally *conditional* freedom, conditioned by a ruling structure of relations and thought. This structure is internalized by the *good* subjects, with its real meaning hidden to them. Individual definition through conditioned acts means, of course, that existential freedom does not define history, but is limited by it in a structured way.

Althusser goes one step further: he argues that the ideological apparatuses are not the realization of ideology *in general*, nor even the conflict-free realization of the ideology of the ruling class. "The ideology of the ruling class does not become the ruling ideology by the grace of God, nor even by virtue of the seizure of state power alone. It is by the installation of the ideological state apparatuses in which this ideology is realized itself that it becomes the ruling ideology" (1971, 185).

The installation of the ideological State apparatuses, in turn, is the stake in the class struggle. It is the victory of the ruling class in the ideological State apparatuses that permits their ideology to be installed in the apparatuses. Once this ideology is installed, we have seen that Althusser has it take on the attributes of an ideology *in general*, and in that sense the individual in his actions is no longer the point of reference for understanding the functioning of society, but rather the individual is a subject, defined in terms of the ideological apparatuses and their practices.

Now that we have discussed the construct of ideology *in general* in Althusser's analysis, and seen that this focus on ideology and superstructure argues that the reproduction of the relations of production takes place through ideology that, in the capitalist mode of production, is *in the last instance* carried out in the context of class struggle, we can turn to Althusser's analysis of the ideological State apparatuses in that model.

Althusser makes four main points in his essay. First, every social formation (such as capitalism) must reproduce the conditions of its production at the same time that it produces, in order to be able to produce. That is, for feudalism or capitalism or socialism to function as such, it must reproduce the productive forces—the land, labor, capital, and knowledge that enter into production *and* the existing relations of production that are inherent in that production system—the hierarchy of power and control among landowners and serfs (feudalism), capitalists and labor (capitalism), or directors or party officials and workers (socialism). "As Marx said, every child knows that a social formation which did not reproduce the conditions of production at the same time as it produced would not last a year" (Althusser 1971, 127).

These productive forces, Althusser suggests, are not reproduced at the level of firm but at the level of *class*. For example, in capitalism, the capitalist class, as a class, reproduces labor power by paying workers wages with which they can feed themselves and raise the next generation of workers. The level of wages paid is determined by class struggle over the length of the working day and the hourly wage. But workers have to be reproduced as more than just homogeneous workers. They have to be "diversely skilled and therefore reproduced as such" (1971, 131). This diversity is defined by the sociotechnical division of labor—its different jobs and positions.

The second point of Althusser's essay concerns how the reproduction of the division of labor and skills is carried out under capitalism. Here Althusser discusses an issue left obscure by Marx and Engels, who treated labor as "homogeneous" (undifferentiated) except in terms of Engels's conception of an "aristocracy" of the working class, paid off by capitalists as a means to divide workers against themselves. Althusser argues that unlike social formations characterized by slavery or serfdom, this reproduction of the skills of labor power tends "decreasingly to be provided for 'on the spot' (apprenticeship within production itself), but is achieved more and more outside production: by the capitalist education system, and by other instances and institutions'' (1971, 132).

Reproduction here is not the same issue that Gramsci and also Althusser, below, raise about the function of education (schooling) in reproducing the *relations* of production (the norms, values, and conception of society). Rather, in this instance, Althusser brings education into the reproduction of the division of labor—the development of particular production skills for particular people. As we shall discuss in more detail below, this ''know-how'' is divided into different categories for students according to their different future roles as workers; furthermore, the schools also teach different children different rules of behavior depending on the type of job that they are likely to hold. Thus, ''the reproduction of labor power reveals as its *sine qua non* not only the reproduction of its 'skills' but also the reproduction of its subjection to the ruling ideology or of the 'practice' of that ideology, with the provision that it is not enough to say 'not only but also' for it is clear that *it is in the forms of ideological subjection that provision is made for the reproduction of the skills of labor power*'' (1971 133).

Now, what about the reproduction of the *relations* in production? How is this reproduction secured? As the third point of his essay, Althusser answers: ''I can say: for the most part, it is secured by the legal-political and ideological superstructure.'' Furthermore, he argues that again ''for the most part, it is secured by the exercise of State power in the State Apparatuses, on the one hand the (Repressive) State Apparatus, on the other the Ideological State Apparatus'' (1971, 148). He says ''for the most part'' because the existing relations of production are first reproduced by the reward and punishment system of production itself—by the materiality of the processes of production. But repression and ideology are, of course, present in production.

Althusser's conception of reproducing the relations of production is almost identical to that of Gramsci's hegemony, except that for Althusser the State has a much more important role in reproduction than for Gramsci (''for the most part'' versus the ''first line of trenches''). For Althusser, the State attains an overwhelmingly important position relative to the effects on reproduction of the production system itself and its related ''private'' institutions, both in the reproduction of labor power (not discussed by Gramsci) and in reproducing the *relations* of production. And the most important single institution in the State used to carry out these two types of reproduction is the school:

This reproduction of the skills of labor power . . . is achieved more and more outside production: by the capitalist educational system. (1971, 132)

I believe that the ideological State apparatus which has been installed in the *dominant* position in mature capitalist formations as a result of a violent political and ideological class struggle against the old dominant ideological State apparatus, is the educational ideological apparatus. (1971, 152)

Like Gramsci, Althusser roots superstructure in structure. The superstructure is determined "in the last instance" by the base: "The upper floors (the superstructure) could not 'stay up' (in the air) alone, if they did not rest precisely on their base" (1971, 135). He goes on to say that the determination of the superstructure by the base "in the last instance" is thought of by the Marxist tradition in two ways: (1) there is relative autonomy of the superstructure with respect to the base and (2) there is reciprocal action of the superstructure on the base—changes in the superstructure affect the base, as well as the more traditional concept that changes in the base affect the superstructure.

The State, then, is rooted in the base. It is, in the fourth point of Althusser's essay, also the "machine" of repression, which "enables the ruling classes to ensure their domination over the working class, thus enabling the former to subject the latter to the process of surplus-value extortion" (1971, 137). He therefore returns initially to the original Marxist conception of the State as the "essential point": "The State apparatus, which defines the State as a force of repressive execution and intervention 'in the interests of the ruling classes' in the class struggle conducted by the bourgeoisie and its allies against the proletariat, is quite certainly the State, and quite certainly defines its basic 'function' " (ibid.). Althusser also argues that Marx's conception of the separation of State power and the State apparatus is correct; the State apparatus can survive intact even with a change in State power (i.e., a change in the class that holds State power). The objective of class struggle concerns State power and the use of the State apparatus for class objectives; thus, in the Marxist-Leninist tradition, the proletariat must seize State power in order to destroy the bourgeois State apparatus, replace it with a proletarian State apparatus, and then destroy the State—the famous withering away of the State (the end of State power and of every State apparatus).

To this traditional conception, Althusser adds Gramsci's contribution of the ideological State apparatuses (ISAs). The repressive State apparatus contains the government, the administration, the army, the police, the courts, the prisons, etc., all of which "function by violence," at least ultimately. The ISAs are defined as the religious ISA (the system of churches), the educational ISA, the family ISA, which is also responsible for the reproduction of labor power, the legal ISA, which also belongs to the repressive State apparatus, the political ISA (the political system including the different parties), the trade union ISA, the communications ISA (press, radio, television), and the cultural ISA (1971, 143).

The differences between the ISAs and the repressive apparatus hinge on the singularity of the repressive apparatus versus the plurality of the ISAs—the repressive apparatus is entirely public, it is "unified" (although Althusser does not deal with the possibility of conflicts and contradictions within the repressive apparatus), while much of the ISA is private—churches, political parties, trade unions, families, private schools, newspapers, etc. What, Althusser asks, do the private ideological apparatuses have to do with the State? He relies on Gramsci for the answer: "The distinction between the public and the private is a distinction internal to bourgeois law, and valid in the (subordinate) domains in which bourgeois law exercises its 'authority' . . . [T]he State, which is the State *of* the ruling class, is neither public nor private; to the contrary, it is the precondition for any distinction between public and private" (Althusser 1971, 144). It is unimportant then whether the ISAs are public or private; it is their *function* that matters; it is what they do and for whom they do it. In a sense this is the same point brought out by Galbraith (1973): the planning sector is undifferentiated as to State or private, except as defined by law.

Furthermore, although both the repressive State apparatus and ISAs contain repressive and ideological elements, the former functions "massively and predominantly" by repression while functioning secondarily by ideology. Even the army and police use ideology to "ensure their own cohesion and reproduction" (Althusser 1971, 145). The ISAs, on the other hand, function primarily by ideology and secondarily by repression: even the churches and schools use repressive punishment systems, disciplining "not only their shepherds, but their flocks" (ibid.).

In developing the nature of the ISAs, Althusser falls back on Gramsci: the diversity of the ISAs is unified beneath the ruling ideology, and "no class can hold State power over a long period without at the same time exercising its hegemony over and in the State Ideological Apparatuses" (1971, 146). Control of these ISAs, however, is not only necessary for the class trying to hold power, but is necessary in the face of the ISAs as a site of class struggle. As Gramsci pointed out, the superstructure—the hegemonic apparatus—controlled by the ruling class, also gives rise to a counterhegemony. In Althusser's terms,

> The class (or class alliance) in power cannot lay down the law in the ISAs as easily as it can in the (repressive) State apparatus, not only because the former ruling classes are able to retain strong positions there for a long time, but also because the resistance of the exploited classes is able to find means and occasions to express itself there, either by the

utilization of their contradictions, or by conquering combat positions in them in struggle. (1971, 147)

Control of the State apparatus, therefore, is useful for the class in power insofar as it permits that class to use the repressive apparatus to enforce the law (a body of law that exists or is altered to fit the needs of the class in power), and insofar as it is able to exercise its hegemony through the ISAs. Althusser agrees totally with Gramsci that the State apparatus without hegemony means a State without long-term power, even if those who control the State apparatus also control the repressive apparatus. In this sense, he (like Gramsci) shifts attention to the possibility of contesting State power (and therefore the power of the ruling class) not through the contesting of the repressive State apparatus (war of maneuver or frontal strategy) with a counterforce based on *violence*, but through the development of a counter-ideology, an ideology that becomes so pervasive among the subordinate classes that it destroys the ideological hegemony of the ruling groups, thereby (according to this analysis) making it impossible for these groups to rule in the long term. This means—in Gramscian terms—*surrounding* the State.

NICOS POULANTZAS: THE ORGANIC RELATION BETWEEN STATE AND BASE

Althusser's structuralist reading of Marx was first applied to an investigation of the State by Nicos Poulantzas. Unlike Althusser, Poulantzas makes his central focus social classes and politics rather than Marxist theory as a whole. Yet, if we accept the Gramscian proposition that superstructure has a prominent place in understanding social structure and change, Poulantzas's studies of the State encompass most of the crucial elements in a theory of society.

Poulantzas's principal contribution to the debate on the capitalist State is his analysis of the State in relation to class struggle. His work focuses on the nature of social classes, the role of the State in shaping and defining class conflict, and the effect of this conflict on the State itself. Out of this analysis, we find a State that is inserted in and defined by class relations (the "structures" of capitalist society), at the same time that it is a factor of cohesion and regulation of the social system in which it functions.

However, Poulantzas's theories changed significantly between the publication in France of *Political Power and Social Classes* in 1968 (translation published 1974), and *State, Power, Socialism* in 1978 (translation published 1980). The early work was definitely structuralist. In it, the State reproduces the class structure because it is an articulation of economic class relations in the political "region." The State's form and function is therefore shaped by the structure of class relations. In this early work, Poulantzas also argues that although there is no all-encompassing theory like the Hegelian ideal, transcendental State. The State is *specific to the mode of production*—for example, the capitalist State, the feudal State, and so forth. Moreover, in *Political Power and Social Classes*, he uses Althusser's concept of the "relative autonomy" of politics and economics to argue that the capitalist State is at once a class State and must also be relatively autonomous from the class struggle in production to function effectively as a class State. But the relatively autonomous State serves as the site of the hegemonic group's organization of the fractionated *capitalist class*. Labor's struggle only shapes the State insofar as it is part of class relations in production.

In his later work, Poulantzas abandons the structuralist State for a State shaped by class struggle itself. As early as 1973, Poulantzas argued that there is a different relation between social classes and the State, depending on the *stage* of capitalist development. So changes in capitalist relations of production shape political institutions; the "structure" of the capitalist State is not a "structure" at all, but rather apparatuses shaped by class struggle and by corresponding changes in capitalist production. In *State, Power, Socialism* ([1978] 1980), the "relative autonomy" of the State is made dialectic: there is the possibility of class struggle within the State apparatuses because of the very contradictions inherent in "autonomy." It is these contradictions and the role of social movements in shaping the State that become important in the latest works.

Thus, Poulantzas's State becomes much more than the site of the dominant group's organization of dominant-class power. The State is more than the unifier of capitalist-class fractions and individualizer/isolator of the working class. It is, in this last work, a site of class conflict where political power is contested: the State, for Poulantzas in 1978, is shaped by struggles in production and *within the State*. Yet he retains his notion of the class State and its origins. We will therefore begin with this earlier version of the State theory and then show how it changed to its present form.

EARLY POULANTZAS

Poulantzas argues in *Political Power and Social Classes* ([1968] 1974) that the capitalist State is *part* of class relations in production. Specifically, in capitalist production, the separation of the direct producer from his means of production does not lead to his individualization and isolation per se, but rather to a *socialization* of productive forces (labor) and to a concentration of capital. The political separation (isolation) of workers from each other (preventing class cohesion) is *not* the result of capitalist production itself, but of the juridical-political superstructure of the capitalist State.

It is in production that the *structure* of the labor process is determined. It is the separation of the direct producers from the means of production that determines the "setting-up of agents as juridico-political subjects, *in that it impresses a determinate structure on the labor process*" (1974, 129). This determines their class relation. The State here is an *activist*: within this determined structure, the State individualizes and personalizes workers, preventing class struggle.

For Poulantzas, then, the process of capitalist production—in the civil society—defines the formation of classes. But it is the State that redefines workers and capitalists politically into individual subjects as we observe them in capitalist society. The "absence" of cohesive classes, particularly a cohesive working class, is therefore a result not of the separation of labor from its tools and product, but of a juridical political apparatus that individualizes workers.

He contends that in the last instance, the juridical and ideological structures are determined *by the labor process*. They change the nature of the class struggle by intervening to conceal from the newly created individual-subjects (agents of production) that their relations are class relations (1974, 130).

> This effect of isolation is *terrifyingly real*: it has a name: *competition* between the wage earning workers and between the capitalist owners of private property. It is in fact only an ideological conception of the capitalist relations of production which conceives them as commercial encounters between individuals/agents of production on the market. But competition is far from designating the *structure of capitalist relations of production*: it consists precisely in the effect of the juridical and the ideological on *socio-economic relations* . . . [this relation] conceals from the agents of production their class relations in the economic struggle. (1974, 130-131)

This point is crucial to Poulantzas's early and later analysis: it is the State that isolates workers and capitalists into "individuals,"[2] not the class-structured capitalistic production (which inherently moves both capitalist and workers to class identification). Competition is developed among mem-

---

[2] Of course, competition among capitalists in production already isolates and individualizes them. But the capitalist State's juridical apparatus ostensibly prevents official collusion among them. Claus Offe argues that the State does quite the opposite: it organizes the class project for inherently competitive (in production) individual capitalists (see Chapter 5 below).

bers of the same class by the juridical-political apparatuses of the State, while those same apparatuses diffuse the inherent conflict *between* production-based classes by "concealing the class relation." The capitalist State appears as the political *unity* of an economic struggle. The State presents itself as representing the "general interest" of competing groups— it is the national-popular class State.

If the State tends to diffuse class conflict between inherently hostile economic classes (workers and capitalists) by isolating people as individuals and then reunifying them as the popular nation-State, how, according to Poulantzas, does the capitalist class come to dominate the State? Since Poulantzas claims that the State promotes competition among individuals through its juridical-political apparatus, how do the competing capitalists come to use the State for their own purposes against the equally individualized working class? For it is precisely this (in early Poulantzas) that the capitalist class comes to do. Poulantzas calls this the *political class struggle* (1974, 136). He argues that the political struggle is *relatively autonomous* from the economic struggle—it has to be, in order to conceal class relations in the economic struggle from the agents of production. Yet it tends to constitute *class unity* for the capitalist class out of the isolation of the economic struggle, a class unity that serves the reproduction of economic class relations. In other words, the State allows for the unity of the individualized capitalists, and their dominant (economic) class is able "by means of a whole political-ideological operation of its own," (1974, 137) to constitute its strictly political interests as representative of the people-nation, an ideological construct intended to encompass members of different social classes as individuals stripped of their class identity.

This is the principal problematic for Poulantzas's early work: once economic struggle is mediated in the particular way outlined by the State, the relatively autonomous political struggle itself is dominated by the dominant class(es). In order to explain how this happens, Poulantzas relies on Gramsci's concept of hegemony, and on Althusser's ideological apparatuses. Hegemony indicates, for Poulantzas, (a) how the political interests of the dominant class become constituted as representative of the "general interest" of the body politic, and (b) how the fractions of the dominant class can compose themselves into a "power bloc," which reunifies competitive capitals into a dominant class and "controls" the State. For this State, according to early Poulantzas, "presents this peculiar feature, that nowhere in its actual institutions does strictly political domination take the form of a political relation between the dominant class fractions and the dominated classes. In its institutions everything takes place as if the class 'struggle' did not exist" (1974, 188).

Gramsci, Poulantzas argues, introduces a theoretical break between hegemony and domination (see Chapter 3 above). A class can and must become the leading class ideologically before it can become a politically dominant class. It wins hegemony before it conquers political power. Hegemony is a world view that is imposed on a social formation and gains ideological domination *before* the conquest of political power. In that sense power is separated from hegemony, and the political organization of a class is apparently related to the elaboration of a world view that it imposes on the ensemble of society—all this in contrast with the position that a class cannot gain ideological domination before conquering political power.

But Poulantzas contends that Gramsci's formulation (as interpreted by Poulantzas) is not correct. It is here that Poulantzas is at his most Althusserian: a given ideology cannot be separated from the unity of the structure in which it is manifested, and this structure has the domination of a given class as its effect in the field of class struggle. In other words, ideology cannot be separated from the dominance of a given class.

> The dominant ideology, by assuring the practical insertion of agents in the social structure, aims at the maintenance (the cohesion) of the structure, and this means *above all* class domination and exploitation. It is precisely in this way that within a social formation ideology is dominated by the ensemble of representations, values, notions, beliefs, etc. by means of which class domination is perpetuated: in other words it is dominated by what can be called the ideology of the dominant class. (Poulantzas 1974, 209)

Ideology, then, is part of the class struggle, the relation within which class domination functions. That is why the dominated classes necessarily experience their relation to the conditions of existence within the overall framework of the dominant ideology, and the dominant ideology does not necessarily represent only values and norms of the dominant class. Further, the dominant ideology is not necessarily isomorphic with the ideology of the dominant class. But the fact that a certain class is dominant in the class struggle makes the dominant ideology serve that class in the political region (the State), and therefore enables the class to use the dominant ideology as a manifestation of its class power.

One of the particular characteristics of the dominant bourgeois ideology is, according to Poulantzas, the fact that it conceals class exploitation in a specific manner, "to the extent that all trace of class domination is systematically absent from its language" (1974, 214). This specific masking of class domination, combined with the particular role of cohesion that the bourgeois ideology plays under the dominance of the juridical-political system that is part of that ideology, is reflected in the close relation between ideology and the capitalist State. The particular power of this interrelation is that individuals do not seem to be able in one and the same theoretical movement to be unified *and* to attain their social existence, except by means of gaining political existence in the State. Thus, through hegemony, the hegemonic-class leadership is able to present itself as incarnating the general interest of the people-nation and at the same time to condition the dominated classes to a specific political acceptance of their domination. Ideology, by hiding the class relationship and subsequent exploitation implicit in the ideology of individualization and reunification of the nation-State, therefore enables the dominant class to reproduce social relations in such a way that it remains dominant. In other words, ideology *legitimates* the existence and functioning of a class State.

Yet, what about competition between members and subgroups of the dominant classes? How is this competition resolved to produce the translation of dominant ideology into dominant-class power? Poulantzas argues that the relationship between the capitalist State and the dominant classes or fractions pushes them "toward *their political unity under the protection of a hegemonic class or fraction. The hegemonic class or fraction polarizes* the specific contradictory interests of the various classes or fraction of the power blocs by making its own economic interests into political interests and by representing the general common interests of the classes or fractions of the power bloc. This general interest consists of economic exploitation and political domination" (1974, 239).

What is interesting in Poulantzas's formulation is that the hegemonic class or fraction may be in charge of the State, but a class or fraction may be in charge of the State without thereby being hegemonic. Even more, the ruling class or fraction may not only not be hegemonic but even on occasion may not be part of the power bloc. He cites the example of certain social democratic governments in France where the petite bourgeoisie was neither hegemonic nor a part of the power bloc, but was the ruling class—that is, it controlled the State. "In this case the characteristic dislocation between this class and its party representation is generally found: its party plays the role of 'clerk' with a hegemonic class or fraction or even for another class or fraction in the power bloc. The same holds true for the class in charge of the state" (1974, 251).

Within the context of the dominant ideology, then, the power bloc is the political expression of the different fractions of the dominant class. It is through the power bloc that these different fractions are unified to rule; nevertheless, its function is to translate the dominant ideology into concrete action. It is through the power bloc that ideology is transformed into a series of material practices, customs, and morals, which act as cement in the ensemble of social, political, and economic relations. The dominant ideology is thus incorporated into the State apparatuses, which elaborate,

inculcate, and reproduce this ideology. This role is crucial for the reproduction of the social division of labor, social classes, and the domination
of society by a particular class.

In his early work Poulantzas sees the State as being autonomous from
the civil society because of the necessity of isolating workers from the
class consciousness developed in the civil society. The State is autonomous
in the sense that although characterized by hegemonic-class leadership,
the State does not directly represent the dominant classes' economic interests, but rather their political interests: the State is the dominant classes'
political power center as the organizing agent of their political struggle.
The State functions to organize dominant classes and reduce competition
among them, while it increases competition among the dominated classes,
isolating each member of the dominated classes into his or her individual
space, but maintaining its legitimacy in the eyes of the dominated classes
by claiming to be a unifying force and representing mass interests.

In this formulation, the State is not a place of class struggle, but rather
a *product* and a *shaper* of class struggle in the civil society. The dominated
classes have very little influence over the structure and operation of the
State. This equilibrium of political power really does not indicate any sort
of *equivalence* of power among the forces present. (This meaning of
equilibrium must not be confused with Marx and Engels's conception of
autonomy, in the situation where no class has enough power to control the
State.) The equilibrium at issue in early Poulantzas is related to the dislocation of relations of power in the framework of the capitalist State and
the relations of forces in the field of economic struggles within the limits
set by political power. The State is autonomous vis-à-vis the economy: it
is possible to have a social policy that profits certain dominated classes
but also makes it possible to cut into the dominant classes' economic power
without ever threatening their political power. So, although it is true that
the political and economic struggles of the dominated classes impose a
guarantee to protect the economic interests of certain members of those
classes, this is not in any way a constraint on the political power of the
dominant classes:

> The notion of the general interest of the 'people,' an ideological notion
> covering an institutional operation of the capitalist State, expresses a
> *real fact*: namely that this State by its very structure, gives to the eco-
> nomic interests of certain dominated classes guarantees which may even
> be contrary to the short term economic interests of the dominant classes,
> but which are compatible with their political interests and their heg-
> emonic domination.

This brings us to a very simple conclusion but one which cannot be too often repeated. This guarantee given by the capitalist State to the economic interests of certain dominated classes cannot be seen *per se* as restraint on the *political power* of the dominant classes. It is true that the political and *economic struggles of the dominated classes* impose this on the capitalist State. However, this simply shows that the State is not a class instrument, but rather the state of its society divided into classes. The class struggle and capitalist formations entails that this guarantee of the economic interests of certain dominated classes is inscribed *as a possibility* within the very limits imposed by the State on the struggle for hegemonic class leadership. But in making this guarantee, the State aims precisely at the political disorganization of the dominated classes; in the formation where the strictly political struggle of the dominated classes is possible it is the sometimes indispensable means of maintaining the dominant classes in hegemony. In other words, according to the concrete conjuncture a line of demarcation can always be drawn within which the guarantee given by the capitalist State to the dominated class' economic interests not only fails to threaten the political relation of class domination but even constitutes an element of this relation. (Poulantzas 1974, 190-191)

THE MILIBAND-POULANTZAS DEBATE

There have been a number of critiques of Poulantzas' early work, both as a structuralist (see the discussion of the German ''derivationists'' in Chapter 5) and as a functionalist (Clarke, 1977). The best known discussion, however, at least to English-speaking readers, took place in the pages of the *New Left Review* in 1969-1970 (with a later contribution by Poulantzas in 1976), in the form of an exchange between Ralph Miliband and Poulantzas. Ostensibly, the discussion centered on Miliband's book *The State in Capitalist Society* (1969). In that work Miliband both attacks pluralist models of the State and presents his version of a Marxist interpretation of the State's role in reproducing capitalist-class society. This is not the place to go into Miliband's views in detail; they will be discussed more adequately when we deal with American Marxist analysts of the State in Chapter 8. But it is important to note that while the Miliband-Poulantzas discussion has been characterized as a debate between ''instrumentalism'' and ''structuralism'' (Gold, Lo, and Wright 1975), it is a mistake to view Miliband as an instrumentalist—as developing a theory of the State that has the State acting as a *direct* instrument of the ruling class. The debate between Poulantzas and Miliband can be more accurately described in terms of the issues of: (1) method, and (2) the individual as a source of change versus the individual as determined by structure.

On the first issue, Poulantzas criticizes Miliband's work by arguing that Miliband chooses to reply directly to bourgeois ideologies by the "immediate examination of concrete fact. . . . Not that I am against the study of the 'concrete'; on the contrary, having myself relatively neglected this aspect of the question in my own work (with a somewhat different aim and object), I am only the more conscious of the necessity for concrete analyses. I simply mean that a precondition of any scientific approach to the 'concrete' is to make explicit the epistemological principles of its own treatment of it" (Poulantzas 1969, 69).

It is here that Poulantzas states the overall structuralist (Althusserian) position most clearly: he contends that in contesting the notion of plural elites fundamental to bourgeois theory, Miliband should have rejected the very notion of elite. He should have moved "outside" the individual-oriented, empiricist epistemology of bourgeois political science. "For concepts and notions are never innocent, and by employing the notions of the adversary to reply to him, one legitimizes them and permits their persistence. Every notion or concept only has meaning within a whole theoretical problematic that founds it: extract it from this problematic and imported 'uncritically' into Marxism, they have absolutely uncontrollable effects" (Poulantzas 1969, 70).

Poulantzas claims that this methodological error is manifested in Miliband's difficulty in comprehending social classes and the State as *objective structures*, and "their relations as an *objective system of regular connections*, a structure and a system whose agents, 'men,' are in the words of Marx, 'bearers' of it . . . Miliband constantly gives the impression that for him social classes or 'groups' are in some way reducible to *interpersonal relations*" (ibid.).

Poulantzas therefore correctly argues that epistemology, method, and results cannot be separated. How does Miliband respond to this? He launches an essential critique of structuralism. He grants that *The State in Capitalist Society* may be insufficiently theoretical in the sense that Poulantzas demands, but he also thinks that Poulantzas's approach (i.e., structuralism) is "so profoundly concerned with the elaboration of an appropriate 'problematic' and with the avoidance of any contamination with opposed 'problematics,' as to lose sight of the absolute necessity of empirical inquiry, and of the empirical demonstration of the falsity of these opposed and apologetic 'problematics' " (Miliband 1970, 55). Miliband insists that a study of the concrete, which Poulantzas so carefully avoids, is a necessity for any demystification of bourgeois theory.

On the second issue of the debate—Poulantzas's view that Miliband puts undue emphasis on the direct participation of members of the capitalist

class in the State apparatus and government as a means of showing that
the State is tied to bourgeois interests and is an expression of them—
Poulantzas argues that the relation between the bourgeois class and the
State is an *objective relation*. "This means that if the function of the State
in a determinant social formation and the *interests* of the dominant class
in this formation *coincide*, it is by reason of the system itself: the direct
participation of members of the ruling class in the State apparatus is not
the *cause* but the *effect* and moreover a chance and contingent one of this
objective coincidence" (Poulantzas 1969, 73).

Miliband counters by arguing that Poulantzas's *exclusive* stress on objective relations suggests that "what the State does is in every particular
and at all times *wholly* determined by these 'objective relations': in other
words that the structural constraints of the system are so absolutely com-
pelling as to turn those who run the State into the merest functionaries and
executants of policies imposed upon them by the 'system' " (1970, 57).

For Miliband, all this seems to do is to substitute the notion of objective
structures and objective relations for the notion of ruling class, and that
Poulantzas's analysis seems to lead straight toward "a kind of structural
determinism, or rather a structural super-determinism, which makes impossible a truly realistic consideration of the dialectic relations between
the State and the system" (1970, 57). The relationship between the ruling
class and the system, according to Miliband, is much more complex than
this determination by the "objective relations" allows. If the objective
relations entirely determine the functioning of the State bureaucracy, then,
according to Miliband, it follows that there is really no difference between
a State ruled by bourgeois constitutionalists or one ruled by fascists.

The significance of the "debate" is that it poses very clearly Poulantzas's
position at the time and the most important objections to it. The "instrumentalism" versus "structuralism" aspect of the debate with which it has
been labeled, is, in fact, a misreading of the main points being made.
Rather, Poulantzas's structuralism is posed as a scientific method against
Miliband's empiricism, and the State, as conditioned by the structures of
the relation of production and the class struggle inherent in those relations
of production, is posed against Miliband's view that the ruling economic
class finds its political expression directly in the apparatus of the State.
Both writers criticize each other's brand of determinism. Both are probably
correct; neither *The State in Capitalist Society* nor *Political Power and
Social Classes* presents us with a dialectical analysis of the relationship
between the State and civil society, even though both works *hint* at such
a dialectical relationship. Poulantzas, for example, sees in the unifying
function of the State a principal contradiction:

Its principal contradiction is not so much that it 'calls' itself the State of all the people, although it is in fact a class State, but that, strictly speaking, it presents itself in its very institutions as a single 'class' State (i.e., the State of the dominant classes which it helps to organize politically), of a society which is institutionally fixed as one not-divided-into-classes; in that it presents itself as a State of the bourgeois class, implying that all 'people' are part of this class. (1974, 189)

Miliband, when all has been said about the limits and contingent character of civic and political liberties under bourgeois democracy in his analysis, argues that many liberties have indeed been an important part of the landscape of advanced capitalist societies, particularly in the way that they affect the relationship between the dominated classes, the State, and the dominant classes. The point is that some bourgeois freedoms implicitly represent an expression of "power" of dominated classes in bourgeois society, and it is these freedoms that "need to be extended by the radical transformation of the context, economic, social and political, which condemns them to inadequacy and erosion" (Miliband 1973, 239).

It is significant that although neither Miliband nor Poulantzas carried this analysis any further in their earlier work, both had made significant changes in their positions by the late 1970s, Miliband in *Marxism and Politics* (1977), and Poulantzas in *Classes in Contemporary Capitalism* (1975) and *State, Power, and Socialism* ([1978] 1980). In this later work, Poulantzas modifies his earlier construction of the State as being totally autonomous in a civil society because of the necessity of isolating workers from the class-conscious development of civil society. He comes to argue that the State's autonomy is not only couched in the class struggle in the civil society—it not only tries to represent the interests of the dominant classes by mediating the contradictions of that struggle in the civil society, transforming it for individualizing the workers, and legitimating itself through its ideology of unification—but ultimately, in playing that role, *incorporates into its heart the class struggle itself*. Autonomy gives rise to class struggle in the State and the possibility of the dominated classes *taking over* the apparatuses of the State for their own purposes and interfering with the functions of the State reproducing the dominance of the dominant groups. It is here that Poulantzas, much more than in earlier works, relies increasingly on Marx's and Engels's "abnormal" situation, in which the State is analyzed in an instance where no class has enough power to dominate the State. To this, Poulantzas adds the possibility that unlike in the Bonapartist State, the class struggle could ultimately put the State into a position where it acts to modify the relations of production in the civil society.

LATER POULANTZAS: DIALECTICAL STRUCTURALISM

We now turn to a detailed summary of Poulantzas's reformulation of his own work on the capitalist State in the context of class struggle. In this reformulation, he carries forward his concept of the State as both the product and the shaper of objective class relations.

The State and Social Classes

First, he argues that the role of the State apparatuses is "to maintain the unity and cohesion of a social formation by concentrating and sanctioning class domination, and in this way reproducing social relations, i.e. class relations" (1975, 24-25). Political and ideological relations are materialized and embodied, as material practices, in these apparatuses. Furthermore, social classes are *defined* by their relationship to the economic apparatuses—the place of production *and* the State apparatuses. So social classes and the class struggle are part of the economic and political relations in a society: "the apparatuses are never anything other than the materialization and condensation of class relations" (1975, 25). He separates this concept from the institutionalist-functionalist analysis, which has class relations arising from the situation of agents in institutional relationships. Weber, for example, had class relations emerging from relations of power in hierarchical institutions. But Poulantzas contends that State apparatuses do not have "power" of their own—institutions have no "power" as such, nor is power inherent in hierarchical relations. Rather, the State "materializes and concentrates class relations, relations which are precisely what is embraced by the concept 'power.' The State is not an 'entity' with an intrinsic instrumental essence, but is itself a relation, more precisely the condensation of a class relation" (1975, 26). It is therefore not hierarchy that creates classes, but social classes that produce the particular configuration of power in the State apparatus. At the same time, the State apparatus is inherently marked by the class struggle—class struggle and the State apparatus cannot be separated.

The second formulation defines the relationship of the State to the *dominant* class. Since the State apparatuses are the "materialization and condensation of class relations," they attempt, in some form, to represent the interests of the dominant class. Poulantzas describes this representation as two stages of capitalism: one is the competitive stage, and the other, the more recent monopoly capitalism. In both stages, the State is "separated" from the economic structure, giving it the appearance of having relative autonomy from the dominant class. This separation is carried out, according to Poulantzas, as part of the relative separation of the political from the economic that is a specific to capitalism. It derives from the "separation and dispossession of the direct producers from their means of production that characterizes capitalism" (1975, 98). He argues that historically, capitalist ideology has promoted the concept of democracy in the political sphere as a sufficient condition for a mass democratic society. One person-one vote has shifted attention away from the class struggles inherent in capitalist production; political "democracy" has *displaced* the struggle from the economic sphere to the voting booth. In the political arena—including the juridical apparatus—all members of society are equal. Rich and poor, old and young, (ultimately) women and men, all have the same power (one vote) to change or maintain the social situation. The inequality of economic relations is thus downgraded in capitalist society in favor of equality in political life. This diffuses conflict in economic matters, because it diverts such conflict into the political arena, into a contest over power in the State apparatus (1974). As in his earlier work, the State, under these ideological conditions, has to "appear" autonomous and neutral while at the same time keeping the dominated classes fractionalized and representing the interest of the dominant classes' power bloc. Relative autonomy is the necessary condition for the role of the capitalist State in class representation and in the political organization of hegemony. But now, more than in his earlier work, with the displacement of class struggle from the economic to the political arena, the State itself becomes subject to the struggle—it becomes, in Poulantzas's words, "the condensation of a balance of forces":

The correspondence between the state on one hand, which ensures the social formation's cohesion by keeping the struggles that develop within the limits of the mode of production and by reproducing the social relations, and the interests of the hegemonic class or fraction on the other hand, is not established by means of a simple identification or reduction of the state to this fraction. The state is not an instrumental entity existing for itself, it is not a thing, but the condensation of a balance of forces. The correspondence in question is established rather in terms of organization and representation: the hegemonic class or fraction, beyond its immediate economic interests which are of the moment or at least short-term, must undertake to define the overall political interest of the classes and fractions that constitute the power bloc, and thus its own long-term political interest. It must unite itself and the power bloc under its leadership. In Gramsci's profound intuition, it is the capitalist state with all its apparatuses, and not just the bourgeois political parties, that assumes an analogous role, with respect to the power bloc, to that of the working-class party with respect to the popular alliance, the 'people.' (1975, 98)

In monopoly capitalism, the State takes on economic functions that it did not have in the competitive stage. Poulantzas argues that the State has a general economic function even in the competitive stage, but this consists of reproducing the general conditions of the production of surplus value; taxation, factory legislation, customs duties, and the construction of economic infrastructure such as railways all constituted the liberal State's intervention in the economy within the context of the class struggle. In monopoly capitalism, however, the relation of separation between the economic and the political that we described above is modified: the difference between politics and ideology (the conditions of production) and the economic space (the relations of production) becomes much less clear. The State enters directly into the relations of production—into the valorization of capital (1975, 101). Thus, in the monopoly stage of capitalism, the functions of the State are extended directly into production as a result of the crises of capitalist production itself.

It is here that Poulantzas goes "beyond" Althusser and Gramsci on two grounds. First, he argues that we can distinguish certain apparatuses that are part of the State and can be designated "ideological apparatuses of the State," such as the schools and other ideological apparatuses that conserve a "private" juridical character (but are closely allied with the State), such as the Church (private), media (State and private), cultural institutions (State and private), etc. We can also think of a "separate" *repressive* apparatus of the State for analytical purposes. Yet, this conception of distinct ideological and repressive apparatuses can only be descriptive and indicative. It is true that the repressive apparatus has had a *certain manner* of expressing ideology—the exercise of *legitimate* physical violence—but the repressive apparatus has an ideology and is ideologically bound. According to the forms of the State and the phases of capitalist reproduction, certain apparatuses can move from one sphere to another, from the ideological apparatuses to the repressive and vice versa. Poulantzas cites the example of the army which, in certain forms of military dictatorship, becomes directly an ideological-organizational apparatus functioning principally as the political party of the bourgeoisie (1974, 1980). Similarly there is a constant ideological role played by the justice system, the penal system, and the police. Thus, the ideological and repressive functions and apparatuses of the capitalist State are often difficult to separate.

Second, and more important, however, Poulantzas claims that the conception of the ideological and repressive roles of the State as developed by Gramsci and systematized by Althusser rest on the presupposition that the State only acts, only functions, by repression and ideological inculcation. That is, the State only acts *negatively* as a preventer, excluder, controller, etc. This conception:

considers the economy as a self-reproducible, self-regulating instance, where the State only serves to pose *negative rules* of the economic "game." Political power is not present in the economy, it only frames it; it isn't engaged in its own positive way because it only exists to prevent (by its repression and ideology) disturbing interferences. (1978, 33; my translation)

To analyze the State solely with the categories of repression-prohibition and ideology-mystification necessarily leads one to *subjectivize* the reasons for consent (by the masses) . . . and to situate these reasons either in ideology (in the sense that the State fools and cheats the masses) or in the wish for repression and love of the Master. (1978, 35; my translation)

Poulantzas cannot agree that the State acts only negatively; to the contrary, he contends that the State is engaged at the heart of the capitalist reproduction process: "the State also acts in a positive fashion, *creating, transforming and making* reality" (1980, 30). The economic functions of the State simply cannot be captured in the ideological-repressive dichotomy—these are not preventive actions, but the development of positive alternatives to other possibilities, possibilities that could have serious negative implications for the reproduction of capitalist production.[3]

He concludes, then, that Gramsci's formulation of the State's political space in terms of the repressive and ideological apparatuses *did* enlarge the State's sphere of operations, *did* include a series of apparatuses—often private—in the dominant class's hegemonic apparatus, and *did* insist on the ideological action of the State, but it restricted this sphere to negative actions, leaving us with a very *restrictive* notion of the State, one in which the actions of the State are unidirectional and in which the State apparatus itself contains no conflict or contradictions.

Poulantzas extends Gramsci's concept of a State that is part of the (ideological) hegemony of the dominant class plus the repressive apparatus. Poulantzas's concept carries on both of these functions in the context of a class struggle (therefore the State is part of and the result of the class struggle)—and plays an economic role in reproducing the general conditions of the relations of production. And in the monopoly phase of capitalist development, the State enters directly into production itself *as part of its reproductive role.*

---

[3] This analysis disagrees completely with Buci-Glucksmann's concept of Gramsci's State as an active *expander* of dominant-class power (see "Hegemony and the State" in Chapter 3 above).

The State and Class Struggle

In his last book ([1978] 1980) before his untimely death, Poulantzas expanded these two major formulations of the State as product and shaper of objective class relations into a detailed analysis of the capitalist State. He develops the concept of the "separation" of the political and economic spheres through the State into four parts: the division of manual and intellectual work, individualization, the law, and the nation. These he sees as the major elements in the State's functioning to displace the class struggle from the economic to the political arena. Before going on to explore these elements in detail, it is worth noting again that class structure and the class struggle for Poulantzas are the fundamental definers of relations in a society. Political power, even though founded on economic power, is primary in the sense that its transformation conditions all change in other areas of power (here he agrees with Gramsci), and political power is concentrated and materialized in the State, the central point of the exercise of political power (1978, 49). Thus, the apparatuses of the State are not simply appendices of power—the State is "organically present in the generation of class powers" (1980, 45). (It is here that he is in total *disagreement* with the concept of power as developed by Foucault—e.g., see Foucault 1978.) Note also that Poulantzas answers the question of why the bourgeoisie chose the representative, national-popular, modern State for the expression of its political power by arguing that this particular kind of State most successfully separates the worker from the struggle over the means of production and hence most successfully reproduces capitalist relations in production. Thus, the State is neither just "political" nor just juridical in the sense that it reproduces or enforces the legal bases of capitalist exchange. Rather, it is fundamental to the conditions under which the bourgeoisie can accumulate and control capital, displacing struggle and conflict to the political from the economic sphere. What are the details of this separation?

The division of knowledge and power. Capitalist production, Poulantzas points out, is marked by a social division of labor that separates intellectual work from manual work by a separation of technology from the process of work itself, by the use of science and technology to *rationalize* power, and by an organic relation between this separated intellectual work and political domination—a relation between knowledge and power. The State incorporates this division into all of its apparatuses. "It is within the capitalist State that the organic relationship between intellectual labour and political domination, knowledge and power, is realized in the most consummate manner" (1980, 56). This State is the corollary and the product of this division, also playing its own role in the division's constitution and reproduction.

These apparatuses . . . imply precisely the setting up and control of knowledge and discourse (whether directly invested in the dominant ideology or erected out of dominant ideological formations from which the popular masses are excluded). . . . It is the permanent monopolization of knowledge by this scientist-State, by its apparatuses and its agents, which also determines the organizational functions and the direction of the State, functions which are centralized in their specific separation from the masses. . . . It is equally evident that a series of institutions of representative democracy—that is indirect democracy—(political parties, parliament, etc.), in brief, institutions of the relations between the State and the masses, arise from the same mechanism. (1978, 61-62; my translation)

The State takes knowledge and participates in its transformation into language and rituals that serve to separate knowledge from mass consumption and from manual work—from the process of direct production. This legitimizes a particular ideology—the dominant bourgeois values and norms—by changing that juridical-political ideology into a set of technocratic "facts" and decisions based on "scientific" studies, on "expertise," etc. But, Poulantzas argues, the knowledge-power relation is not only an ideological legitimization: the capitalist separation of intellectual from manual work also concerns science itself. The State incorporates science into its mechanisms of power—intellectual "experts" as a body of specialists and professionals are controlled through their financial dependence. They have largely become functionaries, in one form or another, of the State. For example, in the United States, a very high percentage of *all* professionals (about 30 percent) are directly employed by federal, state, or local government (many in education), while another 20 percent depend indirectly on State expenditures for their livelihood (e.g., on defense or research contracts in private universities). Research is heavily influenced by such government contracts, and they also have an important effect on new technology.

The State not only has an important hold on the generation of new knowledge in the society, but also on how that knowledge is used. Poulantzas argues that the discussion in the State apparatus—the discussion that is separated from the masses by the relation of power and knowledge—is a discussion of action, of strategy. Knowledge used by the State is part of a strategy for political action within the dominant ideology. It is this discussion that is nourished by the knowledge available to the State through its "experts." The State helps define expertise by financing and employing intellectuals, then uses this expertise in a particular way to reinforce the exclusion of the masses from decision-making while at the same time legitimizing its role as the center of power and decision-making.

Where Poulantzas differs from Gramsci on this point should now be clear. Although Gramsci analyzed the role of intellectuals in the organization of the dominant-class hegemony and recognized that the bourgeoisie was the first class in history that needed, in order to make itself the dominant class, a body of organic intellectuals—intellectuals who helped maintain and extend dominant-class hegemony (for example, the role of Enlightenment philosophers was fundamental to the bourgeois revolutions), Poulantzas puts these intellectuals at the heart of the modern capitalist State itself.[4] It is the State that is crucial to new formations of the division of knowledge and its uses, as well as legitimizing the separation of intellectual work from manual work. It is also in the State where an important part of the strategies for maintenance and expansion of dominant-class hegemony—based on "expertise"—are developed. Furthermore, Poulantzas sees such uses of knowledge—expertise carried out in the State—as part of a class struggle, so State-influenced expertise has to develop strategies of compromise, of how to maintain dominant-class hegemony in the face of subordinate-class demands. How many of these "strategies" and uses of knowledge respond directly to subordinate-class demands depends on the power relations in the society. Poulantzas's point is that one cannot talk about technology or knowledge without talking about power. The process of developing counterhegemony is part of the process of class struggle, including the struggle within the State apparatuses.

Individualization. Through its juridical (legal) system and political ideology, Poulantzas theorized in 1968, the capitalist State isolates both workers and capitalist managers from their antagonistic class-conflict position in production (1974). It considers and treats each member of society as an individual, whether worker or capitalist. This treatment tends to separate both workers and capitalists from their respective production-based social classes. Each individual, whether worker or capitalist or manager, competes in production with other members of his or her class. The State then reunifies these isolated (in the economic sphere) individuals within the political sphere under the aegis of the nation-State. The State claims to represent the collective will of workers and capitalists. Thus, neither the production-based class interests of capitalists nor of workers is supposed to be represented in the workings of the political system. But, in fact, says Poulantzas, the State is not neutral. It functions to keep workers from

---

[4] The situation portrayed here reaches its most extreme levels in the French State, with its intellectual bureaucracy. Nevertheless, to one degree or other, all modern capitalist States incorporate intellectuals, who seem to have an unmitigated desire to be near power.

organizing *politically* as a class (keeps them isolated from their class interests) while it simultaneously helps to bring capitalists and their managers back from their isolated position (an isolation that the State has helped to create) in order to reassert their dominant position through the State.

The "individualization" of class members—their separation from their class by the capitalist State—is a fundamental tenet of Poulantzas's exploration of why the bourgeoisie has chosen the modern, "democratic" State as the expression of its class power. But the earlier version had functionalist overtones, which Poulantzas corrected in his last book ([1978] 1980). In this last version, the individualization of the worker has its roots in the separation of the worker from the means of production in the capitalist mode. This separation—this isolation—that is the basis of the extraction of surplus value by owners of capital and their managers and creates a work force in which individual workers become appendices of machines, also is the basis of the institutional materialism of the capitalist State. In the State apparatus, the division of labor is also based on the atomization of functions. Yet, the State is not only a reflection of the division of labor in the rest of capitalist society; it is a crucial factor in the *organization* of the social division of labor by *reproducing* the social "fractionalization-individualization" inherent in that division. This is part of the ideological apparatus of the State: "This ideology of individualization not only serves to mask and obscure class relations (the capitalist State never presents itself as a class State), but also plays an active part in the divisions and isolation (individualization) of the popular masses" (Poulantzas 1980, 66).

For Poulantzas, then, the individualization and privatization of the society is the result of the exercise of State power, which divides people from their production-based social classes, isolates them, and then reunites them under the aegis of the nation-State—recollectivizes them, as it were, in the image of the State itself. The State refashions individuals, redefines them, homogenizes them, and places them in a new division of labor consistent with the social space as defined by the nation-State. Nevertheless,

if the private individual is not a limitation on, but a channel of the power of the modern State, this does not mean that this power has no real limits; rather, the limits are not defined by the private individual. They arise in popular struggles and in the power relations between the classes, because the State is also the material and specific condensation of a given relationship of forces, which is itself a class relationship. This private individual appears equally as the *result* of this relation of forces, and of its condensation in the State. If private individuals do not have an intrinsic essence that places, as such, absolute external barriers to the power of the State, they do limit this power through being one of the privileged modern representations of the class relationship *within* the State. We are familiar with this limit: it is called representative democracy, which as much as it is truncated by the dominant classes and by the materialism of the State, is nonetheless inscribed at the heart of this materialism, of popular struggle and resistance. If it is not the only limit to State power, it is nonetheless decisive. (Poulantzas 1978, 80; my translation)

The individual is transformed by the State and ceases to be a threat to State power in his previous form, the form in which he controlled the means of production and was rooted in a private collectivity—the village, the land, or the family production unit. The new individual is homogenized in terms of his new functions in the capitalist production system, separated from his tools and appended to others' capital. He is normalized and fitted into the new hierarchies, the division of labor associated with modern capitalism. It is in this form that the State re-creates the individual and stresses individuality—individual rights, equality before the law, individual consumption, individual expression, individual political power (voting)— within the context of the nation-State. It is the State that assumes the expression of collective will, using the "expert knowledge" produced by the division of intellectual from manual skill in the form of intellectuals who are themselves homogenized into the new "normalized" individual. But in this context, as well, the State gives power to the individual through representative democracy, and it is in this form that the normalized individuals can, as part of *political* class struggle, make gains of power within the State itself. By holding up the individual as the source of power, the modern capitalist State *allows representative democracy to be an arena of struggle*.

The law. Poulantzas has two basic formulations concerning the role of law in the capitalist State and the reproductive function of that law. In the first, he discusses the relationship between the law and repression; his principal point is that there is no dichotomy between law and repression in the capitalist State, but rather that law and repression are intimately entwined. In the second, he argues that the law constitutes the formal cohesive framework for individuals separated from their means of production; the law defines the political space into which these individuals are reintegrated and the *way* they are reintegrated. Thus, it is the law that defines the normalization process discussed above, which includes, for example, a system of examinations in school, rules of property (relations between capitalist and worker), and the rules of conflict (e.g., the rights and obligations of labor unions).

The first formulation is crucial to Poulantzas's argument, discussed earlier, that the repressive and ideological apparatuses should not be analytically separated (as they are in Gramsci's work on the one hand and by Foucault, on the other). It is also crucial to understanding why the dominated masses "consent" to the rule of the bourgeois State. Gramsci argues that the dominant-class hegemony is internalized by the masses, who thus consent to dominant-class rule. Although Marx saw this as "false consciousness" that could be broken down by a vanguard, conscious, working-class party, Gramsci understood that the State was actively involved in the *expansion* of dominant-class hegemony by entering directly into the ideological formations and reinforcement of this hegemony, which included bourgeois law. Furthermore, although Marx viewed bourgeois law and the juridical-political system as part of the repressive apparatus of the State, Gramsci tended to view it much more as part of the ideological apparatus. If the dominant-class hegemony came into crisis, Gramsci argued, it was then that the repressive forces were brought into play by the bourgeoisie.

Poulantzas rejects Gramsci's argument that the increase of the ideological apparatuses and their techniques for maintaining and extending dominant-class power implies a reduction of physical repression, that the two forms of using power are substitutes for each other rather than complements.

For Poulantzas, the capitalist State neither separates law from violence nor substitutes mechanisms of manipulation-persuasion (ideology) for repression. To the contrary, the capitalist State develops a monopoly on legitimate physical violence; the capitalist State's accumulation of the means of corporal control goes hand in hand with its character as the State of law and order. This monopoly "underlies the techniques of power and the mechanisms of consent; it is inscribed in the web of disciplinary and ideological devices; and even when not directly exercised, it shapes the materiality of the social body upon which domination is brought to bear" (1980, 81). Thus, he goes on, disciplinary institutions and the emergence of ideological institutions like the parliament and the school *assume* the monopoly of violence by the State, and this violence, in turn, is obscured by the displacement of legitimacy toward "legality" and the law. Not only that, but the major instrument of legal violence—the army—serves as the model for the organization of schools and bureaucratic hierarchies both within the State and in the private corporations.

We turn now to Poulantzas's second formulation of the role of law, which *defines* the individual in the capitalist nation-State, the State itself (as the law) incarnating and representing the unity of the people-nation.

Capitalist law, according to Poulantzas, does not obscure real differences among peoples, rather, it defines and legitimizes these differences (both individual and class).[5] The law consecrates individualization itself, simultaneously making everyone equal before the law—so individuals are held to be different and separate but within a framework of *homogeneity*, of equal treatment under uniform law and the unity of the people-nation. Under feudalism, the religious precepts of the Church assigned a piece of divine truth to each individual. But they also limited individuals' earthly power—statutes and privileges were based on *natural law*. Under capitalism the law embodies the capitalist relation of power and knowledge: there is neither knowledge nor truth in individuals except as it is defined by bourgeois law.

In keeping with his general dialectical model, Poulantzas sees in both these formulations the contradictions that shape the class struggle. First, law displaces the class struggle from the economic to the political arena by defining the rules of conflict away from a struggle over property to a struggle over the State apparatus. This was intended originally to permit the possibility of power struggles among different fractions of the bourgeoisie (workers, women, and other subordinated fractions of the working class did not have the right to vote), but it ultimately permitted the participation of dispossessed groups (through their struggle to participate), the modification of power relations in the State itself, and also provoked certain "interpretations" of law that favored the working class.

> Capitalist law appears as the necessary form of a State that has to maintain relative autonomy of the fractions of a power bloc, in order to organize their unity under the hegemony of a class or a fraction of a class. . . . But capitalist law also rules the exercise of power for the dominated classes. Confronted by the struggle of the working class in the political arena, law organizes the framework of a permanent equilibrium of compromise imposed on the dominant classes by the dominated. This law also rules the exercise of physical repression: the juridical system, its "formal" and "abstract" liberties are also, we have to emphasize, the conquests of the popular masses. It is in this sense, and only in this sense, that modern law *poses limits* on the exercise of power and the intervention of the apparatuses of the State. (Poulantzas 1978, 100-101; my translation)

[5] One example of the kind of institution spawned by the capitalist juridical-political system is schooling and school exams—these legitimize differences among individuals that serve as the basis for the division of labor, but more than that, they define incorporation into the social body and treatment before the law.

Bourgeois law, then, is tied directly to the monopoly of physical violence by the State, to the dispossession of the means of production from the worker and his reincorporation as an "individual" equal before the law. The individual worker is defined, legitimately, by institutions whose hierarchies of power are still rooted in the unequal class production system (including the State). Thus bourgeois law also has to allow the struggle over power in the State, a struggle that in and of itself allows the possibility to limit the exercise of power against the dominant classes.

The nation. Poulantzas's theory of the State contends that through law, the capitalist State legitimizes the dispossession of the worker from the means of production, and that the State reunifies the individual under the umbrella of the people-nation, a nation that (like the State) did not exist in societies without classes and continues to exist (like the State) in societies where the division of classes is "eliminated." This nation is not the same as the State; the capitalist State may incorporate several nations, such as the Austro-Hungarian Empire (1980, 94). Even so, the capitalist State seems, in particular, to be a *national* State; it works actively to establish a *national* unity, and modern nations generally move toward forming their own States.

For these reasons, the nation and the meaning of the nation become an important fourth element in Poulantzas's analysis of the State. He rejects the traditional Marxist notion that nations were formed under capitalism to unify the internal market for the facilitation of bourgeois development. This does not explain—according to Poulantzas—why this unification took place precisely at the level of the nation, or why the territorial boundaries that were chosen for the definition of the internal market were necessarily "national," or why it was organized around the concept of "unification" (1980, 96). Furthermore, why are territory, language, and tradition all part of this "national" definition of internal market?

Poulantzas formulates the problem in two parts: (a) in terms of territory, and (b) in terms of tradition. Territory, for Poulantzas, is the modern space in which the wage worker—fractionalized, isolated, separated from his means of production and the space defined by them (deterritorialized)—is reincorporated and assimilated. The modern nation redefines *inside* and *outside*: "within this very space are inscribed the movements and expanded reproduction of capital, the generalization of exchange, and monetary fluctuations" (1980, 104). The modern State's apparatuses—army, school, centralized bureaucracy, and prisons—materialize this spatial matrix. He argues that the people-nation of the capitalist State is the objective and essence of the State, whose frontiers are the outline of the material foundation of power. So, for the State, territory defines the borders within which it must reunify the deterritorialized workers resulting from capitalist production, just as law abstracts the conditions under which the individual is reunified into a homogeneous, but redifferentiated whole. The national State realizes this unity of individuals in the people-nation in the same motion, as it were, by which it forges their individualization and their reseparation. This State doesn't unify a previously defined internal market, but installs a national unified market when it defines the national borders, borders that also define the inside as compared with the outside. At the same time, however, Poulantzas argues that the power which allows the State to define national borders, also allows it to extend those borders through the extension of capital, markets, and territories. And the other side of the coin is that it is not possible to extend national limits without first defining an *inside* (a homogenized, unified nation) that can then be extended infinitely (even into outer space).

The second element of Poulantzas's formulation of nation is "common historical tradition." He calls this the "temporal matrix of historicism," since under capitalism (he argues) the temporal matrix changes from a precapitalist concept of time that was homogeneous, reversible, repetitive, and not universally measurable, to a concept that is segmented, serial, divided into equal moments, and cumulative and irreversible (because it is oriented toward production, and through production, time is oriented toward an enlarged reproduction, a reproduction for universal goals).

In precapitalist societies, the sense of *present* was attributed to the sense of *before* and *after*. To understand origins of things in precapitalist times did not mean to retrace the history of accumulation (of experiences, of knowledge, of events) or progress that led to the present, but rather to attain the original omniscience. The beginning and the end, the before and the after, were wholly co-actualized in the always present divinity. Truth was immutable and progressively revealed, not cumulated. Power was embodied in the sovereign. The body politic did not emerge historically; rather, it resided in a continuous and homogeneous historicity, in which power itself was uninterrupted. Only the human body that incorporated that power changed. The territory associated with this temporal space had no definition, no inside and outside: "Pre-capitalist territories have no historicity of their own, since political time is the time of the prince-body, who is capable of extension, contraction, and movement in a continuous and homogeneous space" (1980, 110).

On the other hand, capitalist time is measurable and strictly controlled by clocks, chronometers, and precise calendars. This type of time poses a new problem: it has to be unified and universalized; there has to be created a unique and homogeneous measure of time that unifies the very separate temporal rhythms (worker time, bourgeois time, economic, social, and political time)—separated by the capitalist production process and its extensions, the capitalist social system (classes), and political systems (the State)—into a "universalized" capitalist concept of time. "This matrix for the first time marks out the particular temporalities as *different temporalities*—that is to say, as rhythmical and metrical variations of a serial, segmented, irreversible and cumulative time" (1980, 110).

The nation, as developed in the capitalist State, together with its territory, tradition, and language, is a form of unification of people divided by capitalist production into classes—segmented, separated, individualized and isolated—into a new concept of space and time, a concept that is intended to keep the dominated class from realizing who and why it is. Instead, members of that class focus on the new individual's consciousness, on the commonality each has (under the State) with other members of the people-nation; he or she is *inside* the same territory, has the same historical goals, and is engaged in the same process of change as all other members of the people-nation. In addition, each individual is treated equally by the law.

The State as an Arena of Class Struggle

With the understanding of these four elements in Poulantzas's formulation of the capitalist reproduction, we can analyze briefly the logical continuation of this formulation. Capitalism and production separate and individualize workers. The State reintegrates these individuals into the people-nation under a set of institutions that homogenize and normalize them, differentiating them under a new set of rules, norms, values, history, tradition, language, and concepts of knowledge that emanate from the dominant class and its fractions. This same reintegration takes place in the context of class struggle, and all the institutions of society, including the State, are the product of that struggle. This is Poulantzas's particular contribution to theories of the State. He shows how the capitalist State provides the framework for struggles among fractions of the dominant class, and reintegrates the working class, as individuals detached from their means of production and their class, into a nation and a unifying set of rules and institutions. At the same time, the State provides the political space for class struggle, and so—just as the capitalist State emerged from a struggle—the State becomes *shaped* by class struggle. The State is key to the reintegration of workers (and bourgeoisie) into a unified whole that will be reproduced as capitalist society—as a class structure—from generation to generation, even while the working class remains separated, alienated, isolated, and exploited. Yet, contradictions arise in the superstructure itself—in the State—as their integration is taking place.

Poulantzas's analysis of these contradictions is divided into two parts:

(a) the relationship of the State to the dominant classes, and (b) the relationship of the State to the masses and their struggle.

Before this analysis, a word is necessary about contradictions internal to the State and how Poulantzas distinguishes his concept from two others (reviewed above). For Lenin, the State is fused with monopoly capitalism and is at the service of monopoly capitalists. It has neither autonomy nor *any political relevance* of its own—the State is reduced to an appendage of the power of the monopoly bourgeoisie (hence Popper's [1945] critique). This is what Poulantzas calls the "State-object." On the other hand, as the "State-subject," the State is autonomous in an absolute way; its autonomy is derived from its own will as a "rationalizing instance of civil society" (Poulantzas 1980, 129). This is the "institutionalist-functionalist" view.

The "State-object" view argues that politics are determined by the State's position subordinate to the power of a single fraction of the bourgeoisie—monopoly capitalists. Contradictions in the State are secondary, the monolithic State changing only as a result of changes in the relative power of one fraction or another of the bourgeoisie. Contradictions take place *outside* the State in the "State-object" view.

The "State-subject" has its own power, an absolute autonomy with relation to social classes, always outside of the class structure, imposing "its" policy—that of a bureaucracy or of political elites—on the divergent and consensual interests of civil society. In this theory of the State, internal contradictions, Poulantzas claims, are also secondary, accidental, and episodic, due to friction among political elites or bureaucratic groups—contradictions external to social classes.[6]

Now we can turn to (a) Poulantzas's view of the relation between the State and the dominant classes, most of which is preserved from his earlier work. The State has principally an organizational role with regard to these classes. "It represents and organizes the dominant class or classes; or more precisely it represents and organizes the long-term political interests of a *power bloc*, which is composed of several bourgeois class fractions. . . . The State is able to play this role of organizing and unifying the bourgeoisie and the power bloc insofar as it enjoys *relative autonomy* of given fractions or components, and of various particular interests" (1980, 127).

For Poulantzas, as we have shown, the capitalist State is not an intrinsic

---

[6] It is evident that Poulantzas considers such contradictions "secondary" in the sense that they are defined as independent of class structure and because they do not affect the fundamental development of capitalist production. But, as we have pointed out, differences between elite groups are considered "primary" by institutional functionalists—for one thing, they exclude any basic difference between "worker" interests and "capitalist" interests. So "primary" conflicts reside within the bureaucracy of the elite.

entity, but "a relation, more exactly a material condensation of the relation
of conflicts between classes and fractions of classes as they are expressed
. . . in the heart of the State" (1978, 141; my trans.). Therefore, the
establishment of State policy has to be considered as the result of "class
contradictions inherent in the structure of the State itself" (1978, 145; my
trans.). Class contradictions constitute the State, are present in its material
framework, and in turn frame its organization. The diverse fractions and
classes in the power bloc participate in political domination only to the
extent that they are present in the State. And "however paradoxical it may
seem, the play of these contradictions within the State's materiality alone,
makes possible the State's organizational role" (1980, 133). For it is the
State as *unifier* that enables it to act as a reproducer, and unification means
the existence of contradiction, of conflict, between different groups. In the
first instance, the bourgeois State is structured to allow conflicts only among
dominant groups who are in the power bloc. The politics of the State is
therefore established by intra-State contradictions—the State is the institution where the fractions of the power bloc resolve their conflicts. This
gives a chaotic and incoherent image to the State, each fraction trying to
gain at the expense of others.

At any moment of time, Poulantzas points out, one fraction is dominant,
and the State produces a global strategy that favors this fraction.

> But this unity of power of the State doesn't establish itself by monopoly
> capitalists physical take-over of the State and their coherent will. This
> centralization-unity is inscribed in the hierarchic-bureaucratized structure
> of the capitalist State, the result of the reproduction of the social division
> of labor in the heart of the State (and included under the manual work—
> intellectual work form) and the result of its specific separation from the
> relations of production . . . also . . . of the predominant place of that
> class or hegemonic fraction in the heart of the State. . . .
>
> . . . [U]nity is established by a whole chain of subordination of certain
> apparatuses to others and by the domination of one apparatus or branch
> of the State (the army, a political party, a ministry) which crystallizes
> the interests of the hegemonic fraction over the other branches or ap-
> paratuses, centers of resistance of other fractions of the power bloc.
> (1978, 150-151; my translation)

Poulantzas therefore describes a State where conflict not only takes place
over State power, but among apparatuses of the State and *within* each
apparatus. The centralized unity of the State, he argues, doesn't reside in
a pyramid whose summit has to be controlled in order to control the State—
various State apparatuses could be controlled by the bourgeoisie, for example, even if the Left were to control the legislature (or, in the Chilean

case, the executive branch). *"The State is not a monolithic bloc but a strategic battlefield"* (1978, 152; my trans.; italics added). In this later work, Poulantzas does for the State what Gramsci did for civil society: Poulantzas takes the Gramscian concept of dominant-class hegemony in all its complexity and pervasiveness and articulates it for the State. The State itself becomes an arena of struggle.

Proceeding to (b) the relationship of the State to the masses and their struggle, the State, then, not only resolves conflicts among fractions in the power bloc but also between the power bloc and the dominated classes. Poulantzas rejects the Leninist (and Gramscian) idea that the contradiction between dominant and dominated classes stay outside the State. In that concept, the dominated classes can only exert pressure on the bourgeois State. He does agree that power and mass struggle originate outside the State, but as far as they are political struggles, they have to include the State. For Poulantzas, the structure of the State—its hierarchical-bureaucratic organization—includes the specific presence of the dominated classes and their struggle. In other words, it is impossible to understand the organization and functions of the State without including its role of mediating conflict between dominant and dominated classes, particularly its attempts to divide and disorganize the dominated masses (but at the same time compromising with many of their demands).

However, Poulantzas also argues that it is false to conclude that the presence of popular classes in the State signifies that they can stay there very long without a radical transformation of the State. "But the popular classes have always been present in the State, without that ever having changed anything of its hard core" (1980, 143). "[The State structure] does indeed retain the dominated classes within itself, but it retains them precisely as *dominated classes*. . . . The action of popular masses within the State is a necessary condition of its transformation, but is not itself a sufficient condition" (1980, 143).

Furthermore, even though the contradictions between the dominant and dominated classes are mediated by the structure of the State (and the power relations expressed in that structure), there is not necessarily agreement at any given time among the fractions of the power bloc on how to deal with such contradictions and the struggle with the masses. All this is condensed in the internal division and contradictions in the State, *among* its diverse branches, networks, and apparatuses, and *within* each one.

Thus, the State, in all its functions (ideological, repressive, and economic) is marked by contradictions, because class struggle takes place *in the heart of the State* even as it tries to maintain an external dominant-class hegemony. Poulantzas insists that the State is neither an instrumentalist depository (object) of dominant-class power, nor a subject that possesses an abstract power of its own outside the class structure. It is rather a place for the dominant class to organize itself strategically in its relation to the dominated classes. It is a place and center of the *exercise* of power, but it does not possess its own power. Furthermore, under monopoly capitalism, the ideological and repressive functions of the State (according to Poulantzas) are less important than under commercial capitalism. *"The totality of the operations of the State are currently being reorganized in relation to its economic role"* (1980, 168). The State not only reproduces labor power and the relations of production through ideology and repression, it intervenes directly in the crises of production by investing in private production (in the military industry in the United States, for example) and by producing itself, rescues sectors of industry that have become unprofitable but are crucial employers and domestic suppliers of particular goods. This makes even the class struggle in production enter the State apparatuses, since the State is a producer.

CONCLUSION

Poulantzas's work reflects the development and transformation of a structuralist view of the State into one that is more historical-specific and where social movements play a key role. Structuralism was and is widely criticized for its ahistorical and deterministic view that the State corresponds to a mode of production, its form and function determined by the structure of the class relations, and, as Althusser saw it, in the capitalist mode, determined by *economic* class relations. Poulantzas originally applied such a theory to the capitalist State, accentuating the ideological role of the State determined by the class relations of production. This necessarily "relatively autonomous" class State appears above class struggle when in fact it reproduces the dominance of the capitalist class. For Poulantzas as structuralist, the State in the capitalist mode of production is "determined" in fulfilling this reproductive function, not by direct control of the capitalist class, but rather by the *class nature* of the ideological and repressive State apparatuses. Poulantzas could argue that in capitalist production, capital (and labor) is fractionalized, but a fraction (or fractions) of capital can—specifically through the class State—organize its hegemony. And because the State *is* a capitalist-class State, labor necessarily *cannot* use the State in the same way.[7]

The criticisms of this position came quickly. In England, from Miliband;

[7] Poulantzas has fractions of the capitalist class establishing hegemony through the State. He does not argue, as does Offe (see Chapter 5) that the State organizes class interests *for* the fractionalized capitalist class.

in Germany, from the derivationists and Offe (see Chapter 5); in Italy, from Ingrao (see Chapter 6); and in America, from James O'Connor (see Chapter 8). Poulantzas's reaction to these criticisms was to retain his fundamental analysis of relative autonomy and the State's roots in class relations, but to abandon the determinist, structuralist nature of that autonomous class State. This he did in two important ways.

First, he argues that as capitalism developed, the capitalist State changed. Thus, capitalist relations of production, the class structure, and the State are historical-specific within the capitalist mode of production. There is no "structure" for the State; rather, the form and function of the State is shaped by class struggle in capitalism and the State's role in that struggle.

Second, he argued that the "displacement" of the class struggle from production into the State brings that struggle into the "heart of the State" (1978, 141). The forms and functions of the State are not determined by the economic class relations in some abstract sense, but by the historical expression of those relations in the form of struggle. The subordinated classes therefore also shape the State even while it is a class State, and even while it is used by the dominant fraction to establish and extend dominant capitalist hegemony.

A State contested by subordinate classes may become dysfunctional as a site where the dominant classes can establish their hegemony. In that case, the State may have to be changed drastically (e.g., become authoritarian rather than democratic). Poulantzas became convinced that democracy is a crucial issue in the transition to socialism, for it is democracy (even "bourgeois" democracy) that is simultaneously a working-class victory and a principal form of subordinate-class contestation in the class State (see Chapter 6).

There exist a number of difficulties even in this last work, primarily in understanding how autonomous the capitalist State is and what the relationship is between nonclass movements, class struggle, and the "class" State. Is the State a site where dominant capitalist fractions organize their hegemony, or where an autonomous State bureaucracy develops and extends capitalism for capitalists in their long-term interest? As nontraditional class social movements redefine the civil society (and the State), and class struggle in the State changes social-class relations, how is the nature of class struggle itself affected? These are key questions that Poulantzas did not answer even though his analysis certainly led to asking those questions. Furthermore, he retained in his work an abstraction that is not only common to Althusser but to the French philosophical tradition. But Poulantzas's structuralist origins accentuated this tradition's ahistorical, aspecific characteristics. Others, like Cardoso and Faletto (see Chapter 7) in Latin America showed that an historical-structural approach to understanding the State applied to specific case studies adds important dimensions, lacking in Poulantzas's more abstract formulations, to State theories. Despite these important limitations, Poulantzas gives us a solid theoretical reference point for current discussions of class and State.

CHAPTER FIVE

The German Debate

AT THE SAME TIME that the structuralist discussion developed in France around Althusser's and Poulantzas's work, a similar interest in the State emerged in Germany. German State theories are influenced significantly by earlier attempts in the 1950s to incorporate changes in capitalist forms into orthodox Marxist theory. "State monopoly capital" theory, as these attempts are called, argued that as a result of the general capitalist crisis of the 1930s and capitalist imperialism, and as a response to the expansion of socialism after World War II, the capitalist State had to intervene increasingly in the economy to maintain the dynamic of capitalist development. Although there were a number of versions of this theory (see Jessop 1983), they have in common the introduction of a *political* variable in the heart of orthodox theory. Capitalist development is no longer simply deduced from market (production) relations, but represented as a much more complex class struggle in which base and superstructure are intertwined. Also, a basis was laid for regarding the socialist struggle as inherently antimonopoly and antibureaucracy, hence fundamentally "democratic" (see Chapter 6).

But State monopoly capital formulations continued to suffer from the instrumentalism of orthodox theory. State intervention was interpreted as exclusively serving the monopoly fraction of the capitalist class—that is, viewing monopoly capital as using the State for its own purposes. The theory consists largely of describing the connections between various capitalists and the government, the financial dependence of political parties on finance capital, and the manipulation of the media by monopoly interests. None of the *limits* on State intervention is discussed; rather, the State is characterized as having an unlimited number of possibilities to solve capitalist (production) crises unless an antimonopoly coalition is capable of overthrowing it (Laclau 1981).

The main problem of the State monopoly capital work was that it never developed a theory of the State's position in monopoly capitalist society. It was precisely this challenge that was taken up by the Germans, but in rather different ways. The capital logic (or "derivationist") school developed a theory of the State from the concept of capital, while Claus Offe—influenced by the Frankfurt School, with its Hegelian overtones, and by Max Weber's analysis of bureaucracy—took a "political" view of the State, focusing on it as a relatively autonomous subject of study.

There are several variants of the capital logic school. One, associated with Elmar Altvater, attempts to deduce the necessity of the State from the competition among capitals—exactly the opposite starting point from State monopoly capital theory. The State, for Altvater, assumes the function of reproducing capital as a whole, providing infrastructure investment, the regulation of conflict between capital and labor, helping to expand national capital in world markets, and regulating a fractionalized capitalist development with fiscal and monetary policy. We will see the similarity between some aspects of Altvater's and Offe's theories. Another variant, on which this chapter will focus, argues that the origin of the capitalist State is in the relation of wage labor to capital. The struggle of labor against capital pushes profits down, and requires State intervention to offset falling rates of profit. But in this version, the strict derivation of the State finds its limits, since the contradictions of State intervention are reproduced inside the State itself. These contradictions severely limit the possibility of the State to oversee capitalist interests.

For the "derivationists," the principal issue in the Miliband-Poulantzas debate was not whether the bourgeoisie controls apparatuses of the State directly (State monopoly capital—the State acts to insure and promote the domination by the monopoly capitalist class) or indirectly (the State in capitalist society incorporates the class struggle inherent in corporate production, but remains a mechanism of capitalist-class rule). Rather, the issue is the separation of the political from the economic in analyzing the State. Can the political be constituted as an autonomous and specific object of science? Such a position is rejected by the derivationists.[1]

> [They see] in Marx's great work [*Capital*] not an analysis of the 'economic level' but a *materialist critique* of political economy, i.e., a materialist's critique of bourgeois attempts to analyze the 'economy' in isolation from the class relations of exploitation on which it is based; consequently, the categories elaborated in *Capital* (surplus value, accumulation, etc.) are seen not as being specific to the analysis of the 'economic level' but as historical materialist categories developed to illuminate the structure of class conflict in capitalist society and the forms and conceptions (economic or otherwise) generated by that structure. From this, it follows that the task is not to develop 'political

[1] The derivationists claim that only by deriving political relations from economic relations can this separation be avoided, but John Keane (1978), a friendly critic of Offe's, has called the return to Marx by the derivationist view "thought in retreat," precisely because, according to Keane, it separates civil society and the State.

concepts' to complement the set of 'economic concepts,' but to develop the concepts of *Capital* in the critique not only of the economic but also of the political form of social relations. (Holloway and Picciotto 1978, 4)

Claus Offe, on the other hand, argues that the State is comprised of the institutional apparatuses, bureaucratic organizations, and formal and informal norms and codes that constitute and regulate the public and private spheres of society. As the materialization of relations of domination, the State apparatuses consist of a set of complex, differentiated organizational structures whose unity resides in their claim to legitimate authority and their monopoly of coercive forces. In keeping with Marx's early views of the State (see Chapter 2), and the subsequent Weberian interpretations of bureaucracy's relation to civil society, Offe's analysis emphasizes the relative *autonomy* of the State to the degree that bureaucracy becomes the "independent" mediator of the class struggle inherent in the capitalist *accumulation* process. Contradictions arising from the various mediating roles of the State itself (and the inherent characteristics of bureaucracy) make the State the principal arena of crisis (the "crisis of legitimation") and the place where the crisis is resolved or exacerbated.

In Offe's political view of the State, the analysis centers on the functions of the State administrative apparatus and its relations to various actors in the political arena, including State bureaucrats themselves; in the "mediator" or "derivationist" view, however, the investigation of the State must begin with an analysis of the capital accumulation process—the form of capital, the movement of prices, class differentiations, the international system, etc.—and from this changing structure of capital relations, to "derive" concretely the functions and modes of functioning of the State apparatus.

The issue, then, centers on the concept of a theory of politics in Marx's writings. Offe, we have mentioned, presents us with a highly autonomous State and concentrates on the functioning of the State's relatively independent bureaucracy; the derivationists claim that Marx's materialist critique of political economy, through its illumination of class conflict in capitalist society, provides the essential elements of that political theory and therefore the basis for a theory of the capitalist State.

There is yet another interesting aspect to the German debate. Because of some derivationists' (notably Hirsch's) focus on the process of capital accumulation as central to understanding the functions of the State, there is a corresponding emphasis on the "economic" role of the State, that is, on its fundamental function of counteracting the tendency for the rate of profit to fall, and distributing the surplus among different capitals and between capital and labor. While providing a specific theory of the political, Offe also emphasizes these direct economic State interventions, and like the derivationists, deemphasizes the ideological-repressive State functions. This is in sharp contrast to Gramsci, Althusser, and Poulantzas (and even Miliband), who see the State's important role as much more ideological-repressive than economic.

In this chapter, we discuss these positions and their contribution to understanding the capitalist State. Although a number of writers have been involved in the debate (see Holloway and Picciotto 1978 and Broady 1980 for summaries of various aspects of the discussion), we will focus on two principals: Claus Offe, representing the "political" view, and Joachim Hirsch, representing the "derivationists."

OFFE'S THEORY OF THE STATE IN LATE CAPITALISM

For Offe, the State develops in capitalist societies in response to periodic crises arising from the basic contradiction in capitalist production: the increasing socialization of production (the incorporation of labor into production as wage labor) and continuing private appropriation (surplus extraction by capitalists). The crises give rise to the development of adaptive mechanisms both internal to the market (oligopolization and monopolization) and through expanded State functions. Offe sees the State as a mediator of capitalist crises—a crisis manager. In this context, he addresses two fundamental issues: (1) what is the relationship of the State to the dominant capitalist class, that is, how is it guaranteed that the State will represent the social interest of capital—the reproduction of the capitalist social relations of production—while at the same time appearing to be a neutral arbitrator of competition among capitals and between capital and labor; and (2) what are the limits imposed on the State's crisis-management functions by inherent necessity to reproduce capitalist relations of production? (Sardei-Biermann et al. 1973).

The Class Nature of the State

In dealing with the first of these issues, Offe *rejects* two principal theories of the class nature of the State, "influence theories" (instrumentalism) and "constraint theories" (structuralism). In describing the principal elements of instrumentalism and structuralism, Offe is apparently discussing the works of Miliband (1973), Poulantzas (1974), and Domhoff (1967). What Offe calls "influence theories" ascribe direct control of the State to the capitalist class through the influence of corporations on the executive and legislative branches of government, regulatory agencies, and the media, as well as through the capitalist threat of an investment strike. "Constraint theories" insist that there is evidence of a "structural limitation to the possible courses of action, of the lack of sovereignty of political institutions and processes. . . . that the institutions of the political system cannot in any case effectively become the instrument of any non-capitalist interest whatsoever" (Offe 1974, 2-3). Both theories, Offe insists, assume that the action of the State (policy-making) is externally determined, which gives public policy its capitalist content. The State—in these theories—is regarded as a neutral instrument, one that could potentially be used by any social class.

In particular, Offe argues that both theories assume that special interests of individual capitals or groups of capitals are translated into policies that have a *class-interest* quality. "The concept of class interest as contrasted with the mere special interest of individual enterprises or capital groups clearly presupposes that the definition of interests possesses a 'degree of rationality' which allows the creation of a conception cleansed of situational and particular coincidences and divergencies" (Offe 1974, 4). But the "anarchy" of competition-geared capitalist production makes it highly unlikely that such a standardized concept of capitalist-class interest would ever be created. What is much more likely is that any particular State policy serves a particular interest rather than the class interest as a whole. Furthermore, even those policies that can be shown to be functionally important for the conditions of surplus-value creation frequently "cannot be genetically traced back to the interest-oriented influence of groups or authorities advocating them" (Offe 1974, 5).

Secondly, Offe criticizes the theories with regard to their assumptions about power relations. He argues that their view of power is mechanistic, and that in order to show that there exists a power relation between two subsystems (the production sector and the State), it must be shown that their structures display a minimum of reciprocity or complementarity.

Any proof of the "capitalist," class-bound character of a State governance organization therefore stands or falls by whether it can uncover structural analogies between the State and the capitalistically organized economy . . . [T]he State, which is supposed to be the "ideal collective capitalist," would only have to be organized analogously to capital but at the same time would also have to be a structure which presents itself to the particular and narrow interests of individual capitalists and their political organizations as a supervisory, tutelary force . . . since it is only through the State's becoming independent in this way that the multiplicity of particular and situation-bound special interests can be integrated into a class-interest. (Offe 1974, 6)

Given these critiques, Offe proposes that the capitalist State is not a set of institutions that can be easily separated from other "private" institutions, but is "a historically accumulated network of legal and institutional formalisms covering and conditioning (almost) all of the processes and interactions that go in a society . . . a [capitalist] state [is] the structure of *those* historical societies which reproduce themselves through competition and exploitative commodity production" (Offe 1976, 4). He proposes that the common interest of the ruling class is best expressed in those strategies of the State apparatus that are not initiated by outside interests but by the very routines and formal structures of the State organization itself. Actual influence by particular interest groups, far from serving the interests of the capitalist class as a whole, would tend to violate that interest by creating conflicts within capitalist society, which would disrupt the mediation of overall crises in capitalist development.

In these circumstances, which internal structures within the political system guarantee the implementability of initiatives and interests arising from the process of exploitation? How, he asks, is the success of exerting influence structurally assured? "One can speak of an 'ideal collective capitalist' (the State) only when it has been successfully proved that the *system of political institutions displays its own class-specific selectiveness* corresponding to the interests of the process of exploitation" (Offe 1973, 6-7). Offe sees this class-specific selectiveness neither in the direct control by a capitalist class over the State nor in the structural limitations on the State's political space, which prevent any anticapitalist policy. Rather, the capitalist State *must and will fulfill certain conditions to reproduce itself*; this is what guarantees its class-specific selectiveness. These four conditions follow.[2]

First, the State cannot order production or control it—it cannot initiate noncumulative production in private enterprises or halt production that is cumulative. Accumulation takes place in private accumulation units and the State cannot interfere to begin or end such accumulation. The State includes organizational formalisms that prohibit any actor in the State from making decisions about the concrete use of the same production.

Second, the actors of the State apparatus depend for their survival (as

---

[2] As will be argued below in more detail, the nature of the capitalist State as described by these conditions is much more like Poulantzas's later analysis than is usually assumed. The principal difference is that Offe's State is more tied to the accumulation process than the reproduction of the *relations* of production. But if accumulation is considered the sine qua non of reproduction, the Offe position is not all that different from Poulantzas's.

well as for any political goals they want to achieve) upon resources derived from the private accumulation process, primarily through taxation. This reliance on the taxation of wages and profits means that each interest of the personnel of various branches and agencies can be pursued only if it is in accordance with the imperative of maintaining accumulation. Accumulation acts as the most powerful constraint criterion (but not necessarily as the determinant of content) of the policy-making process.

Third, the State therefore not only has the authority but the mandate to sustain and create *conditions* of accumulation. In order for resources to flow to the State, depending on sources that are not owned by the State, the State apparatus must promote the general accumulation process. It must do so in the face of threats that cause problems of accumulation, threats from competition among accumulating units, both domestically and internationally, and from the working class. The function of creating and maintaining conditions of accumulation means establishing control over these destructive possibilities and events.

Finally, since the personnel of the State apparatus do not have a power base of their own, they need some mandate for action derived from an alternative source of power. This mandate for action must come from the concept of the State as representing the common and general interests of society as a whole. "This is to say that the State can only *function* as a capitalist state by appealing to symbols and sources of support that *conceal* its nature as a capitalist state; the existence of a capitalist state presupposes the systematic *denial* of its nature as a *capitalist* state" (Offe 1973, 127). Poulantzas poses essentially the same condition: to be legitimate, the capitalist State must appear to allow (unlike private production) equal access to power and to be responsive to all groups in the society. A source of power for the State is therefore based on the symbolism of mass participation in the selection of State personnel. Although this gives the State its alternative source of power, it also means that to maintain itself as a capitalist State, it needs to be legitimate in the eyes of those masses who give it power.

This, then, is Offe's formulation of how "the state *gains* power, *applies* this power in a way conducive to and maintaining the conditions of accumulation, *without* thereby subverting its own existence as a capitalist state" (Offe 1973, 127). In his view, the capitalist State can represent the general interest of capital through the relationship between the State and the accumulation process plus the legitimacy afforded the State by mass participation in the selection of its personnel. But the State, in this formulation, cannot represent specific capitalist interests without endangering its overall function of representing the social interest of capital. Neither can it appear to represent capital to the detriment of its mass-based support, for in that case it endangers its legitimacy—its alternative source of power.

The Limits Imposed on the State

In Offe's model, the limits on State functions emanate from the problem of dynamically reconciling the requirements of capitalist accumulation on the one hand and legitimation on the other:

> The key argument that I wish to pursue here is that the process of formation of state policies is determined through the concrete difficulties of *reconciling those four constituent elements.* The motive force of all policy formation is the problem of reconciling these elements; policy-making of the state is nothing but the process in which these elements are reconciled, and rather than assuming some instance which pressures or manipulates the policy process from the "outside," the key explanatory concept which we want to suggest is the *institutional self-interest* of the actors in the state apparatus which determines policy outputs and outcomes. (Offe 1976, 6)

Offe views government policy-making as the attempt to establish a dynamic equilibrium among constituent elements. Implicit in this argument is the pervasive role of the State in the capital accumulation process. For Offe, the State in advanced capitalism is intimately involved with the accumulation process such that private accumulation becomes a function of bureaucratic State activity and organized political conflict. In his long review of Offe's work, John Keane writes: "No longer are they as superstructure to base. Rather, capitalist relations of production have been repoliticized. The (potential) antagonism between socialized production and particular ends has reassumed a directly political form. The realization of *private* capital accumulation . . . is now possible only on the basis of an all-encompassing *political* mediation" (Keane 1978, 56).

The solution to the problem of accumulation and the legitimacy of the State is the "condition of universal and permanent exchangeability of all units of value. As soon as the commodity form actually does govern all social relationships permanently, there is neither a problem of accumulation (which is nothing but the by-product of equal exchange of equivalents between labor and capital) nor a problem of legitimation (which would be provided by the 'justice' of the market place, namely equivalent exchange)" (Offe 1976, 6-7). This means that the State apparatus must ensure that labor power is employable and is employed "on the market" and that individual units of capital find it profitable to employ this labor—that the rate of profit is high enough to promote increased investment and economic expansion. The advanced capitalist State—as opposed to the liberal capitalist State, which could be legitimated by noninterference with private markets—must exercise its power (declare itself as a power) and intervene in the accumulation process. It must, at the same time, practice its class character (promote private capital accumulation), but act as if it were representing mass interests: the existence of a capitalist State presupposes the systematic denial of its nature as a capitalist State.

The problem arises when there are difficulties of accumulation, when owners of money capital fail to spend it on factors of production, and of legitimation, when needs are not satisfied through exchange processes. Offe argues, therefore, that the capitalist State will, out of its institutional self-interest, attempt to increase the employability of labor and to promote the investment of money capital. This is a policy-making process in which the State solves its *own* problems as they result from the discrepancies of the four constituent elements—the personnel of the State try to ensure their own jobs and hence ensure the continued existence of the State apparatuses. There are groups, however, namely individual owners of money capital, who are in a position to obstruct successful policies. "What this class basically does is to decide upon the volume, place, time and kind of exchange processes to take place. Seen in this way, the political power of the capitalist class does not reside in what its members *do politically* (exert 'power' and 'influence' in the decision-making process, etc.) but it resides rather in what its members can *refuse to do economically* (namely initiate exchange processes through buying labor power and fixed capital, i.e., invest)" (Offe 1976, 8-9).

The State faces obstruction in its project of reconciling the four constituent elements and stabilizing the commodity form or production value. The competition among capitals leads to monopolization and a constant tendency for the organic composition of capital to increase, and therefore for the unemployment of labor to become an increasing problem. With monopolization, the self-expansion of capital becomes more and more contingent upon giant investment projects, huge capital outlays, and growing social overhead costs. Under these conditions, there is a permanent underutilization of capital and lack of investment outlets. The State must both socialize capital and social overhead costs to promote investment, and at the same time pay unemployment benefits to labor and extend training programs to it that make it more employable. All of this puts tremendous fiscal pressure on the State. "The real source of fiscal problems lies in the asymmetry between the growing socialization of capital and social overhead costs by the State and the continuing private appropriation of profits" (Keane 1978, 64).

Furthermore, from the point of view of accumulation, underemployment of labor and capital is more threatening, the more welfare rights have already become institutionalized as legal "rights" of the unemployed or "unemployable." The existence of organized labor also makes the existence of a high level of unemployment more threatening for the legitimacy of the State. Solutions to class conflict instituted by the State at an earlier point in time to assure its legitimacy (for example, welfare State measures and the integration of labor organizations into the political process), now make the problem of unemployment more serious in terms of the legitimacy of the State, and hence have to make the State even more sensitive than in the past to the failure of the commoditization of labor power.

In this sense, Offe translates economic crises (both past and present) into political crises, through the pervasive presence of the capitalist State in the accumulation process. Contradictions in the private accumulation process become political crises as the State attempts to ensure capital accumulation in the State's *own institutional interest*. And the more the State institutionalizes its intervention in the exchange process, the more sensitive becomes its interventionist role.

There is yet another limit on the capitalist State, and this one is internal to its own operation. Offe points to the impossibility of the State becoming an "ideal collective capitalist"—that is, directing or supplanting private accumulation—because of structural limits upon its attempts at centralized, bureaucratic, middle-range planning for the reproduction of capital (Keane 1978, 65). In order to analyze why this is so, we have to discuss the *strategies* by which State policies attempt to reconcile the constituent elements. Offe calls these "allocative" and "productive."

Allocation, he says, is a "mode of activity of the capitalist State that creates and maintains the conditions of accumulation in a purely authoritative way" (1973, 128). Resources and powers that intrinsically belong to the State and are at its disposal are allocated. Such powers are the rights to tax and spend, and to make laws and administer (enforce) them. These are *legal* rights, powers vested in the State through a constitution or other legal and widely (if not universally) accepted documents that constitute the social contract. State authority to allocate resources and power is politically legitimated, and thus political power is the sole criterion and determinant of allocation.

Productive State activity requires something different from the allocation of resources and power that the State already has under its control. In addition to the State-organized framework of production and accumulation, some physical input into production is required in order to maintain accumulation. This type of State activity is required when the conditions of private production are such that the capitalist cannot capture the full value of the product. The resulting situation would be the failure of private capitalists to produce commodities on which the accumulation of other capitalists depends (in neoclassical economics, this is posed as the problem of "external economics").

> The novelty of productive policies is that they seek the provision of "inputs of accumulation (e.g., reconstructing labour skills via programs of vocational training) in *anticipation* of disturbances within the domain of "privately" controlled accumulation. Thus, productive policies strive to bolster sagging supplies of both variable and constant capital, where such capital is either not provided, or provided in inadequate supply by private market decisions. . . . The rationale . . . is to "restore accumulation or to avoid or eliminate perceived threats to accumulation." (Keane 1978, 58)

The decision rules by which the State operates in allocative and productive activities must differ, according to Offe. The rules for allocation are directly derived from politics, and so the problem is relatively simple; directives on how to allocate can be derived from the power relationships emanating from the political process itself. But in order to respond to an *anticipated* danger, a different set of rules is necessary—there is no clearcut course of action. An additional set of decision rules is required that determines *policies*. The bureaucratic mode of operation of the State apparatus, which seems to be well suited and sufficient to administer the allocation process, fails, according to Offe, to operate adequately in productive State activities.

> The problem is that the application of predetermined rules through a hierarchical structure of "neutral" officials is simply insufficient to absorb the decision load that is implied by productive state activities. In other words, the administration of productive State activities requires more than the routinized allocation of state resources like money and justice. Additional questions have to be answered in order for productive State activity to begin, for example: What is the final product, or purpose, of state production? How much of it is needed in a particular situation? What is the most efficient way of producing it? Who should receive it? At what point in time and for what length of time? How should it be financed, and what priorities should be followed in case of cost increases and/or revenue decreases? All these questions are beyond the scope and the responsibility of a bureaucracy in the strict sense. (Offe 1973, 136)

The fact that bureaucracy is inadequate for the productive type of State activity flies in the face of Weber's hypothesis that the bureaucratic structure has a superior efficiency. Offe (and others) claim that bureaucracy is *inefficient* and *ineffective*.

What are the alternatives for the State, given its increasing productive role? Offe argues that the State could turn to a purposive-rational structure or one based on democratic conflict and consensus. The purposive-rational structure would make government apparatuses in their internal procedures like the private production structures. However, the choice of ends in industrial production is set by market forces, and no such mechanism exists for setting the goals of State production. The variety of needs and interests appearing in the environment of State activity is contradictory, and the State, in its specific capitalist form, is not able to impose its own definition of goals. Offe concludes that the obstacles to instrumental rationality are such that "the adoption of this principle cannot be considered as an adequate and viable solution to the structural problems of the capitalist state and its internal organization" (Offe 1973, 139). The second alternative is to allow a highly decentralized process of political conflict and consensus to determine the production process. Inputs and outputs would be determined simultaneously by the clients of State administration and the recipients of its benefits. The logical distinctions between politics and administration and the State and society would be negated. Of course, under such an alternative there would be great difficulty for the State to function as a *capitalist* State: a policy process that is directly dependent upon democratic pressures would not be consistent with the functions of the State required in capitalist society. The adoption of social conflict and consensus as the basis for policy production does, according to Offe, invite more articulated demands and interests than can be satisfied under the fiscal and institutional constraints for the capitalist State.

Part of the problem of the capitalist State in reconciling the four constituent elements is how to establish and institutionalize a method of policy production that constitutes a balance (or reciprocity) between required State activities and the internal structure of the state. Given the difficulties, if not impossibilities, of moving out of a bureaucratic mode, the State is unable to perform the productive functions required to maintain and promote accumulation, the condition of universal and permanent exchangeability of all units of value. The capitalist State is constantly trying to reconcile and make compatible the need to maintain both accumulation and legitimacy with its internal structure, or mode of operation (bureaucracy).

But what is equally real is the fact that there is neither visible nor to be anticipated a strategy that actually *does* reconcile these functions and thus achieves a balanced integration of the State and the accumulation process, that is a reliable and workable strategy of "systems maintenance" (as many radicals believe). The reality of the capitalist state can thus be best described as the reality (and dominance) of an unrealistic attempt. There is no method of policy formation available that could make this attempt more realistic, at least if it is true that [the state's function for accumulation] spells—under conditions of advanced capitalism—the need for productive State activities. (Offe 1973, 144)

Offe's capitalist State cannot resolve economic crises in a permanent way. Although called upon to intervene in the capital accumulation process in a way that will preserve capitalist relations of production, and willing—through its own institutional interest—to do so, it is beset by the interests of individual capitals obstructing this intervention, and by the demands of the working class and other labor constituencies on whom it relies for its source of power. The State is constantly trying to fulfill its capital accumulation function while maintaining its legitimacy. "The contradiction—the functional need to pursue systematic needs of an economic and power structure which successfully resists the fulfillment of those needs—explains why reformist policies of the capitalist state seem to display the cyclical pattern of motion in which no point of 'balance,' 'compromise' or 'equilibrium' is arrived at" (Offe 1976, 22).

HIRSCH'S DERIVATIONIST VIEW OF THE STATE

The central theme of the German derivationist view of the State is that the development of the State form and the structural limitations and possibilities of State action can only be approached through an analysis of the relation between the State and the contradictions of capitalist accumulation. In criticism of Poulantzas and Offe, derivationists insist that an analysis of the State requires a systematic analysis to the changing forms of State-society relations and of the State itself, particularly of the changing nature of capitalist accumulation—that is, the changing nature of capitalist exploitation of the working class, and the constraints and limitations that the nature of capitalist accumulation imposes on State action. The analysis of the relation between State and society must be based on the *derivation of the State form* from the contradictions of capitalist society (Holloway and Picciotto 1978, 16). This is not seen as a position of economic determinism, but rather as a view that sees in Marx's *Capital* not an economic analysis, but a materialist critique of the economic form.

Just as the social relations of the capitalist mode of production have given rise to the economic form and the categories of political economy, so they have given rise to the political form and the categories of political science. Thus the investigation of the relation between the economic and the political begins not by asking in what way the 'economic base' determines the 'political superstructure' but by asking: what is it about social relations in bourgeois society that makes them appear in separate forms as economic relations and political relations? (Holloway and Picciotto 1978, 18)

Some derivationists derive the State from the inability of capital (in its existence as many competing capitals) to reproduce the social nature of its own existence. To reproduce, capital requires a State that is not subject to the same limitations as individual capitals. But, as Hirsch points out, a State that is the institutionalization of capital's interests in general is given a power and a knowledge that it cannot possess—it cannot carry out the function assigned to it, since it cannot possibly know what the general interest of capital is. Also, this formulation says little about the State as a form of class domination—what Offe calls the legitimation problem or what Poulantzas describes as the class nature of the State. In part, these problems arise because early derivationists were responding to the instrumentalist position (the State as a tool of the ruling class), but they are also a function of an interpretation of capitalist development that focuses on antagonistic relations between individual capitals rather than the antagonistic relations between capital and labor (Holloway and Picciotto 1978, 22).

Hirsch argues that the specific form of the bourgeois State is derived not from the necessity of establishing the general interests of capital in a society marked by competition among capitals, but from the necessity of abstracting the relations of force from the immediate process of production. So, far from representing in any concrete form the "general interest" of capital, the structural relations of the State to society reproduce the contradictions of capitalist society in the State apparatuses—a position identical to that argued by Poulantzas. But Hirsch goes a step further. Even though the State does not represent an institutionalization of the general interests of capital, its continued existence as a particular form of social relations depends on the reproduction of capital accumulation: the State's activities are bounded and structured by the necessity of ensuring the continued accumulation of capital (Offe's position). For Hirsch, the dynamic force behind the capital accumulation process and therefore behind the development of the State itself is the *tendency of the rate of profit to fall*, which in turn represents a condensation of the contradictions inherent in accumulation (class exploitation). The development of the State is derived from the falling rate of profits and the *need to develop countertendencies* against that decline. Because of its form as an institution separated from the immediate process of production, however, the State can only react to the development of the process of accumulation—it *mediates* the contradictions inherent in capital accumulation in a reactive way. The *form* of the State is bounded and structured by the precondition of its own existence—the need to attempt to ensure the continued accumulation of capital. The *content* of State activities develops through a process of mediated reaction to the development of accumulation.

These, then, are the three components of Hirsch's formulation of the capitalist State. First, a theory of the bourgeois State must be developed from the analysis of the basic structure of capitalist society. Therefore, the bourgeois State is a specific historical form of class rule and not simply a bearer of particular social functions. That State is an autonomous apparatus raised above the reproduction process.

> The contradictions of the capitalist process of reproduction in which the bourgeois state apparatus has its source and continuing basis, give rise to the apparent inconsistencies in its mode of appearance and activity. As the authority guaranteeing the rules of equal exchange and of commodity circulation, and autonomous from the social process of reproduction and the social classes, it acquires—a particular form of the mystification of capital—the appearance of class neutrality free from force, which, however, can and must be transformed into an overt use of force, both internally and externally, if at any time the foundations of the reproduction and self-expansion of capital and of exploitations are threatened. (Hirsch 1978, 65)

Second, it is implicit in the particular form of the bourgeois State that the State apparatus must clash not only with the working class but also with the interests of individual capitals and groups of capitals. "But this means that—just as the bourgeois state does not originate historically as a result of the conscious activity of a society or class in pursuit of its 'general will' but rather as the result of often contradictory and short-sighted class struggles and conflicts—its specific functional mechanisms also evolve in the context of conflicting interests and social conflicts" (Hirsch 1978, 65). The *concrete activities* of the State emerge not as the result of some abstract logic of a given social structure but only under pressure of political movements, as interests succeed in pressing home their demands.

The existence of a bourgeois State is derived from the basic structure of capitalist society. Its possibility of existence depends on its separation from bourgeois society and its being able to guarantee the general and external conditions of reproduction that cannot be created by private capitals, and to intervene with force against the encroachments of workers and individual capitals. The possibility of the bourgeois State's existence, therefore, lies in raising it above the production process, and in its maintaining the capitalist reproduction process. In this way, *its material basis is secured.* "This will necessarily manifest itself as the specifically political and bureaucratic interest of the direct holders of state power and their agents in the safeguarding of capital reproduction and capital relations. This is why the bourgeois state must function as a class state even when the ruling class or a section of it does not exert direct influence over it" (Hirsch 1978, 66). The parallel with Offe is clear. The possibility of the State depends on maintaining a material base, and maintaining that base requires the reproduction of capital accumulation.

Third, the *necessity* of State intervention results from the fact that the capitalist process of reproduction structurally "presupposes social functions which cannot be fulfilled by individual capitals" (Hirsch 1978, 66). This, for Hirsch, is the key to moving beyond some general determinations of the functions of the bourgeois State. What are these social functions that cannot be fulfilled by individual capitals? Hirsch argues that to answer this requires an analysis of the concrete historical development of the capitalist reproduction process and of the changing conditions of capital valorization and class relations, an analysis based on a theory of the capitalist accumulation and crisis. "An analysis of the capitalist accumulation process must above all explain how the capitalist production process, *on the strength of its inherent laws and through the technological transformation of the labor process and the development of the productive forces,* itself produces the barriers to the valorization of capital in which the capitalist crisis itself becomes the necessary vehicle for the actual implementation of state interventions to safeguard reproduction" (Hirsch 1978, 67; italics added).

The specificity of the forms and content of the bourgeois State resides, according to Hirsch, in the *tendency of the rate of profit to fall,* which emanates from the inherent struggle of labor with capital. Capital tends toward crisis and toward collapse. But why, asks Hirsch, has this collapse not occurred? What concrete developments have modified and continue to modify the operation of the general law? He quotes Marx: "The same influences which produce a tendency in the general rate of profit to fall, also call forth counter-effects, which hamper, retard and partly paralyze this fall" (in Hirsch 1978, 71). The most important countertendency, based on the technological transformation of the labor process, is the associated increase in the productivity of labor. The fact that the same causes that cause the rate of profit to fall also generate a countertendency, makes it "difficult to assess quantitatively, let alone predict, the extent and the speed of the change in the rate of profit" (1978, 72). The rate of profit is also influenced by other factors that revolve around the labor-capital struggle: the length of the workday, speedup, and other efforts of capital and labor to lower and raise wages. "Thus, it is clear that the 'counter-tendencies' to the fall in the rate of profit should not be understood as the sum of isolated factors but are rather the expression of a *social complex of conditions of production*, and assert themselves in an increasingly crisis-ridden manner and in any case not merely in the normal course of the accumulation process and in the expanded reproduction of capital relations by capital itself" (1978, 73). The course of capitalist development, Hirsch argues, is not determined mechanically, but by the actions of actors and classes struggling within the context of capitalism's general laws. This tendency toward crisis and collapse, which marks the historical development of capitalist society, can only be counterbalanced by the permanent reorganization of production and relations of surplus extractions. The reorganization of the conditions of production means concretely changing the form of capital itself (monopolies, types of financing, etc.), the expansion of capital into the world market, and the acceleration of scientific and technical progress.

For Hirsch, the investigation of the State must be carried out in the context of the attempt by capital to reorganize production and the relations of exploitation. The State comes to play an increasingly important function in this reorganization, a continuing attempt by capital to counterbalance the tendency to crisis and collapse.

Only the systematic derivation of these movements on the "surface" (changes in the form of capital [monopoly], the establishment or non-establishment of an average rate of profit, the movement of prices, class differentiations, the existence of only partly capitalist countries, movements of the world market, and so on) from the 'central structure' of the capital relation, allows us to analyze concretely the functioning and the modes of functioning of the State apparatus. The logical and at the same time historical concretization of the movements of capital and the way in which they shape class struggles and competition must thus be the starting point for any investigation of political processes if it is not to relapse into the failing of mechanical economic determinism or abstract generalization. (Hirsch 1978, 81)

The capitalist State is interventionist, but interventionist in the context of capitalist laws of motion. We can derive the possibilities of the State from logical deduction, but to understand the particular nature of the capitalist State, we have to analyze in terms of the laws of motion of capitalist development. This means, to Hirsch, that such an analysis cannot proceed abstractly from an objective logic of development processes but must focus on the development of class relations and class struggles mediated by the transformations in the economic base, and the resulting conditions for securing burgeois political domination. This domination has required, he says, concrete intervention by the State apparatus in the material preconditions of the production process and in the conflicts between classes to keep economic reproduction (capital accumulation) in motion and the class struggle latent. Intervention has changed as the production structure changes. First, the State intervened to impose the capitalist-class structure and develop the proletariat as a class, at the same time making the mass of the population dependent materially on the capital accumulation process (as determined by the capitalist class). Then the State intervened to help centralize and monopolize capital and form the imperialist world market. Finally, the State has intervened in the process of technological revolutionization of the labor process as part of counteracting the falling rate of profit.

This is the methodology that Hirsch proposes to use to study the State. With it, he critiques both Offe's and the early derivationists' position directly. For, Hirsch argues, it is impossible to separate the particular functions and operations of the State apparatus without a clear historical analysis of the mediation of competition and class struggle. It is the laws of motion of capitalist development that define the nature of State intervention. "In itself the derivation of objective determinants of the function of the State apparatus from the laws of reproduction tell us nothing decisive about whether and in what form certain State activities result from those determinants. In addition we need to know how the objective determinants are transformed into concrete actions of competition and class struggle" (Hirsch 1978, 83-84).

Given this methodology, Hirsch goes on to analyze what he views as the main trends in capitalist development and the role of the State over approximately the last fifty years. He finds that the mechanism of State interventionist regulation of the reproduction of capital is thoroughly contradictory: the expanding system of State redistribution of revenue for the purpose of guaranteeing and equalizing profits on capital and for the purpose of pacifying wage labor by means of welfare State measures generates the opposition of those capitals that are hurt by the State's policies. At the same time capital as a whole puts up permanent resistance to an expansion of the State's share in the social product because this reduces the margin for private accumulation. Furthermore, increased direct taxes and downward pressure on real wages both by firms trying to increase the profit rate and by indirect taxation (inflation) promotes struggle by the working class against the State itself. Under these circumstances, maintaining accumulation (as Offe points out) becomes increasingly crucial for the maintenance of the State's material base. Hirsch also argues that the tendency of the rate of profit to fall through the technical transformation of the labor process leads historically to a change and to a tendency for the general conditions of production to expand. The State becomes increasingly involved in providing infrastructure services, including, most recently, its expenditures on technological development itself (although in America, with land-grant colleges having already been funded in the middle of the last century and the development of agricultural technology in those colleges in the early twentieth century, this is a long-established tradition).

In summary, Hirsch emphasizes that the bourgeois State inherently cannot act as regulator of the social process of development; it cannot provide a general social interest to capital in the face of competing individual capitals, but must be understood as a reactive mediator of the "fundamentally crisis-ridden course of the economic and social process of reproduction. The developing state interventionism represents a *form* in which the contradictions of capital can temporarily move; but the movement of capital remains historically determining" (Hirsch 1978, 97). We can see here the agreement and disagreement that Hirsch has with Offe's analysis. He agrees with Offe that the State is a reactive mediator; indeed, there is even agreement that the personnel of the State act in their own interest to promote the capital accumulation process. But, on the other hand, Hirsch argues that: "State measures 'to manage the economy' and their success can only be really evaluated in such a context (the class struggle) and not as detached strategies of political instance, understood finally as being indeed 'autonomous,' i.e., as obeying independent laws of motion and as thus subjected to specific capitalist 'restrictions' " (1978, 99).

Although this disagreement is an important one at a methodological level—Hirsch puts much more emphasis on developing empirical data on the process of capitalist development as a precondition of analyzing the reactions of the State apparatus to the contradictions of capitalist development—it seems that the contradictions in late capitalism identified by Offe are close to Hirsch's analysis, and Offe's view of the State as a reactive mediator also agrees with Hirsch's. What Offe does comparatively better than Hirsch is to provide us with a conceptual framework where the State not only faces contradictions in its dealing with individual capitals as it attempts to maintain capital accumulation, but also faces contradictions in securing the continued domination of the bourgeoisie as a class in the face of working-class demands. The fact that the personnel of the State must have a base of power that is not in production (since the State is above reproduction) requires legitimacy with the masses—those who select the State's personnel. Furthermore, Offe provides us with insights into the organizational contradictions associated with a multifunctional bureaucratic State as the crises of capitalist development intensify.

The strength of Hirsch's analysis lies in his very derivation of the State's intervention in the laws of motion of capital accumulation. By studying these laws of motion, it is possible to understand how the nature of State intervention will *change* over time as capital changes the nature of reproduction of accumulation. Seeing the State as a mediator of crises means that understanding the nature of mediation requires an understanding of changes in the nature of the crises, keeping in mind the underlying basis for those crises and for the existence of the capitalist State. We have examined only a small part of his overall analysis of these changes here, but the main point is that understanding the functions of the State at any moment in time cannot be separated from the history of the crises in the capitalist development of that society.

In a sense, then, Offe's and Hirsch's work represents two ends of a spectrum. On one end, Hirsch provides us with a detailed analysis of the laws of motion of capitalist development and their implications for the particular form and functions of the State. His analysis enables us to understand the source and pattern of changes in these forms and functions. As he argues, by analyzing the movements on the "surface" in the form of capital from the "central structure" of the capital relation, we can analyze concretely the functioning and the mode of functioning for the State apparatus. At the other end of the spectrum, we have Offe, whose analysis provides us with little understanding of *changes* in the form and functions of the State apparatus, but gives a detailed understanding of the laws of motion of the State apparatus itself, an understanding not at all divorced from economic relations, but lacking a theory of *change*. Where the two overlap is in their analysis of the relation of the State apparatus to capital accumulation, and in their general view of the possibility and necessity of the bourgeois State's existence. In the present crisis of late capitalism, Offe's and Hirsch's analysis of the relation between the contradictions of capitalist development and the State are quite similar. They both agree that the State does not serve the social function of resolving for *individual capitals* conflicts among those individual capitals in the general interest of capital, for such a general interest is unknown. What is known, they agree, is that capital accumulation must continue and that the State depends on that capital accumulation for its survival. For that reason, it must mediate both differences among individual capitals and the struggle between capital and labor.

OFFE, HIRSCH, AND POULANTZAS

The derivationists' critique of Offe's "political" analysis is also applied to Poulantzas's earlier work: "the central problem of the Marxist theory of the state, the problems of the development of the State form, of the structural limitations and possibilities of state action, which can be approached only through an analysis of the relation between the state and the contradictions of capitalist accumulation, are necessarily passed over in Poulantzas' work'' (Holloway and Picciotto 1978, 6). The very same argument we have given above in terms of a spectrum of analysis can be repeated here: since Poulantzas's work does not analyze the material foundations of the State, changes in the forms and functions of the State are necessarily incomplete. "By severing his study [Poulantzas 1973] from the analysis of the contradictions of accumulation . . . he cuts himself off from the principal source of change in capitalist society—the development of those contradictions, powered by the revolutionary struggle of the working class'' (ibid.).

According to the derivationists, Poulantzas and Offe commit the same error—they "take for granted" the laws of motion of capital and the tendency of the rate of profit to fall. "Relegated to the economic sphere, the analysis of the political can proceed in isolation from the necessities and limitations imposed on the political by precisely those laws of motion'' (Holloway and Picciotto 1978, 6). But Poulantzas's class-based analysis not only fails to understand the *development* of political forms (as does Offe's), it cannot analyze systematically the *limitations* imposed on the State by the relation of the State to the process of capital accumulation (something that Offe somehow achieves without a derivationist approach).

For Poulantzas, the crucial dynamic is class struggle and the displacement of that struggle into the political arena. The development of political forms is therefore couched in class struggle, both among fractions of the power bloc—among individual capitals—and between the working class (and its fractions) and the power bloc as a whole. And the limitations imposed on the State are also related to those struggles. Where this analysis failed in its earlier form (Poulantzas 1974) was in elucidating the mechanism by which personnel of the State, recognized by Poulantzas as not necessarily belonging to the capitalist class, and certainly not directly controlled by the capitalist class (the State being an arena of class struggle), inherently reflect the domination of the bourgeois class. Poulantzas, as we have seen, argues that this mechanism is couched in the *objective relation* that the State has to the bourgeois class. The objective relation, specifically, is ideological—the State's ideological apparatuses are necessarily an articulation of dominant-class hegemony, part of that hegemony in the political sphere. For Poulantzas, as for Gramsci and Althusser before him, the functioning of the State bureaucracy, at least in this earlier formulation, can be explained by its role in extending and developing dominant-class hegemony, where hegemony gets its quality and dynamic from ideology.

Offe and Hirsch, to the contrary, place primary emphasis on understanding the State through its economic role, particularly (Offe) on capital
accumulation (extraction of surplus *and* reproducing the relations of production) and (Hirsch) on offsetting the tendency to a falling rate of profit
(surplus extraction), and the contradictions that emerge in the State as it
attempts to perform its economic functions. The class struggle formulation
developed by Poulantzas is still important in Offe and Hirsch for understanding *changes* in political forms, for, as Hirsch recognizes, it is class
struggle that is the basis for crises in capital accumulation and therefore
the basis for the laws of motion of the State apparatuses. And, as Offe
shows, class struggle must be the basis not only for crises in capital
accumulation (although this is much less clear than in either Hirsch or
Poulantzas), but also for crises of legitimacy.

Yet, Offe's and Hirsch's focus on capital accumulation has its dangers.
There is a notable absence in the German debate of any discussion of the
ideological and repressive functions of the State. Although Offe discusses
the useful notion of "legitimation," legitimacy in his analysis depends
solely on material gains by the working class. The ideological means
available to the State (and to the private sector) to legitimize worker
exploitation and State action against the working class and individual
capitals is not discussed by either Offe *or* Hirsch. In his seminal article
on the State, Hirsch's comment on the ideological and repressive functions
of the State is limited to one sentence: "What must be borne in mind,
however . . . is that state regulation of the economic reproduction process
is only an (albeit important) form with which capital is temporarily able
to break through the self-posited barriers to its valorization, and that the
use of the state apparatus as an apparatus of ideological and physical force
in the class struggle represents a quite essential 'functional equivalent'
thereto'' (Hirsch 1978, 100).

The absence of discussion of ideological functions, in particular, leaves
Offe's and Hirsch's capitalist State depending entirely on *economic* resources. For example, Offe describes the allocation powers of the State
entirely in economic terms—the power to tax, to erect tariffs, to subsidize,
etc. Thus, the State is analyzed solely in terms of its capability to resolve
class conflict through economic means, because the class conflict is located
concretely in capital accumulation. From the Gramscian perspective—and
it is in this tradition that Poulantzas develops his theory of the State—the
State is part of dominant-class hegemony, which means that it can affect
the *terms* of the class struggle. Offe and Hirsch would see downward
pressure on wages (in order to counter the tendency in the rate of profit
to fall) as intensifying the class struggle, or, in Offe's terms, as delegitimating the State. The State, in order to retain legitimacy, would have to

provide the working class with some material benefits to offset the falling wages. But Poulantzas would argue that there are other possibilities for the State (short of repression), particularly through its ideological apparatuses. The State could attempt to get the working class to accept lower wages as part of a "national effort." (This, in fact, is implicitly what Reaganomics proposed.) The countertendencies to the falling rate of profit include ideological struggles in which State personnel not only take action to promote capital accumulation, but to justify "unpopular" actions (e.g., increased unemployment, lower real wages) with dominant-class ideology. Indeed, as Poulantzas points out, the State's role in the dominant hegemony is part of the capital accumulation process: the ideological apparatus of the State is situated in that process and in the class struggle that characterizes it.

Nevertheless, Poulantzas's earlier work lacked Offe's coherent analysis of how the State bureaucracy, autonomous from the production sector and the capitalist class, secures the domination of that class. In particular, the concept that the State acts in the interest of the capitalist class even if the personnel of the State are not from that class, implies (in Poulantzas's analysis) that there is some close relationship between State policy and capitalists, a relationship that allows capitalists to establish hegemony through the State, while the working class is kept divided. Offe suggests, however, that the State's interest in capital accumulation does not mean cooperation with the capitalist class or the fragmentation of the working class (as long as it is not necessary to repress it). The State may very well conflict with individual capitals *and* the working class in attempting to assure the reproduction of accumulation. Such potential conflict of the State with capitalists is an important contribution to understanding the concrete actions of the State apparatus, an understanding that was missing from Poulantzas's earlier analysis.

Poulantzas moved to correct that deficiency in his last book ([1978] 1980). His analysis there argues that class struggles "traverse and constitute the State; that they assume a specific form within the State; and that this form is bound up with the material framework of the State" (1980, 154). And class contradictions are also inscribed in the State through the internal divisions of the State personnel and through the fact that although this personnel is not in and of itself a class, it is a social group that has a class place (defined by its place in the social division of labor) and is therefore internally divided. Thus, while the dominant ideology acts as the *internal cement* of the State apparatuses and their personnel (contrast this with Offe's "economic" cement), with the "neutral" State attempting to appear as the representative of the general will and interest and the arbiter among struggling classes, the struggles of the popular masses "constantly call into question the unity of the State personnel as a category in the service of the existing power and hegemonic fraction of the dominant classes" (1980, 155). "What frequently brings them (the State personnel) into conflict with the dominant classes and the upper reaches of the State is the hold of big economic interests over the State, which they see as threatening its role as guarantor of socio-economic 'order' and 'efficiency' and as destroying state 'authority' and the function of the traditional state 'hierarchies' " (1980, 136).

However, Poulantzas argues, this also means that the State personnel, even in defending the "interests" of the popular masses, do so in the context of reproducing the social division of labor within the State apparatus and within the division between rulers and ruled that is embodied in the State. These are the limits imposed by the material framework of the State (the objective relation between the dominant class and the State); these limits can be changed only *if the institutional framework itself is transformed* (1980, 157). The question then remains: would the personnel who swing over to the popular masses help transform the State apparatus itself? Poulantzas suggests that the wish to provide a *continuity* for the State apparatus, which is at the core of the swing to the popular masses on the part of some personnel in the first place (to defend the "independence" of the State in the face of challenges to that independence by big economic interests), could persuade these State personnel to *go along* with transformations elsewhere by transforming the State apparatus.

On the point of relative autonomy of the State apparatuses, then, Poulantzas's recent work comes remarkably close to Offe's: "It is true that the state bureaucracy also seeks to defend interests peculiar to its own position, so that we can speak of an 'interest in stability' characterizing the entire personnel" (Poulantzas 1980, 157-158). But, as both Poulantzas (1980) and Hirsch (1978) suggest, autonomy is not the essential point, even though it is important in dealing with their own analysis of bureaucracy. Rather, in one form or another, the very material framework of the class structure and struggle imposes limits on the State and on the process of defending the bureaucracy's "autonomous" position. This, according to Hirsch (1978), is where Offe's theory is *incomplete*: he locates power outside of the State (in the popular vote that maintains or replaces political actors and in the capital accumulation process that is the source of the State's revenue), but he does not supply us with a theory of *why* the crises to which the State must respond to maintain itself occur in the first place. Government strategy for Offe is described in terms of technical responses, not in terms of class relations and their dynamics. Are problems in capital accumulation just the result of competition among capitals or rather, of class struggle? Offe views the State as the primary moment of State theory, but that State only *reacts* to capitalist accumulation crises and class movements without steering them. According to Hirsch, Offe ignores the fact that the capital accumulation process must be described in terms of class conflict, subject to objective, regular developments. For Poulantzas and Hirsch, the power relations between classes and among fractions of the dominant class determine the content of the State interest and the concrete actions of government groups toward reorganizing class relations. Offe's description of the State mechanisms can only be useful and relevant within a theory that can decode the State as a specific form of class power and analyze State-administered actions as movements of ideological and repressive developments of exploitative relations.

CHAPTER SIX

The State, Democracy, and the Transition to Socialism

ALTHOUGH MARX's early writings were concerned with democracy (Draper 1977), the issue has not been a central theme in Marxist discussion of the State until recent years. Marx's work on the Paris Commune ([1871] 1978), cited so extensively by Lenin in *The State and Revolution*, is an exception to the more pervasive view in Marx's, Engels's, and Lenin's writings that sees the State as necessary only in a class society, to repress the dominated classes and to reproduce the class relations of production. Without class struggle, such repression and reproduction are unneeded: thus, the "withering away of the State." Democracy, in a communist society, would be part of the classlessness (equality) of the society. Political democracy developed in the context of the State has been, for Marxist-Leninists, a conceptual contradiction. The politics of the transition from capitalism to socialism in Marxist literature is vague, except in terms of eliminating the bourgeoisie as a social force, and, by definition, eliminating the bourgeois State. Whereas remnants of this State might remain during the transition, its functions are antithetical to building socialism. Hence, the fundamental social changes are to come from *outside* the transition State bureaucracy, enabling it to wither away.

Rosa Luxemburg (1961) questioned the position Lenin had taken on the dictatorship of the proletariat, emphasizing the contradiction of attempting to build socialism by suppressing (because they were and are considered elements of a class State) free speech, free press, and other characteristics of bourgeois democracy. Her analysis raised the *process* issue of the transition: how the revolution develops has to affect its institutions. Politics matters. But it was Gramsci and his increasing influence on Marxist analysis in the post-World War II period that began to open the way for serious discussion of the capitalist State as a site of class struggle, not merely as the bourgeoisie's repressive apparatus. Furthermore, his idea that the superstructure is a crucial arena of conflict allowed Marxists to discuss a theory of the transition State—a theory of politics—that includes emphasis on the *nature* of institutions emerging from the building of proletarian hegemony and how they relate to the subsequent proletarian State.[1] Concretely, Gramsci's notion of "passive revolution" (see Chapter 3) forms the basis of the current debate on whether new forms of democracy can transform the relationship of the individual to the State and go beyond the formal limitations of liberal democracy (Showstack Sassoon 1980; Buci-Glucksmann 1979; Gorz 1968).

There is also the reality of the Soviet Union, and the growth of "socialism" in the post-1945 period. The bureaucratic Soviet State and the obvious lack of democracy in the socialist bloc raise serious questions about the politics of the transition. When placed next to the Soviet State, "bourgeois" democracy in advanced capitalist societies has appeal even for their proletariat (see Przeworski, 1979). The State does not seem to be withering away in "socialist" societies. Rather, it has enormous economic and political control over people's lives and when threatened—as in Poland—by workers trying to dismantle it, attempts to repress them. Thus, the whole basis of orthodox Marxist political theory runs into difficulties: What if socialism does not lead to the withering away of the State, but instead the State is here to stay? Is the State a necessity of modern economic and social life where, even in a socialist world, representative democracy at local, regional, and national levels is the probable political decision-making form? What if the very process of building socialism without basic bourgeois personal freedoms would (as Rosa Luxemburg foresaw) form barriers to socialist development? The transition State would then become a real issue, not one to be swept under the withering-away rug.

But can democracy be extended *through* the bourgeois State; can representative democracy and the rest of the bourgeois State apparatus be transformed into a "mass" State without first destroying it? The existence of social democracy in Scandinavia (and milder versions since World War II in Great Britain and Germany), the failure of democratic socialism in Chile and Portugal, and the growth of an electoral Communist Party in Italy and a Common Program in France have all affected the present lines of this old discussion (even before the events in Poland and the Socialist Party victories in France, Greece, and Spain).

There are today several significant Marxist positions on democracy that deviate from the orthodox denouement of the bourgeois State as a democratic "facade," a bourgeois "invention" consciously designed to fool the people. Not surprisingly, since Gramsci had already opened the doors

[1] Although Gramsci does not go beyond a critique of parliamentary democracy to consider its place in socialist strategy, "he perceives all of its fragility and his analysis is never reduced simply to the denunciation of its class character, according to the classical schema" (Buci-Glucksmann 1982, 124).

to this discussion in the 1920s, three views have appeared in what might be called the "Italian debate" on democracy and the transition to socialism.[2] A fourth position emerges from the debate on socialist/communist political strategy in France in the mid- and late-1970s.

The first position (in order of chronological appearance) is taken by Lucio Colletti (1972). Throughout his career, Colletti has developed a consistent left-wing critique of Italian Communist Party (PCI) politics and of the Soviet position in the Party. Colletti's work, like that of his teacher, Della Volpe, takes a sharp anti-Hegelian position in interpreting Marx's work, which, among other things, poses Marx's view of the State in opposition to Hegel's idealism rather than Adam Smith's, Bentham's, or Mill's utilitarianism. But more interesting for us is his "rereading" of Lenin's *The State and Revolution* (similar to Althusser's rereading of *Capital*), especially his reinterpretation of Lenin's view of democracy and his defense of that view in light of post-revolutionary Soviet developments.

The second position is Norberto Bobbio's. For more than twenty-five years, Bobbio has been a PCI critic from a class perspective. In 1975, Bobbio wrote a series of articles in *Mondoperaio* under the title, "Does There Exist a Marxist Theory of the State?" (Bobbio 1977a). Bobbio's conclusion is that there does *not* exist such a theory of the transition to socialism except in the vaguest terms (thereby pointedly disagreeing both with the orthodox Communist Party view and with Colletti). He argues that not only does "bourgeois" democracy represent real working-class victories in a struggle over the form of the capitalist State, but that the alternatives to representative democracy all ignore the fundamental importance of political emancipation as a *precondition* of economic emancipation. Democracy, even in its bourgeois form, he insists, must be the starting point for the *extension* of democracy, either politically or in the economic sphere. It is the democratization of the State itself that must form the basis for the overall democratization of society.

The view represented by Pietro Ingrao (1977, 1979) and Nicos Poulantzas's last work (Ingrao's influence is evident there) contrasts with both Colletti's and Bobbio's positions. Ingrao insists that the bourgeois State *is* a class State and therefore the *content* of the democratic rules of that State is determined by the structural conditions of capitalist development. He agrees with Bobbio that it has been the working class who has given democratic content to liberal representative institutions, but for that very reason authentic change has to come with the eruption of the masses— with mass struggle. While representative democracy in capitalist societies

[2] The term "Italian debate" emanates from the discussion begun by Norberto Bobbio on Marxist theories on politics in the pages of *Mondoperaio* in 1975.

may be a favorable terrain for organizing popular forces, the parliament will not allow change in and of itself unless rooted in a mass movement from which that democracy receives its power. Furthermore, it is unclear what the form will be of democratic institutions rooted in such a movement, particularly when economic democracy is combined with political. It is to the details of these positions that we now turn.

COLLETTI ON LENIN

In his interpretation of Lenin's position on the State and democracy in *The State and Revolution*, Colletti (1972) spells out a structuralist version of the necessity of destroying the bourgeois State as a prerequisite to social and political change. The issue, he argues, is not whether the overthrow of the capitalist State must be violent—the traditional-Communist Party position until Stalin's death—but whether the State must be destroyed. For Colletti, this is Lenin's essential point: the old State machine must be destroyed because "the bourgeois State depends on the *separation* and *alienation* of power from the masses. . . . A socialist revolution that maintained this type of State would keep alive the *separation* between the masses and power, their *dependence* and subordination" (Colletti 1972, 220). Power must be transferred directly to the people, and that is impossible if this "diaphragm that separates the working classes from power" (1972, 220) is not first smashed. The destruction of the old machine is the destruction of the limits imposed on democracy by the bourgeois State. "And, adds Lenin, 'full democracy is *not*, qualitatively, the same thing as incomplete democracy.' Behind what might seem formally a difference in quantity, what is actually at stake is a 'gigantic replacement of certain institutions by other institutions of a fundamentally different order' " (Colletti 1972, 221).

For Lenin, the revolution is not only the transfer of power from one class to another, it is also the passage from one type of power to another. The revolution destroys the difference between the governors and the governed, bringing the working class to govern itself. Any theory of State seizure, Colletti insists, that does not contain this element of both destruction and transformation of power oscillates between two poles: "a reckless subjectivism that sees the essence of the revolution and socialism in the promotion to power of particular *political personnel*, who are, as we know, the party bureaucracy; and an inter-class conception of the State" (Colletti 1972, 223). According to Colletti, then, Lenin's attack on the bourgeois State is an attack on the fundamentally *undemocratic* nature of that political formation. But not because the bourgeois parliament is a "fraud." Rather, the State's growth is organically linked to the growth of the capitalist socioeconomic order—the State in capitalist society is structurally a class State, hence *must* act as a separator of power from the masses.

Yet, Colletti goes much further. He argues that in *The State and Revolution*, Lenin discovers that the "dictatorship of the proletariat" is not the dictatorship of the party but of the Paris Commune.

> The difference between the two view-points is so radical that whereas in the first case the critique of parliament becomes a critique of *democracy*, in Lenin's case, on the contrary, the critique of parliament, i.e. of *liberal* or *bourgeois* democracy, is a critique of the *anti-democratic* nature of parliament—a critique made in the name of that infinitely "fuller" (and hence qualitatively different) democracy, the democracy of the soviets, the only democracy that deserves the name of socialist democracy. (Colletti, 1972, 224)

Parliament is suppressed by Lenin to be replaced by institutions of proletarian democracy—by the self-government of the mass of producers. Nevertheless, this still implies the withering away of the State: the more democracy develops (that is, the more the self-government of the masses is extended) the "further the withering away of the State has advanced" (Colletti 1972, 226). This implies that the socialist State itself—insofar as socialism needs a State—is a remnant of the bourgeois State (primarily because of the continued existence of the bourgeois "right" to be remunerated according to labor instead of need).

What, then, explains that socialism today has so little to do with Lenin's democratic ideals and his Marxist theory of politics (as Colletti presents them)? Colletti contends that this is due to the incompleteness of the world socialist revolution: it is not Lenin who is outdated, it is national socialism—the construction of socialism in one country—that is outdated. For the Leninist vision of democracy to exist, the revolution must be worldwide and communism must have a "world-historical existence" (Colletti, 1972, 227).

So, for Colletti, Marxist-Leninist political theory not only exists, but nothing written since in the Marxist literature is "pervaded with such a profound democratic inspiration as that which animates Lenin's text from beginning to end" (1972, 224-225). The capitalist State must be destroyed in order to achieve socialist democracy, and this democracy is the direct control of the governed by the governed themselves. It is some form of the soviets; yet the State itself must eventually also disappear. Does this mean that the soviets disappear? Is the capitalist State by definition the only form of the State; is complete democracy only possible with the State's disappearance? If the development of socialism is measured by the level of development of democracy, and communism (the final form of socialism) is marked by the withering away of the State, then democracy and the State are contradictory terms. One grows at the expense of the other, and there is nothing that can be called a socialist State. All revolutionary politics must be aimed at State destruction.

BOBBIO ON ALTERNATIVES TO REPRESENTATIVE DEMOCRACY

In his initiation of the "Italian debate" (eight years after the appearance of Colletti's essay on Lenin), Bobbio attempted to establish that the "retaking" of the democracy issue by socialism is fundamental to socialism's political future, *and* that democracy in capitalist societies is, in fact, not the result of capitalist stratagems, but of "conquests that have cost blood and tears to the worker movement" (Bobbio 1977b, 39). Furthermore, the socialist claim to democracy cannot be based on Lenin's views (even a reinterpretation of them) because of "what has happened . . . after Lenin." We cannot place the theoretical ideas of even Lenin before the "hard facts, as Hegel has said, of history" (Bobbio 1977b, 39).

The present problem for socialism lies in the socialist reality of the Soviet Union and the Eastern European bloc countries and the concomitant failure of history to provide an example of the transition to socialism except in the most negative terms: we are presented with a rigid Soviet-style bureaucracy as one possibility and the specter of the 1973 bombing of Chile's presidential palace (and the death of Allende) as the other. In this he and Colletti agree. But Bobbio goes much further. He argues that, except in the vaguest terms, there does not exist a Marxist *theory* of the transition. In large part, this is the result of Marx's fundamental view of the State as a "necessary evil," not necessary for society's overall welfare but only as the instrument of a dominant class. Thus, Marx rejects Hegel's position that the State's monopoly on legal violence is a force for morality and ideals, and replaces it with one that puts the State squarely in the hands of one social group dominating another, not for the common welfare (as other realists had assumed), but for the interests of the dominant group. Thus, Marx was the first philosopher to argue that the State is "not only an instrument, an apparatus, an ensemble of apparatuses, among which the principal and determinant one is the monopoly on the exercise of force, but that it is an instrument which serves particular (class) interests, not general ones" (Bobbio 1977b, 46).

Once the State is defined this way, Bobbio contends, it is logical that Marx should see the State as always "bad," and that for him and Engels (and Lenin), the problem of good government cannot be resolved by replacing a bad form of the State with a good one. The only good State is one that has no political function. In fact, Bobbio goes on, this was not only a necessary stage in the development of State theory, but much more important in understanding Marx's views than his "too famous" analysis of the Paris Commune experience (Bobbio 1977b, 46). Thus, we are left with no critical political analysis comparable to the economic critique in *Capital* with which to develop a socialist theory of the democratic State.

This established, Bobbio attempts to fill the gap by beginning from his own view that bourgeois democracy, as it exists at any historical juncture, is as much the result of working-class victories as of bourgeois hegemony. He defines democracy as what we observe in today's advanced capitalist societies (but not limited to what we observe): majority rule, freedom of information, freedom to vote, minority rights, and so forth (Bobbio 1977a, 50). The significance of his position is that although he may consider democracy in capitalist societies to be "restricted," it is still democracy, a valid form of political participation *won by the working classes* and valued by them in their struggle against bourgeois dominance. So democracy as it appears is not complete, but *must be included* in any concept of socialist politics. Although the co-optation of the working class through corporatist unions and bourgeois-dominated political parties is, in Gramsci's terms, "passive revolution," which maintains bourgeois hegemony, Bobbio implies that so-called bourgeois democracy itself (and its expansion) is not bourgeois, but counterhegemonic, and contributes to breaking through capitalist social relations.

He is totally opposed to Colletti's argument that representative democracy is "alienating" and "separating" as part of the alienation and separation of capitalist society (and therefore must be destroyed in order to create "real" democracy). Indeed, the concept of direct democracy (Lenin's soviets, for example) put in opposition to representative democracy, he argues, is a straw man, for in modern societies, direct, mass democracy is not really the issue. Rather the issue is the extension of existing participation in the face of increasing pressure to reduce such participation, whether in representative or direct form.

Bobbio's argument hinges on his contention that the objective conditions of modern capitalist development are increasingly less democratic. Hence democracy is increasingly posed *against* the dynamic of capitalist development and therefore represents a crucial element in the countertransformation of capitalist society.

He poses four paradoxes of modern democracy. First, people are constantly asking for more democracy in objective conditions increasingly less favorable for it. That is, nothing is more difficult than for large organizations to respect the rules of the democratic game, and such organizations, including the State itself, are not only growing in size but are dominating more and more aspects of society. So the conditions for creating a working democratic society are more difficult today, in the era of large bureaucracies. Second, the modern State, like private corporations, has also grown both in terms of size and in the number of functions it performs. These increased functions have produced a growth of bureaucracy, which is characterized by a hierarchical, nondemocratic structure. Democracy (and even more, increased socialism) has been characterized until now by an increase in bureaucracy, and not—since the great suffrage victories—by increased participation.[3] The problem is how to build democracy and socialism without increasing hierarchical structures. Third, industrial societies, whether capitalist or socialist, have increased—in an accelerated way—problems that require technical solutions, which can be found only by highly skilled technocrats. There is a temptation to govern through technocrats and technocratic solutions, in other words, through technocracy. This type of government, Bobbio argues, is the opposite of democracy; it is a contradiction of industrial society that technocracy is a government of those who know a single thing but know it well, whereas democracy is a government of all, of those who must decide not on the basis of competency but of existence itself. "The protagonist of industrial society is the scientist, the specialist, the expert; the protagonist of the democratic society is the common citizen, the man in the street, the *quisque e populo*" (Bobbio 1977b, 56). Is it not contradictory, asks Bobbio, to demand more democracy in a society that is constantly more technical? "To ask for more democracy means asking for an extension of decisions requiring competency by someone who is, by the objective conditions of development of modern societies, increasingly more incompetent. This happens most of all in the production sector, precisely in the sector that, as much in capitalist as in socialist economies, has been withdrawn from all forms of popular control and is the one in which the democratic game is won or lost" (1977b, 57). Fourth, democracy presupposes the full and free development of the human faculties. The effect of "massification"— the growth of a mass society—is generalized conformity: "The characteristic indoctrinization of mass society tends to repress and suppress the sense of individual responsibility, the base on which democratic society is ruled" (1977b, 57). Thus, the mass society—and this includes socialism—generates the decline of individuality, and individuality—particularly individual responsibility—is fundamental to democratic decision-making.

With these paradoxes in mind, Bobbio examines the possible relation between socialism and democracy, in other words, a theory of the State for democratic socialism. As Bobbio has defined it, of course, socialism

---

[3] Alan Wolfe (1977) develops this argument for the United States, emphasizing reduced participation in the context of a legitimacy crisis of the State (see Chapter 8 below).

is more democracy—at least in a theoretical political model of the State. Despite Marx and one hundred years of socialist practice, he says, the fundamental problem for modern man, a problem that has not been resolved and may not even be solvable, is how the individual can—at one and the same time—give up his liberty to the body politic of which he forms a part, and be freer than before.

Furthermore, the democratic socialist model as an alternative to the liberal democratic one (the parliamentary democratic State) does not exist— at least it does not exist in all the "perfection of details" of the bourgeois political system. While the form of the State developed in the socialist bloc *is* an alternative to the representative, parliamentary bourgeois State, it is not an *acceptable* alternative for those who believe in democracy itself. A dictatorship, according to Bobbio, even a socializing one,"always represents, to the masses who suffer, nothing but a change of bosses" (1977b, 62). No one, he continues, and this is perhaps his strongest statement of the problem for a democratic socialist theory of the State, has seen a regime that has suppressed its parliament and been able to maintain individual liberties; nor has anyone seen a regime that both has allowed a parliament to have political power and has been able (or willing) to suppress individual liberties.

The Left has criticized parliamentary (representative) democracy by arguing that it is not enough, that the only "true" democracy is direct. Bobbio feels that the weakness of this argument is that the Left has made direct democracy a fetish without asking whether it is possible to achieve it, and without asking what it consists of or what its relation is to indirect democracy. The problem, he contends, is not in parliamentary democracy per se, but in the fact that such democracy has not been allowed its full expression.

> That which we briefly call the representative State has always had to deal with the administrative State, which is a State obeying a completely distinct logic of power; descending, not ascending; secret, not public; hierarchical, not autonomous; tending to inertia, not dynamic; conservative, not innovative, etc. . . . citizen sovereignty is limited by the fact that the relatively big decisions like economic development policy, never reach the representative institutions, or if they reach them, the decisions are actually made in another place; a place where the majority of citizens have no voice. . . . In a capitalist society, the sovereignty of the citizen as such, independent of whether he/she is a capitalist or worker, bourgeois or proletarian, is also a member of the political community equal to all the rest. This is a *mediated* sovereignty, at least as

long as the separation between civil and political society lasts. (1977b, 70; italics added)

But despite this reality, Bobbio argues, there is also the reality that the area of citizen sovereignty does coincide with the representative institutions at all the different levels, and it is in these institutions that the citizen can exercise his or her sovereignty to the extent that he or she can influence decisions at all.

Bobbio is convinced that democracy flows from the political system to the economic. For example, he contends that the two democratic models posed as alternatives to the parliamentary State, guild socialism and soviets, both require that democratic control has to be extended from the political institutions to economic. The logic behind this demand is the same that gave birth to the democratic State itself, that is, the extension of democratic control (popular democratic control) to the institutions of society. The error always made by advocates of industrial democracy, he says, is "believing in the possibility of resolving political democracy by economic democracy, the citizen self-government by producer self-government" (1977b, 71). The error lies in believing that there do not exist problems of the citizen that are distinct from those of the producer. But it is precisely the problems of liberty—civil and political liberties—whose undervaluation is one of the poorest inheritances of Marxist thought. According to Marx, Bobbio points out, political emancipation is not human emancipation. However, for Bobbio, if political emancipation is not sufficient, it is, however, always necessary, and there can be no human emancipation without political emancipation. "This emancipation requires the development, the extension, the reinforcement, of all the institutions which gave birth to modern democracy, whose suspension—even momentary suspension—does not bring any advantage" (Bobbio 1977b, 72).

The implications of Bobbio's analysis are clear. He insists that democracy, even in its "bourgeois" form, has to be the starting point for the extension of democracy, either politically or in the economic sphere. To create democratic institutions requires *being* democratic, and representative democracy should not be destroyed for its bourgeois origins, but rather made—in Marx's words—into a "working parliament," in which the masses are represented, and in which the most important decisions are made. In addition, of course, democracy should be extended into the economy, but this, according to Bobbio's paradoxes, is becoming more and more difficult. Does that mean that socialism may have to settle for political democracy but State-bureaucracy controlled, nondemocratic enterprises?

Nothing could be farther from Colletti's defense of Lenin's destruction of the bourgeois State. Colletti sees the State as inherently antidemocratic; Bobbio believes that representative democracy as we observe it in advanced capitalist societies must be the starting point for achieving democratic socialism. For Colletti, it is the *absence* of the political State that is democratic socialism; for Bobbio, the bourgeois State, although limited in its democratic possibilities, still contains elements that have developed as *part of the struggle for socialism*: all democracy, even in limited forms, is a step toward socialism. So, although both writers agree that democracy and socialism are intimately intertwined, Colletti defines democracy in a society dominated by the capitalist relations of production as part of that domination. Bobbio, on the other hand, claims that democracy, even in a capitalist society, is an outgrowth of the struggle by the working class for power. The State, for him, is not only an arena of class struggle, it is the *all-important* arena; the necessary precondition of human emancipation is winning and extending political rights within and through the State, using the power of the State to extend democracy from there to other institutions. Bobbio makes democracy the key element in a working-class "war of position," one that is forced to take the field against modern organizational, psychological, and technological factors that are the new, inherently antidemocratic forms of the bourgeois "passive revolution" crucial to the maintenance and expansion of bourgeois hegemony.[4]

DEMOCRACY AND CLASS STRUGGLE

Other Marxists, inside and outside Italy, obviously have found Bobbio's position extremely controversial. The most well-developed theoretical response to both Bobbio's and Colletti's analyses comes from Pietro Ingrao, one of the high officials of the Italian Communist Party and president of the Italian Chamber of Deputies, and, in France, from Nicos Poulantzas, whose work we have already reviewed.[5]

[4] Bobbio's position comes remarkably close to Karl Kautsky's, and for many of the same reasons. Kautsky maintained that any project of direct democracy was doomed to failure in a society dominated by large-scale industry, that is, dominated by a mode of production that inherently required long-term planning and coordination with State policies and that, along with the State itself, was increasingly characterized by bureaucratization and technocratization (compare this with Bobbio's "paradoxes"). These tendencies in the bourgeois State (and subsequently in the Soviet form of socialism) could only be corrected by bringing them under the control of parliament and other democratic institutions. Socialism was not a historical necessity for Kautsky, but a possibility to be realized through political organization and practice, and democracy a necessary and decisive condition for the possibility of socialism (see Salvadori 1979).

[5] It is not by accident that I group these two writers together: Ingrao's work had a significant influence on Poulantzas's political views, as we shall show.

Ingrao and Democracy of the Masses

Ingrao established in his earlier work (1977) a view of the capitalist State as a product and shaper of class struggle, a site where the masses make and win demands that alter capitalist development, just as the class State itself attempts to intervene in behalf of such development. Thus, for example, he sees the welfare State as an attempt to solve the economic crisis of the thirties and (in Europe) to create a successful post-World War II capitalist development. But this State was and is not simply an economic operation. It was and is also characterized by new forms of connections and interrelations between the productive and political processes of the private economy and the State, including new forms of international connections. The welfare State created a new concept of progress based on the dynamic of large, oligopolistic corporations and, at the same time, a new definition of personal rights: guaranteed employment (or unemployment compensation), the reduction of income and schooling inequalities, and old-age and health support. In other words, both capitalism and labor are redefined by the State (Ingrao 1979). Mass struggle in the capitalist economies and the success of the Russian Revolution led to a *new concept of well-being* that included many ''rights'' for workers in capitalist production that did not exist before. Dominant capitalist groups—faced by such struggle or the threat of it—had to look for forms of government and hegemony that were much more exposed to mass-movement pressure than previous forms (the recognition of labor unions as official bargaining units, for example). But at the same time, political parties, unions, and other popular organizations changed to limit popular participation. It was the welfare State itself that became the connection between new forms of production and new social values. Today's crisis is that solution to the previous crisis (of the 1930s), is therefore, for Ingrao, a *hegemonic* crisis rather than an economic one. We are not in the throes of an economic depression, but in an historic moment where the State and capitalism cannot deliver what they have led two generations to believe in. At the same time, mass consciousness of a different kind of life—long-term increases in real income, low unemployment, and State support for the poor and old— remains unchanged. Indeed, the very past success of the welfare State has created new kinds of consciousness in minorities and women. All of these are posed against the decline of that solution.

For Ingrao mass movements *are* democracy, and, in accord with Bobbio, representative democracy, as well as the new concept of well-being, are working-class victories. But unlike Bobbio, Ingrao does not view representative democracy as the only (or even primary) form of democratic (mass) expression. Ingrao's State is a class State in which representative democracy allows the masses to exert political power, but only within the limits set by class relations in the society as a whole. So although Bobbio argues that the procedures of representative democracy are the best there are, and socialists should start with them, following the rules of political democracy, imperfect as they are, Ingrao says that the real problem is situated in the structural conditions that give *content* to these rules. Voters are not equal when many are workers and a minority are owners and managers—when, as Bobbio admits, the major economic decisions are made by "private power." Are we dealing here with a sector of society that is outside the site of political participation and struggles (including the democratic institutions), or is this private power in the center of the whole productive, social, and political mechanism? If it is the second of these, says Ingrao, then "we find ourselves not before an external limit [to democracy], but an internal one that moves inside the whole representative democratic system, and provides the character and value to these same 'rules' with which Bobbio measures democracy" (Ingrao 1977, 200). Ingrao agrees with Colletti that representative democracy cannot be separated from the class relations that permeate capitalist society, but he disagrees with the idea that the bourgeois State is simply an instrument of the ruling capitalist class. It is a site of struggle, and representative democracy is a working-class victory in that struggle. Nevertheless, such democracy is necessarily limited by the partial nature of that victory, demonstrated by the continued existence of class relations in production and other institutions (that is, the continued hegemony of the dominant capitalist class).[6]

Along this same line, Ingrao contends that the main contribution of the Marxist theory of the State has been to discover the mechanism whereby liberal bourgeois democracy does not represent the kind of democracy that

[6] Ingrao's disagreement with Bobbio stems largely from Ingrao's much more faithful adherence to Gramsci's notion of extending democracy and the role of the revolutionary party and counterhegemony in that extension (see Showstack Sassoon 1980a, 1980b). In that notion, true democracy in the transition is not built primarily through the bourgeois parliament but through the party and mass movements—institutions that are "outside" bourgeois hegemony. Although Gramsci says little about the internal organization of those institutions, he does indicate that the "party whose aim is to create a new *type* of State must itself be a new type of party" (Showstack Sassoon 1980a, 228). It is therefore in the party and the mass movements that the new democracy is defined, through the very task of conducting politics "based on creating the conditions for active political intervention by the mass of the population and aimed at the abolition of the division between rulers and ruled" (Showstack Sassoon 1980a, 229). As we have noted in Chapter 3, there are more Leninist interpretations of Gramsci's political writings, but Ingrao has obviously taken Gramsci's general views on counterhegemony and incorporated them (as has Showstack Sassoon) into a strategy of transition through expanded democracy. Bobbio, on the other hand, as we have already pointed out, is closer to Kautsky's social democracy.

would obtain under socialism. It has always been workers' movements that have had to fight against the tendency of representative democracy to reject social change and to support the needs of the dominant power in the economic structure. It has been the working class that has given democratic content to liberal representative institutions. "Bobbio says: democracy is subversive. I would add that modern democracy is subversive in as much as it reveals its incompleteness and asks to be completed" (Ingrao 1977, 202). This is also Alan Wolfe's point in the United States—democracy in capitalist societies only exists in its complete form as a vision. Capitalist reality is characterized by both the existence of participation and the constant revelation of limits placed on participation. It is this contradiction that is at the heart of the issue.

It is logical for Ingrao to ask whether, in a capitalist society, the social system can be changed while giving equal political rights to everyone in the society, both the dominated, exploited worker, and capitalists and managers: "Is it possible to change the social structure if there is equal political citizenship . . . for those who enjoy the advantages of determining economic power and have on their side the tradition, the existing social stratification, the structure of knowledge, and a whole network of international alliances?" (1977, 202-203). Historically, the bourgeoisie has not accepted social change gracefully, at least not any change that threatened to take away its economic (and therefore political) power. It has fought back with all the violence at its disposal. At the same time, Bobbio's point that a Marxist theory of the State must provide a strategy for achieving *democratic* socialism is still valid, for it is only with political democracy that human emancipation can be achieved. So the issue becomes one of analyzing whether representative democracy is only the most favorable terrain for organizing popular forces, or whether it is the possible political form for a transition from capitalism to another socioeconomic formation. The main difficulty, of course, is that an elected socialism has to co-exist for a long period of time (during the transition) within and with the old class structures; it has to maintain itself in State power and change the old structures at the same time. This was partly (partly, because the Popular Unity government did not have a majority in the legislature) the situation of the Allende period in Chile (which ended in disaster), and is the situation of the present period in France, Greece, and Spain.

On the other hand, Ingrao does not agree with Bobbio's obstacles ("paradoxes") to building the new socialist democracy. Those barriers, Ingrao contends, are part of an incorrect analysis of the evolution of capitalist society. Was the State more accessible or less separated from the masses a century ago than it is now? Was there less conformity in the past? Didn't tradition act to control people's behavior then more than the political mechanisms and ideological apparatuses do today? And as far as modern bureaucracy is concerned, he claims that it is in part the manifestation of mass action, the result of a working class demanding equality and justice in the economic system—it is an expression of the class struggle and cannot be separated from it. Likewise, technocracy is the result of a crisis in the structure of knowledge, in the way that decisions were made in the past. It is an expression of intellectuals' failure to produce the masses' desired social and economic conditions. "Is this technology harmonious with those interests that monopolize the large economic decisions? Or are there conflicts between groups inside and outside the State that permit new possibilities in the very heart of the State machinery?" (Ingrao 1977, 206).

The paradoxes should not prevent us—according to Ingrao—from "deciding for *what* Parliament we are fighting (with which powers, for example, within the overall production sector)" (1977, 207). Nor does he see the distinction in a class society between direct democracy (he calls it democracy of the base) and representative democracy, or something that comes after or apart from it. "The existence of a factory council is necessary to have a particular kind of Parliament, one that is capable of programming the fundamental objectives of the economy, and at the same time, the factory council, with more than just salary objectives . . . needs— in order to survive—a really unified national political assembly" (1977, 207).

The transformation of the State is connected with the social process. It is here that Ingrao sees Gramsci's work as particularly useful, since it shows us how political mediation is a "structural construction," and therefore democracy, its values, and its development must all be based "in the reunification and recomposition of the social body" (1977, 208). And despite problems of separation between institutions and masses within political parties, even mass-based parties, Ingrao—disagreeing with Bobbio—argues that mass-based parties are essential to organize the "democratic dialectic" and to avoid handing over politics to "specialists" and a State that is something external to the social process. It is still the party that makes "order" out of mass-based politics and brings the struggle into the State (and outside the State) in some coherent way.

In the last analysis, he argues, authentic social change (and there have been many such changes in the last century) has come with the eruption of the masses, with their struggles and revolutions. Even the authoritarian collectivist regimes of Eastern Europe—themselves the result of social revolution—have had an important influence on the extension of democracy through mass-based movements in the rest of the world. Unless representative democracy is based in such a movement, it will not allow change, and hence will not expand social and political rights.

The Poulantzas View

In France, Poulantzas ([1978] 1980) also entered the debate on democratic socialism, using Rosa Luxemburg's critique of Lenin. Poulantzas raises three major points.

First, like Colletti, Bobbio, and Ingrao, he assumes that democracy is socialism and there is no true socialism that is not democratic. The first part of this assumption stems from the historical struggles that have won mass political liberties under capitalism. These struggles have universally been the political battles of workers to extend and deepen bourgeois representative institutions. If these institutions are not democratic today, it is because the subordinate classes have not been able to gain substantially enough to make them so.

The second part of this assumption about socialism and democracy goes to the heart of the meaning of socialism, to the debate between Rosa Luxemburg and Lenin, to the discussion of the relationship of the masses to the State, and to the meaning of the State itself. In this regard, Poulantzas attacks the Leninist concept of "double power," so eloquently defended by Colletti, in which the bourgeois State can only be confronted (and destroyed) by building a parallel apparatus of power (the soviets) that serves as the proletarian "State" alongside the bourgeois State until the moment that the proletariat can take control of the heights of the State and destroy it. The soviets, in the meantime, are run by the vanguard party, an elite of proletarian intellectuals who dictate policy and direction. Once the bourgeois State is destroyed, it is this "dictatorship of the proletariat" that takes power, with the subsequent decline of the soviets themselves.[7] In this model, Poulantzas argues, it is necessary to take State power first, and once the fortress of the State is taken, the whole State apparatus is destroyed, substituting for it the second power—the soviets—which constitutes a new type of State. But the fact that this new State is controlled at the top by a "single" revolutionary party, whose organization itself is directed by an "enlightened" elite, is the result of distrust by that elite of mass intervention both through the "bourgeois" parliament and through mass-based movements altogether (Poulantzas 1980, 255). The Leninist transition-to-socialism strategy, for Poulantzas, totally avoids the issue: since socialism *is* democracy—a *democratic* socialism is a tautology—the implicit antidemocratic Leninist strategy, despite Colletti's claims to the contrary, cannot come to grips with the central task of a Marxian theory of the State. It is here that we see Ingrao's important influence:

---

[7] The situation in Poland in 1980-1981 could be portrayed as modern-day soviets (in the form of Solidarity) confronting not a bourgeois State but the "dictatorship of the proletariat."

How is it possible radically to transform the State in such a manner that the extension and deepening of political freedoms and the institutions of representative democracy (which were also a conquest of the popular masses) are combined with the unfurling of forms of direct democracy and the mushrooming of self-management bodies? (Poulantzas 1980, 256)

The "withering away of the State" notion, furthermore, historically has obscured the fundamental problem "of combining a transformed representative democracy and a direct, rank-and-file democracy. It is for these reasons, and not because the notion eventually became identified with Stalinist totalitarianism, that its abandonment is, in my opinion, justified" (Poulantzas 1980, 256). So Poulantzas argues that the real basis for rejecting Leninist strategy is *not* that it led to Stalinism, but the fact that it does not reveal a socialist theory of the State; it does not tell us what the nature of a democratic socialism could be, and what should be the structure or essence of democratic socialist institutions—the political relationships that would extend democracy and liberty and *guarantee* that extension. It is these relationships that would describe the socialist State, or at least the transition to that State.

This brings us to Poulantzas's third point, his view of this same transition. "The democratic road to socialism is a long process, in which the struggle of the popular masses does not seek to create an effective double power parallel and external to the State, but brings itself to bear on the internal contradictions of the State" (1980, 257).

Taking State power, according to Poulantzas, does not mean a simple seizure of the State machinery, substituting in its place the second power (the proletarian soviets). Rather, it means winning over the State by *struggling within it as part of class conflict*. For, as shown in Chapter 4, Poulantzas's later work does not separate the State apparatus from the State struggle: "Power is not a quantifiable substance held by the State and that must be taken out of its hands, but rather a series of relations among the various social classes. In its ideal form, power is concentrated in the State, which is thus a condensation of a particular class relationship of forces" (Poulantzas 1980, 257). The State is therefore not a fortress that is penetrated with a wooden horse, or a strong box that is broken into. "It is the heart of the exercise of political power" (1980, 258). The internal contradictions of the State and the resultant crises are moments of the battle that present opportunities for the masses to secure more advantageous positions on the field.

Further, Poulantzas points out that modifying the power relations in the heart of the State means modifying those relations in *all* the apparatuses and their subsystems, not just the parliament or the ideological apparatuses. It means also extending the struggle to the repressive forces of the State. The masses have to restrict and alter the monopoly of the bourgeoisie in the use of legitimate physical violence—the army and police especially.

And all social conflict, whether in the State apparatuses or outside, has its effect on the State apparatuses. This is in keeping with Poulantzas's analysis that the structure, superstructure, and different parts of the superstructure are all organically intertwined, all rooted in the class relations and—even if outside the physical space of the State—always situated in its strategic arena (1980, 260). So, although there may be struggles internal and external to the State, on the road to democratic socialism the two forms of struggle have to be combined. "Authoritarian statism can be avoided only by combining the transformation of representative democracy with the development of forms of direct, rank-and-file democracy or the movement for self management" (1980, 260). For Poulantzas, this twofold strategy implies a pluralistic party system, universal suffrage, and extension and deepening of all political liberties, including those for the adversaries of socialism. It also implies the meaninglessness of the term "destruction of the State." The institutions of representative democracy are permanent and continuous—they have to be extended, not destroyed.

Yet, like Ingrao, Poulantzas recognizes the dangers from bourgeois reactions, both at home and abroad, to a democratic socialist transformation (e.g., Kolm 1977). The important element for survival and success, Poulantzas claims, is the balance between the two processes of representative democracy, and the worker-controlled production units and other institutions of direct democracy. For democratic socialism to prevail, one of these power centers cannot dominate the other. On the one hand, the domination of direct democracy outside the State apparatus makes it impossible for the economy and polity to have a unified direction; on the other, total control by the State apparatus could easily lead to authoritarianism, in which the State becomes an end in itself, *giving* welfare and distributing income as an elite technocracy sees fit (social democracy). How are conflicts between the direct democratic institutions and the representative democratic State to be resolved? Although he cannot answer this question, he does claim that "socialism will be democratic or it will not be at all" (1980, 265).

SOME CONCLUSIONS

Bobbio, Ingrao, and Poulantzas all agree that the democracy we observe in capitalist societies is the result of class struggle, of the working class pushing for the extension and deepening of liberties associated with representative democracy—that is, with State power. The "bourgeois" State is the result of and the place of class struggle; it is no longer (and perhaps never was) the bourgeois State, but rather some bourgeois-dominated State modified to be able to reproduce the relations of production under new conditions. Only a transition to socialism can extend and deepen democracy further under these conditions.

Secondly, all three agree that democratic socialism means maintaining representative democracy as one of the bases of socialist democracy, although Ingrao's and Poulantzas's view of democracy goes beyond existing institutions (where Bobbio stops) to mass-based social movements participating politically inside and outside the State apparatuses—including factory councils, worker control, and so forth. It is these mass-based institutions that would serve to condition and control the State itself.

Thirdly, there is general agreement that the "difficulties" of democracy raised by Bobbio are important, but as both Ingrao and Poulantzas note, they are the result of crises of the State rather than inherent in democracy itself. These crises produce "democracy" as we (and Bobbio) observe it today; it is almost impossible to predict how these characteristics will change in a radically transformed democratic socialist State.

Finally, the essence of these arguments lies in moving beyond the Leninist and Gramscian notions of the State as a fortress to be overthrown (by direct confrontation) and destroyed, or to be surrounded and then destroyed. The State is no longer simply a repressive apparatus or the ideological *and* repressive apparatuses of the bourgeoisie. It is dominated by the bourgeoisie but does not belong solely to the dominant class. It is the product of class struggle and therefore its institutions can be radically altered *as part of the class struggle*, just as they have been altered in the past. The analysis maintains, with Gramsci, that the State and the ideological apparatuses, both State and private, are as important to the political battle as the productive base, but it makes of the advanced capitalist State a site that already contains elements of counterhegemony.

The implications for the debate on the State are subtle. As Ingrao says, "modern democracy is subversive in as much as it reveals its incompleteness and asks to be completed" (1977, 202). Democracy as an ideology is in fundamental conflict with the capital accumulation functions of the State as described by Offe and Hirsch, and plays a particularly important role in limiting new solutions to the decline of the welfare State. Before turning to that conflict as analyzed in the United States, where it has had a special relevance (as the most "successful" of the free enterprise economies), we review the discussion of the State and democracy in the Third World.

CHAPTER SEVEN

The Dependent State

THE STATE in present-day, less-industrialized capitalist societies is generally *not* characterized by parliamentary democracy. Is this the result of leftover feudal elements in lower-income economies? Is it a temporary condition associated with particular phases of capitalist development, such as Napoleon III's dictatorship in France of the 1850s? Or is the State distinctly different in these countries because of their late industrialization and their historical relationship with the already industrialized economies? Does the modern State in Third World countries have binding authority over all the actions taking place under its jurisdiction (as we have assumed it does in the industrialized societies)?

The "leftover" view was central to postwar pluralist theory, which argued, in Schumpeterian (1951) fashion, that as low-income societies became more capitalistic (modern) and less traditional, they would become more democratic (e.g., Lipset 1963; Almond and Verba 1963). The logic of the pluralist model rests on the necessary "rationalism" associated with modernization, or in Hirschman's (1977) terms, on the inherent capability of capitalist social relations to subject human "passions" to the greater power of human "interests" (see Chapter 1 above). The increased penetration of capitalism and the free enterprise system, the pluralists argued, destroys the particularistic, authoritarian political institutions consistent with a feudal economy. Since capitalism makes the economy universalistic and interest (profit)-oriented, and thus subject to a rational discipline, the State can assume the characteristic parliamentary form. With the failure of that prediction to come true, especially in rather highly industrialized countries like Mexico, Brazil, and Korea, the pluralist model has been abandoned by pluralists themselves in favor of more "pragmatic" views that consider the possible inconsistency of liberal democracy with sustained economic development under modern-world capitalist conditions (Huntington 1975; Stepan 1978).[1]

The Marxian debate on the State in low-income countries is also a recent one, and it, too, hinges on issues that have a long history. These issues are part of the Marxian discussion of colonialism, imperialism, and its latter-day manifestation, dependency. In his writings, Marx himself took

[1] See also the discussion of corporatism in Chapter 1 above.

two views of colonialism, one in regard to India, where he considered incursive British capitalism a positive force for change, and the second in regard to Ireland, where he and Engels saw that same capitalism as destructive. Lenin and, later, Mao developed theories that reinforced this second view, and since then, dependency theory has raised that view to its present prominence in neo-Marxist theory.

In keeping with orthodox Marxian theory of the State, none of the earlier theoretical contributions, including much of dependency theory, considers bourgeois democracy as an important goal in itself. Rather, whether the dependent State is characterized by parliamentary democracy or authoritarian regimes, it is, above all, a bourgeois State and represents capitalist-class hegemony. The principal contribution of Lenin and those who came after him was to place this hegemony in the context of a world system. The dominant capitalist class is not necessarily located in the nation, and, it is argued, the dynamic of the dependent State, whether democratic or authoritarian, lies outside the national territory. Since the days of Lenin, then, the principal issue for traditional Marxian theory in less-industrialized economies has been imperialism, not authoritarianism versus democracy (see Warren 1981).

Dependency theory itself, however, is now in flux, and theories of the State in industrializing societies are themselves part of the ongoing Marxian discussion of capitalist development in those societies. Cardoso and Faletto's work (originally published in 1968 and available in English since 1979) placed the discussion much more in the context of *national* historical social struggles. And the recent debate on bureaucratic authoritarian regimes reraises the question of democracy versus authoritarianism in capitalist development.

This chapter concentrates on the recent Marxian debate about the State in such societies and how that State is inherently different or not different from the advanced capitalist State. Yet, to get at the underlying issues of this debate requires some understanding of the Marxian discussion of colonialism and imperialism and the different theories of dependency that emerged from that discussion. Once these theoretical underpinnings are clear, the debate about the Third World State emerges quite naturally.

ANTECEDENTS

Marx's writings on colonialism are largely restricted to India and Ireland, and his views on the two differed considerably (Avineri 1969; Chandra 1980). One common factor in all the ways that he looked at Asian society was his notion of stagnation and immutability that was incapable of change from within. According to Marx, the most important and peculiar feature of Asian society—the characteristic that differentiated it from non-Slavic European societies—was that it was fundamentally without history and social development; it had resisted both disintegration and decline, and further social evolution; and it had remained stagnant, stationary, and changeless since it emerged from the stage of primitive communism (Chandra 1980, 395). Marx had many explanations for this resistance to change, among them the despotic and hypertrophied character of the State, due in turn to the necessity of a centralized power to bring under cultivation—through large-scale irrigation—the arid lands of Asia. At other times, he ascribed the despotic character of the State to lack of private property in land, and the existence of isolated, self-sufficient village communities.

But it was his view of Asian society's stagnation, not the despotism of the State, that gave rise to Marx's conclusions on colonialism's role in India. It was this feature that led him to argue that colonialism performed a revolutionary role in Asian society. Marx wrote in 1853: "England has to fulfill a double mission in India: one destructive, the other regenerating—the annihilation of the old Asiatic society and the laying of the material foundations of Western society in Asia" (in Tucker 1978, 659). The impact and nature of Marx's colonialism were directly related to his views on the society that was being colonized (stagnant, immutable by any other means) and the society doing the colonizing (capitalist and industrial). The positive content of the destructive aspect of colonialism followed from his characterization of precolonial society. Marx thought that British rule, by destroying this stagnant society, had created possibilities for change and development. The regenerative, positive aspect flowed from the very nature of capitalism—capitalism could not exist only in one country and had to expand to encompass the entire world. The capitalism spreading to the colonial societies would be the same as in the colonizing society—full-fledged industrial capitalism, with the same positive (the development of the productive forces) and negative (misery and degradation) aspects as in Britain.

Nevertheless, according to Chandra (1980, 401), Marx's views shifted rapidly from the regenerative aspects of British rule in India to its destructive aspects. Later, in *Capital*, he noted several structural features of British colonialism that negated economic development, particularly a new international division of labor which suited the requirements of the "chief centres of modern industry . . . and converts one part of the globe into a chiefly agricultural field of production, for supplying the other part which remains a chiefly industrial field" (Marx [1867] 1906, 425), and the drain of capital and resources from India to Britain which was crippling the Indian economy. Furthermore, he noted that although the British had disrupted village communities (destructively positive) it had not put in their place a genuine private property system, but rather caricatures of landed estates and small-parceled property (Chandra 1980, 401).

Marx's earlier misunderstanding of the Indian situation and the impact that British colonialism would have on it lay both in his incorrect assumptions about the changelessness of Asian society and the transposition of British capitalism into that society. Marx was a Victorian and indirectly shared contemporary notions about non-Western backwardness. No such illusions entered into his and Engel's analysis of British rule in Ireland. There, they clearly recognized the colonial character of the Irish society and economy. The essence of colonialism in Ireland, they said, was the subordination of the Irish to the British economy and the transformation of Ireland into an agrarian appendage of industrial Britain.

> Ireland [wrote Marx in 1867] was ruled in the interests of English landlords and the English bourgeoisie who wanted to use it as a supplier of raw materials, a market for manufactured goods, and a place for the safe investment of capital in land. Ireland also served other uses for England. It was a supplier of cheap labour and thus it helped to lower English workers' wages as well as their moral and material conditions. The working class in England could be kept divided and politically impotent by promoting national animosities between the Irish and English workers. Similarly, the ruling classes of Britain and the United States used the Irish question to promote national animosity between the two countries whenever they found it politically expedient. (Chandra 1980, 407)

Marx and Engels saw that colonialism was underdeveloping the Irish economy and that this relation served the British bourgeoisie, both in terms of extracting resources from Ireland (agricultural surplus and labor) and in terms of reproducing exploitative relations of production in Britain by posing Irish against British workers. They also saw that the only solution to the Irish social condition was the overthrow of colonialism through the repeal of the Union of 1801 and the voluntary or forcible liquidation of British domination. This would be an agriculturally-based revolution concerned with the struggle for land (Marx and Engels, 1972).

In Ireland, but not in India, Marx and Engels could perceive that British rule promoted the growth of capital, capitalist industry; and capitalist farming, the destruction of the unity between industry and agriculture; and the creation of a working class in the cities and countryside, and that all these were part of a colonialism that underdeveloped the colonized economy. Hence, because Ireland was not stagnant (as India was supposed to be) before colonialism, the "positive" elements of capitalism, transposed in a colonial context, were negative. What Marx failed to understand in the Indian case, according to Chandra, was that the role of the colonial State was almost exactly the opposite of the capitalist State in Europe. In Europe, the State had been the most powerful instrument of capitalist development ''to hasten, hot-house fashion, the process of transformation of the feudal mode of production into the capitalist mode, and to shorten the transition'' (Marx 1906, 703). But in India, the colonial State could not play this role because of its fundamentally different character: ''The colonial State follows, in the long run, anti-industrialization and anti-development policies. And it does so precisely because it is guided by 'the national situation' not of the colony but of the metropolis'' (Chandra 1980, 437). This is the role of the State that Marx and Engels presented in analyzing the Irish question.

Lenin on Imperialism

Lenin was less interested in the situation in the colonies than he was in the economic conditions leading to the expansion of capitalism from the industrialized capitalist economies into a world system. In *Imperialism, the Highest Stage of Capitalism* ([1917] 1966), he argued that imperialism is a *necessary* phase of capitalism—indeed, that it is the logical extension of capitalist development. In the competitive phase of capitalism, the advanced capitalist countries concentrated on the export of goods, but as production concentrated in monopolies, and particularly as the control of decisions by financial interests became the main feature of capitalism in the advanced countries, ''excess'' accumulation led to declining rates of profit and to the export of *capital* to backward areas—the extension of the advanced-country monopolies directly into the backward-country economies. Surplus capital is used for increasing profits by exporting capital abroad to the backward countries. ''In these backward countries, profits are usually high, for capital is scarce, the price of land is relatively low, wages are low, raw materials are cheap'' (Lenin 1966, 216). Investment in the colonies assured control over supplies of new material and their prices. But Lenin does not limit his explanation of the expansion of capitalism into the backward countries to the declining rate of profit in the advanced economies. Imperialism strives to annex not only agrarian territories, but even industrialized regions. As essential feature of imperialism for Lenin is the rivalry between the capitalist powers in the striving for hegemony, that is, for the conquest of territory, not so much directly for themselves as to weaken the adversary and to undermine *his* hegemony. In Lenin's argument these two factors combine to produce a powerful force for overseas expansion.

The critique of Lenin's capitalist imperialism has come from two sources.

Joseph Shumpeter's *Imperialism* (first published in 1921 and translated into English in 1951) introduced the concept of "atavistic impulses," which argued that the explanation of imperialism in the capitalist period is not found in the economic realm, but in psychological forces that are left over from past social and economic structures.[2] And secondly, neo-Marxists like Warren (1980) resurrect Marx's India view that capitalist intervention in the less-developed world is basically a positive, even revolutionary, force: capitalism is the most efficient way to develop the forces of production and worker consciousness necessary for the transition to socialism.

Warren argues that the spread of capitalism into the colonies made possible the economic development of those economies, releasing individual creativity, organizing cooperation in production, and setting the conditions for political democracy, providing "the best political environment for the socialist movement and creat[ing] conditions that favour a genuine learning process by the working class" (Warren 1980, 7). Lenin's work, according to Warren, is historically inaccurate in contending incorrectly that monopoly capitalism was stagnating in the industrialized countries and hence had to seek profits elsewhere. Further, Lenin's *Imperialism* was essentially a political tract, geared—at the height of World War I—to explain the causes of the war and the abandonment of internationalism by the majority of the working classes (Warren 1980, 49). After the Russian Revolution, it was used as the basis of anti-imperialist propaganda and what were thought to be the security requirements of the encircled Soviet state (1980, 8). The "empirically supported" view that "direct colonialism, far from having retarded or distorted indigenous capitalist development that might otherwise have occurred, acted as a powerful engine of progressive social change, advancing capitalist development far more rapidly than was conceivable in any other way" (1980, 9) was abandoned in favor of a nationalistic, anticapitalist romanticism that (1) made imperialism into the major obstacle to industrialization in the Third World rather than the internal contradictions of the Third World itself, and

---

[2] For Schumpeter, imperialism by trading and investment is an impossibility. So it is impossible that capitalist development in non-European societies could be part of an imperialist structure. Since capitalism is by nature anti-imperialist, all institutions associated with the spread of capitalism—wage agriculture and European schools, for example—must be anti-imperialist. Not only do free trade and capitalist relations of production lead to the highest possible rate of growth, but higher levels of ethical behavior are attained. The logical extension of Schumpeter's theory is that capitalism is a *civilizing* force coming from a civilization that rejects war and domination as a means of settling disputes and distributing economic and political power. This idea is the basis of a more recent, generally well-known "development" literature, beginning with Rostow's stages of economic growth (1956) to modernity theory (Inkeles and Smith, 1974).

(2) had little to do with socialist ideology or a socialist critique of capitalism—one that specifically upholds the view that "capitalism serves as a bridge to socialism" (1980, 7).

There *are* a number of problems with the Lenin thesis, but Lenin's insights into the uneven development of capitalist societies, their striving for hegemony, and the conflicts this generates provide a more reasonable explanation for imperialism and world wars than Schumpeter's atavistic impulses. More important for our purposes, however, is the role that the spread of capitalism played in the "backward" countries and, of course, the role of the State in backward societies confronted by that capitalist expansion. It is in that discussion that the Leninist imperialist position confronts Warren's critique head-on. Before turning to an analysis of dependency theory and the dependent State, however, a few words have to be said about Mao and the Chinese Revolution. For although Lenin's *Imperialism* dealt little with conditions in colonized countries, Mao had to deal with the colonial State from within, in the same pragmatic way that Lenin treated bourgeois parliamentarism in *The State and Revolution*. The reality of the Chinese Revolution has had as much or more influence since World War II on Marxist views on the Third World as Lenin's writings.

Mao and the Chinese Revolution

Mao was a member and then leader of a Communist Party organized to establish its hegemony over a *colonized* economy. It is this context of the Chinese Revolution that gave it its particular character, and that has made it particularly relevant to revolutions in other dependent societies. Both Lenin in 1917 and Mao over the much longer period from 1911 to 1949 faced absolutist States in disorganized flux. Tsarism had collapsed in 1917 and the social democracy that replaced it could not mobilize a political base. Mao's revolutionary thought developed after the 1911 overthrow of Chinese absolutism, but as in Russia during 1917, the Chinese gentry (together with a small urban bourgeoisie)—even given a much longer period of time and a certain degree of military control over the country after 1927—was never able to solidify and extend a capitalist development process. In large part, that failure in China was due to China's colonization by the European powers, a colonization that distinguished her sharply from Tsarist Russia and greatly weakened the possibilities of developing in China a bourgeois State.[3]

[3] For an excellent analysis of both the Russian and Chinese Revolutions, see Skocpol (1979).

Mao's theory of revolution, rooted deeply in Leninism but adapted to the Chinese conditions in the 1920s, 1930s, and the war with Japan, had little to say about the capitalist State per se. Nevertheless, from Mao's writings on revolutionary strategy and his analysis of Chinese society, we can infer that Mao saw post-1911, warlord-dominated Chinese polity, as well as the post-1927 Kuomintang State with its bourgeoisie and landowner base (often lumped together in Mao's writings on class), as totally dominated by European imperialists. Mao's revolutionary theory was fundamentally *nationalistic* and *anti-imperialist*. Chiang Kai-shek's weak Chinese State, racked by internal struggles and dominated by foreign economic interests, was certainly an enemy of the revolution, but for Mao, the principal enemy was imperialism. Once the Japanese invaded, that enemy was crystallized in the form of foreign troops; the nationalistic revolutionary struggle became an anti-imperialist war guided in certain geographic areas by revolutionary armies. It was for this reason that Mao, following the anti-imperialist Leninist-Stalinist line, saw the class structure partly in terms of class, but also in terms of collaboration with imperialism. Those elements of any class, including the bourgeoisie, who were willing to take an anti-imperialist position were potential allies in the revolutionary struggle.

This national aspect of revolutionary movements in colonized countries was discussed at length by Lenin and M. N. Roy, the Indian Communist, during a meeting of the Third International in July 1920. Although disagreeing on a number of issues, particularly on who could lead the revolution during its early phases (Lenin thought that the bourgeoisie in colonial countries could be allowed to take the lead), Lenin and Roy did agree that in those countries where the Communists succeeded in establishing their hegemony over the revolutionary movement, they could lead the peasant masses to socialism without passing through a capitalist stage of development. The Third International therefore established the line that the revolution in colonial countries would not be exclusively social as in Europe, but also national, and that it would not be the work of the proletariat alone, nor even of the proletariat and the peasantry. Rather, where an indigenous bourgeoisie existed, and where elements of it were prepared to fight against foreign domination, the Communists should form an alliance with them and even allow them to lead the revolution during its first phase.[4]

---

[4] This shows just how complicated the whole nationalism issue is. On the one hand, Warren argues that Third World socialists should promote capitalist development even if it is foreign-dominated. But in a case like China's, foreign exploitation was so apparent that any reformist movement, whether bourgeois or not, could only gain legitimacy by being anti-imperialist. Indeed, the failure of the first phase of the Chinese "revolution" (1911-1937) was due in

Until 1927 and the almost total destruction of the urban base of the Chinese Communist Party (CCP), this is precisely the line that was followed; indeed, under directions and *financing* from Moscow, the CCP worked within the Kuomintang and together with bourgeois reformists to develop the military-administrative potential and mass base for a reformist/ revolutionary Chinese State. This democratic State was intended to defeat the provincial warlords that had taken over China with the disintegration of absolutism, enabling the Kuomintang to throw out the foreigners as well. Amazingly, despite the purging of Communists from the Kuomintang as soon as the semblance of a national State was effectively established in 1927, the CCP never deviated from its line. Bitter lessons were learned, particularly with the 1927 purges and Chiang Kai-shek's "encirclement-annihilation" campaigns, ending with the "long march" into northwestern China.

But when the Japanese invaded China in 1937, the line was reestablished to form a "united front from below" in order to fight the invader. Thus, although always deeply hostile to Chiang Kai-shek and the Kuomintang government because of the purges and encirclement campaigns, Mao in the late 1930s and early 1940s was able to adhere to the Leninist-Stalinist strategy of trying to build an anti-imperialist alliance with the national bourgeoisie by "separating" Chiang from that class. The conditions in colonized China, then invaded by Japan, continued to dictate that national liberation rather than social revolution had to be the principal revolutionary goal.

This new democratic revolution is part of the world proletarian-socialist revolution; it resolutely opposes imperialism, i.e., international capitalism. Politically, it means the joint *revolutionary-democratic* dictatorship of several revolutionary classes over the imperialists and reactionary traitors, and opposition to the transformation of Chinese society into a society under bourgeois dictatorship. Economically, it means nationalization of all big capital and big enterprises of the imperialists and reactionary traitors, distribution of large landed property among the peasants, and at the same time assistance to private middle and small enterprises without the elimination of the rich peasant economy. Hence,

part to the anticommunism of the imperialist powers, as well as the invasion of China by another capitalist power, Japan. In essence, Warren assumes that anti-imperialism and nationalism became a rallying cry of revolutionary movements because Lenin and the Comintern deemed it so, rather than the just as plausible assumption that these revolutions developed their own dynamic, and that the class struggle was necessarily nationalistic and anti-imperialistic.

while clearing the way for capitalism, this democratic revolution of a new type creates the pre-conditions for socialism. (Mao 1954, 3:96-97)

The most important deviation from the Leninist-Stalinist dicta originated from Mao himself, and gave the Chinese revolution its special character. Whereas Lenin had identified the peasantry in underdeveloped Asian countries as a chief *force* in the revolution, he had also argued that the proletariat, either in the form of an indigenous, urban Communist movement if it existed or in the form of emissaries from the International if it did not, would guide the rural masses. But in early 1927, in his celebrated investigation of the peasant movement in Hunan, Mao attributed to the peasants the capability of *leading* the revolution. He formed the idea that the Communist Party, which directs the revolution, can *issue* from the peasantry (Mao 1954, vol. 1). After the repression of the Party later that year, he set about creating an organization largely of peasant origin, that nevertheless called itself the party of the proletariat, and "proposed to play the role attributed by Lenin to the proletariat and its party as the guiding force of the bourgeois-democratic revolution" (Schram 1963, 34). Nevertheless, this peasant role in the revolution was primarily developed out of necessity rather than any theoretical reasoning. According to Skocpol (1979), it was not until after the Long March that CCP cadres were able to develop methods that permanently transformed village class and political structures in ways "that would allow maximum mobilization of economic resources and peasant manpower" (1979, 255). Indeed, it was not until after the period of the United Front (1937-1940) that these methods were applied, and ultimately resulted in radical land reforms that emerged from new cadres in the villages themselves (Skocpol 1979, 260-261).

Mao's writings refer to a concrete colonized society, and the first socialist revolution in such a society. The fact that a foreign army invaded China in 1937 obviously shaped Chinese Communist Party strategy, as did the powerful influence of the recently successful Russian Revolution. Both theory and practice made foreigners, rather than the national State, the revolution's principal enemy until the very last stage of the military struggle. In addition, Mao turned the peasantry into the shaper of communism rather than simply a force participating in a revolution led by others. The development of a revolutionary peasant army at the core of anti-imperialist forces was necessarily accepted by a weak national State threatened with annihilation by a militarily superior foreign power. It was this acceptance that—after the Japanese defeat—led to the overthrow of the State itself by better organized, mass-based Communist forces.

If we consider the State as an expression of dominant-group hegemony, Mao's view of the post-1911 Chinese State is perfectly understandable.

Whereas warlords had their political and economic base in the local gentry and exploited peasantry, at no time after 1911 and until 1949 could any group establish hegemony over Chinese society. The makings for such hegemony were developing in the Kuomintang of the mid-1920s; mass-base organizing by the Chinese Communist Party combined with a relatively well-organized military brought much of China under a national reformist government by 1927. But it was just at that moment that the bourgeoisie and its allies, particularly Chiang Kai-shek himself, chose to purge the reformist alliance of its revolutionary elements. With that decision, and given the continued strength of local gentry, the Kuomintang effectively restricted its control to the urban areas. Furthermore, it had to rely on foreign capital to finance development and provide government revenues. In effect, the nationalistic Kuomintang continued to be dependent economically on foreigners, and Mao's Leninist view of the State in colonized societies continued to be valid: the Chinese bourgeoisie and the landed gentry were the local agents of foreign domination. The colonial State was an expression of European imperialism.

This was not a State as in Western capitalist societies that developed and extended the hegemony of the dominant bourgeoisie, and one in which there was a close relation between civil society and the State. The Kuomintang of the 1920s and 1930s was incapable of mobilizing the masses or even organizing its direct beneficiaries, the landed gentry. Nor could the Kuomintang crush the Communist "bandits." China continued to be administered by local warlords with their private armies. The State was entirely separated from most of civil society. This weakness and separation of the Chinese State was never clearer than when the Japanese gradually encroached on Chinese territory and then invaded Manchuria; the Kuomintang could not mobilize the various factions of Chinese society even in the face of this direct confrontation with a foreign menace. Mao's notion of the dependent State was borne out historically by the reformist Kuomintang.

This view is not generalizable to all dependent States in every historical period. The purged Kuomintang was unable to organize hegemony over Chinese society for the groups that supported it. Its failure to create a national State reflected conditions particular to Chinese society—a society characterized by an overwhelming peasant population dominated economically and socially by a landed commercial gentry, and a society whose urban centers, in turn, were effectively controlled by foreign commercial interests intent on exploiting China's resources through dominating her external commerce. For all intents and purposes, there was no capitalist reformist group that could alter the nature of this exploitation in the name of national development. The Chinese situation was much closer to Chandra's (1980) view of the colonial State than to the prototypical industrialized, Western (metropolitan) capitalist democracy.

> The colonial State does not represent any of the social classes of the colony; it subordinates all of them to the metropolitan capitalist class. If it gives some of them support and protection, it does so in the interests of its own ruling class, the metropolitan bourgeoisie. Its task is not merely to enable the extraction of surplus from subordinate classes, but also to make the entire economy of the colony subservient to the metropolitan economy, to permit the exploitation of the colony as a whole. (Chandra 1980, 437)

The metropolitan bourgeoisie did not control State power in the colony and its social surplus because it owned the means of production there; rather, it controlled social surplus because it controlled State power (Chandra 1980, 437). The State's function was much more oriented toward the *appropriation* of surplus instead of working with a local bourgeoisie to develop the system of capitalist exploitation inside the colony *and* its appropriation. The repressive forces of the State were more developed for internal control, and the State's administrative apparatuses became enlarged as a necessary means of control, a control that is exercised in the metropolitan economy largely at the place of production.

However, as shown elsewhere (Carnoy 1974), even in the colonial context there are conflicts between the colonial State and the metropolitan bourgeoisie. For example, in early twentieth-century India, this conflict developed over tariffs for renascent Indian textile manufactures. It was in the interest of colonial administrators to raise tariffs in order to raise the revenue they would have available to them for administrative and military expenses. The State itself wished to expand, and, of course, this accorded well with the needs of a small, struggling Bombay bourgeoisie. But at the same time, higher tariffs conflicted directly with the Lancashire textile manufacturers. It is telling that tariffs were *not* raised, which supports the thesis that metropole manufacturers, *through their influence on the metropole State* (this is an important point that Chandra fails to raise), were able to control the colonial State's economic policies. It is also significant that the colonial State was *not* the political committee of the metropole bourgeoisie. Its fundamental interests were allied with that bourgeoisie, but it also had a self-interest in expanding its revenue, and this revenue could be drawn from sources other than the import of goods from and the export of goods to the metropole. Furthermore, the colonial State, in fulfilling its basic role as the mechanism of appropriation, had to develop an extensive local administration, and therefore a colonial educational system. Although the goals of the educational system were clearly consistent with this role of surplus appropriation (Carnoy 1974), that same system also laid the foundations for the overthrow of the colonial State and its replacement with one whose social and economic role related to the development of local capitalism and its productive forces.[5]

The Chinese case provides us with an introduction to the issues surrounding the dependent, or colonial, State. Foreign influence is certainly crucial, and even though, as Warren argues, the national bourgeoisie may use the imperialism issue as a means to deflect the development of a socialist alternative, this does not make the Third World economy or State any less foreign-influenced, nor the working class any less nationalistic. Nor is it clear that in the absence of a well-organized, mass-based, anti-imperialist movement, foreign capital would be as sensitive to its image and its actual surplus extraction and investment policies as it *became* in the post-World War II period. It certainly was not that way in the 1920s and 1930s in China (and many would argue, not that way in the Chile of 1970-1973).

But because of its particular historical conditions the Chinese case tells us little about whether the State in postcolonial, industrializing capitalist societies tends to the "colonial authoritarian" case, where the bureaucracy is politically separated from local classes and negotiates with foreign capitalists and States while repressing the citizenry, or towards the metropolitan model, in which the State and civil society are integrated and the State is able to organize and extend dominant-group hegemony, even though such hegemony is certainly subject to significant crises.

Dependency theorists have debated precisely this issue. With that in mind, we now turn to a detailed discussion of more recent views of the dependent State.

WORLD SYSTEM MODELS AND THE DEPENDENT STATE

Marxist views of the State in less-industrialized countries are debated largely in terms of the nature of development in those countries. The world system view, as expounded by Frank (1978, 1980), Amin (1973, 1980), and Wallerstein (1974) sees the development (rather, underdevelopment) of Third World capitalism in terms of the main internal contradictions that

---

[5] It is worth noting that the development of local capitalism in democratic India, which Warren would argue should have provided the most effective road to building India's productive forces and raising worker consciousness, has built these forces at a much slower rate than has authoritarian, communist China and perhaps also raised worker consciousness much less than in China. It is also questionable whether Indian capitalism will even continue to be politically democratic, thereby reducing further the "best political environment" for raising worker consciousness.

characterize its modes of production as part of the development of world production.

> Any serious inquiry, then, into the differences in origins of the historical experiences and subsequent development paths of the various regions of the New World must begin with an examination of the historical process of capital accumulation on a world scale, since that was the driving force of the various processes in the New World which were integral parts of the world process, and go on to consider how it was mediated through differing modes of production in the various parts of that World which corresponded to the differing—though related—roles these regions played in the worldwide process. (Frank 1978, 43)

Why did the different regions develop differently? According to Frank, because the resources available in the different regions were different. Some regions, like Peru and Mexico, had the gold and silver and the socially organized labor force and technological knowledge that offered the potential for certain kinds of labor exploitation and capital accumulation (in the metropole) that led to the extreme underdevelopment of those regions. Other regions, like New England, did not have the resources to attract that kind of attention. There, the metropoles did not impose a manner of monopolizing and extracting the surplus through low wages and unequal exchange, and did not develop a mode of production that would develop underdevelopment. The present poverty of the formerly rich regions, there- fore, is due in part to the exhaustion of their natural resources, and in part to the dense settlement and erosion of inadequate agricultural lands in mountainous mining regions, but "the principal source of their present underdevelopment is not so much physical as it is the social structure they have inherited from their 'golden years' of export boom, and which is still reflected in their 'archaic customs' " (Frank 1978, 23).

Frank strongly rejects the Ricardian concept of comparative advantage to explain who produces what and the nature of development in each place. The value of resources, first of all, he argues, is determined by the met- ropole economies, and the presence of resources valued by the metropoles determines how societies colonized by them develop (underdevelop). Re- sources determine social structure and the relations of production (mode of exploitation). Resources also determined the colonial relation with the metropolis. The element that enabled this relation to develop in the way it did is the military power of the metropole: that power imposed on the colony the mode of production that suited metropole capital accumulation.

Metropole military power plus periphery resources valued by the met- ropole equaled periphery underdevelopment. Metropole indifference to periphery resources (because they are low-valued) meant the possibility of local development (in New England, for example). Once that development began, it had to be defended by force of arms. On three occasions in one hundred years (1776, 1812, and 1861) New England had to defend its commercial and industrial development against direct and indirect British military force. Pombal's Portugal, Mohammed Ali's Egypt, and Lopez's Paraguay, on the other hand, were unsuccessful in their attempts at autarchic development because "the process of world capital accumulation, capitalist development, and division of labour, not to mention military power, did not permit such development at those times and places" (Frank 1978, 129).

In recent years, however, when conditions in the metropole have demanded it, a new international division of labor is created that *requires* industrial development in the Third World—a substitution of certain kinds of imports for others, consonant with the replacement of consumer goods exports by producer goods and technology exports in the metropole economies. Nevertheless, the most dynamic industries are centered in the metropoles while socialist economies and some capitalist underdeveloped ones increasingly take over the production of no longer leading or highly profitable capital goods and certain consumer goods. And many underdeveloped countries continue to specialize in raw materials that are increasingly essential for industrial development in the imperialist metropolis (Frank 1978, 133).

Frank's (and Amin's) crucial point here is that import-substitution industrial development in the Third World does not create an "internal" market as was created a century before in Europe and the United States, because rather than leading to a rise in wages—to expanding internal market purchasing power as it had in the metropolis and the new settler countries—this dependent capitalist development still depends on the export of raw materials by super-exploited agricultural and mine workers and (later) of consumer manufactures produced by super-exploited industrial workers. The market in which peripheral industrial production is realized again turns out to be in the metropolis, and the peripheral wages, now for industrial as well as primary production, again turn out to be not a source of purchasing power that is to be increased, but a cost factor that must be reduced. The domestic market is still limited to the final consumer demand of the upper and upper-middle classes, and productive consumption. These are both dependent on external sector earnings and their distribution by the State. Instead of periphery surplus being used to develop the forces of production, and thus the internal market, much of it is exported to the center, and the rest goes to fill the luxury-good demand of the social strata that keep this system going: latifundias, commercial comprador bourgeoisie, State bureaucracy, etc. The class alliances that provide the political framework for the reproduction of the system were and are not primarily internal class alliances but rather an international class alliance between dominant center monopoly capital and its subordinate allies in the periphery—"feudal" elements and the comprador bourgeoisie.

For Frank, the imperialist metropoles are the ones that develop this international division of labor and accumulate capital from it. As technological changes and changes in the organization of capitalist expansion (the transnationals, for example) take place, changing tasks are assigned to the underdeveloped countries in that division of labor and in the process of capital accumulation (Frank 1978, 138-139).

Although Amin's conception of underdevelopment in the world capitalist system is similar to Frank's, it also contains important differences. Frank sees all change in the process of periphery development/underdevelopment coming about as the result of the development of productive forces in the metropoles, but Amin argues that it was anti-imperialist liberation movements in the periphery that brought about the transformation in imperialism from the exploitation of primary production labor to a different world division of labor where industrialization could begin in the Third World (Amin 1980, 136). For Amin, it was not the monopolies that planned the transition from the first to the second phase of imperialism; this was not the result of technological change or contradictions in metropole development (economic crises in the centers, for example), but it was imposed by national liberation movements when the peripheral bourgeoisies won from imperialism the right to industrialize (Amin 1980, 141).

Furthermore, this strategy of industrialization transformed the relationship between the periphery bourgeoisie and the center monopolies: the periphery bourgeoisie ceased to be national and became the "junior partner of imperialism by integrating itself into the new division of labor" (Amin 1980, 141). This phase of imperialism is *not* a reproduction of an earlier phase of center development (as Warren would argue), but rather an extension of the first phase of primary goods exploitation: the development process continues to depend on exports, which consist of raw materials or cheap consumer goods or even durables, but all of which depend on low wages (rather than advanced technology), and the dominant-class alliances are still international—the periphery bourgeoisie replaces the old feudal and comprador elements as the subordinate ally of imperialism. Amin considers that changes in that division of labor are in part the function of anti-imperialist struggles in the periphery. The outcome of those struggles for the periphery masses depends in large part on who in the periphery is leading the rebellion. If it is the Third World bourgeoisies, all that will happen is a change in the international division of labor which would perpetuate and aggravate unequal exchange (Amin 1980, 142). True, autocentered development in the periphery would necessarily have to be popular development (Amin 1980, 144).

What is the nature of the periphery State in this dependency view? The State in the Third World economies is an essential instrument for the administration of the dependent role of these economies in the international division of labor and the capitalist world process of capital accumulation. "The exigencies of the process of capital accumulation and the international division of labor, world-wide and in the underdeveloped countries themselves, thus become the principal determinants of the role and the form of the state in the Third World (as well as elsewhere in the capitalist world)" (Frank 1979, 1).

Saul, in part using Alavi's (1972) analysis, argues that there are three points that define the postcolonial State. First, in colonizing the Third World, the metropolitan bourgeoisie had to create a State apparatus that could control all the indigenous social classes in the colony; in that sense, the "superstructure" in the colony is overdeveloped relative to the "structure." The postcolonial society inherits that overdeveloped State apparatus and its institutionalized practices. Second, the postcolonial State also assumes an economic role (not paralleled in the classical bourgeois State) in the name of promoting economic development. Third, in postcolonial societies, capitalist hegemony must often be created by the State itself within territorial boundaries that are artificial once direct colonial rule is removed (Saul 1979, ch. 8).

Is this a "weak" or a "strong" State? Frank and Amin agree with Marini's (1977) contention that the local bourgeoisie in Third World economies is relatively weak,[6] and that the dependent State is relatively strong and autonomous in regard to its local bourgeoisie. But Frank argues that the principal variable here is the relation of the State to the imperialist

---

[6] Amin considers the difficulty that local bourgeoisies have in imposing their hegemony as "the weak link in the imperialist chain" (Amin 1980, 175). However, Amin (1980) does not tell us much about the nature of class relations in the periphery, nor how the dominant classes establish and maintain their hegemony even while they are weak. His principal argument seems to be that the dominant burgeoisie, although not able to construct a national cohesiveness, benefits from the separation of the different ethnic groups constituting peripheral societies (1980, 176). Although this is certainly true for many "nations" in Africa and Asia, it is not generally applicable to Latin America. And even in African and Asian countries torn by ethnic conflict, the whole issue of class and ethnicity is complex. It is difficult, for example, to relate ethnic struggles to social struggle rooted in production if these ethnic conflicts have their roots in precapitalist modes of production—remnants of noncapitalist, nonclass types of conflicts (religious, tribal, or family). On the other hand, Amin's point is well taken: the insertion of ancient conflicts into the objective relations of modern capitalist relations gives the class struggle particular shape and movement, not only manipulable by reactionary forces but also, in those cases where domination and ethnicity overlap sufficiently, by well-organized revolutionary ones.

bourgeoisie of the metropolis, not the local bourgeoisie: "Indeed, this dependent, and in this sense *weak*, character of the state in the Third World—dependent financially, technologically, institutionally, ideologically, militarily, in a word politically, on the international bourgeoisie(s) and their metropolitan states—may be regarded as the fundamental characteristic of the Third World state" (Frank 1979, 5).

The very weakness of the local bourgeoisie relative to the imperialist one leads it to try to strengthen its national State (thereby making the State more autonomous from the local bourgeoisie) as part of the bargaining process between local and imperial bourgeoisies. Nevertheless, in Frank's analysis, the State in the Third World is "far more an instrument of foreign than of local capital" (Frank 1979, 6).

The colonial State in Frank's first and second phases of imperialism (direct colonization, primary good exports) was the appropriator of periphery surplus for the dominant metropole bourgeoisie. Its function was to keep wages as low as possible, if necessary by repression. During what Frank designates the second stage of imperialism (and Amin, the first), the colonial administration in Latin America is replaced by formally independent governments, generally headed by weak local commercial bourgeoisies. These bourgeoisies, according to Frank, after defeating their enemies within their own and other classes, "voluntarily and enthusiastically adopted the free trade doctrine and policy, which elsewhere the metropolitan powers often had to impose by force" (Frank 1978, 165). But the most interesting feature of the Latin American periphery State during this period was its moves to reform Latin American societies to make them more amenable to the process of world capital accumulation centered in the metropoles. Frank argues that these liberal reforms, which took over the lands of the Catholic Church and the communal property of the Indian communities, did not occur simply when liberal ideas had arrived in Latin America from the metropole, but when "the new monoexport of coffee, sugar, meat, wheat, cotton, tin, etc. had expanded sufficiently to account for, say, over 50 percent of total exports. . . . It is this metropolitan-stimulated expansion of Latin American export production that in each country gave certain sectors of the bourgeoisie the economic and political reason and power to undertake the liberal reform" (Frank 1978, 166). The liberal reforms effectively concentrated the seized lands into a few private, and soon foreign and domestic private corporate hands. This forced the indigenous population to work as peons in the rapidly expanding agricultural and mining enterprises or in building railroads (with public capital) to bring those products to metropole markets. If this policy created grave economic problems of underdevelopment that generated political tensions in the periphery countries, the liberals themselves were the first to use political repression to serve their own interests (Frank 1978, 167).

For Frank, the role of the peripheral State in this period is to increase access to domestic resources for metropole capital by mobilizing public funds for infrastructure investment, and by reforming the social and economic structure so that increased labor is available to produce export goods. Whereas the State is ostensibly controlled by the local bourgeoisie, that class views its destiny as deepening its incorporation into the world capitalist system. The result of this deepening incorporation is twofold. The first is the ever greater dependence of local bourgeoisies on the metropolis and the process of world capital accumulation. Exports and the production of goods and services related to exports become the source of capital for local bourgeoisies. The second is the importance of the State itself, since it is the State that is the mechanism whereby the bourgeoisie can make available to metropole capitalists periphery resources. And since this requires the massive underdevelopment of these societies, the State must intervene relatively often to repress resistance to such exploitation. The peripheral State therefore becomes much more crucial to the whole development (underdevelopment) project in the periphery than the metropolitan State is to capitalist development in the metropole.

This view of the State seems deterministic, but Frank does not fall into the trap of claiming that the peripheral State is nothing more than the administration of the dominant imperialist State. He recognizes that differences do exist between the degree to which one country's bourgeoisie turns its resources over to the metropole. He argues that those countries whose major means of production in the export sector fell into foreign ownership suffered a greater weakening of their bourgeoisies, a lower domestic capital accumulation and diversification of the productive structure, and a more polarized society than did those such as Argentina, Uruguay, and Brazil, in which the production, if not the transportation and distribution of exports remained under national ownership (Frank 1979, 171).

But in the same breath, Frank does not view these differences as leading to a more concrete understanding of the process of dependent capitalist development or of the role of the dependent capitalist State in that development. The transformation of the world capitalist economy in the post-World War II period "finally and definitely foreclosed all future possibilities for these economies to achieve quantitatively and qualitatively cumulative capital accumulation and condemned as hopeless all political aspirations of their 'national' bourgeoisies—if they exist at all—to promote economic development within the now *narrow* confines of the national (and even state) capitalist mode of production in the era of neo-imperi-alism'' (Frank 1978, 171).

The periphery State for Frank and Amin *is* different from those in the metropoles. For Frank, its nature is conditioned by an ''underdevelop-ment'' process that is set by the *metropole* bourgeoisies and the power of the metropole States that those bourgeoisies command. It is they who define the international division of labor and therefore the possibilities for the periphery to develop. For Amin, the State is conditioned by foreign economic domination and therefore makes difficult the establishment of local dominant-class hegemony. Effectively, the local bourgeoisie must exploit Third World peasants and proletarians to send surplus abroad, thereby having to rely on the State rather than ideological hegemony to reproduce dependent capitalism.

The most recent turn to authoritarianism is explained, in this model, as a ''logical'' tendency of a weak local financial and monopoly bourgeoisie in response to a world capital accumulation crisis and the struggle between and within classes regarding their participation in and benefits from the international division of labor (Frank 1979, 22). The course of the class struggle as mediated by these Third World States is, according to Frank, ''importantly influenced, if not determined by their contribution—to the process of world capitalist accumulation in its present crisis'' (Frank 1979, 25). It is the pressure from the metropole bourgeoisies and States to increase capital accumulation in the Third World that forces new measures—i.e., militarism—to extract surplus, particularly given the pressure from sub-ordinate classes for an increased fraction of the benefits from production (usually through public spending). This militarism is sanctioned by met-ropole bourgeoisies as a means of restoring ''order'' and increasing capital accumulation. ''The suppression of *all* political interplay thus has the double objective of resolving the principal contradiction [between capital and labor] in favor of the bourgeoisie and to resolve the secondary (intra-bourgeoisie) contradictions in favor of the monopoly bourgeoisie associated with imperialism. . . . The problem of hegemony that the political interplay was unable to solve is now solved through the recourse to authority'' (Vasconi, in Frank 1979, 25).

In the face of the accumulation crisis, Frank argues, when democratic and other forms of the bourgeois State are no longer adequate to meet the needs of foreign and domestic capital, a capitalist coalition acts to replace these forms with authoritarian regimes. He emphasizes the almost deter-ministic role of the metropole bourgeoisies in this process, in that it is the *world* capital accumulation crisis, led by crisis in the metropole economies, that requires increased capital accumulation in the Third World, hence a redistribution of production and the need to impose repressive measures in the Third World.

The authoritarianization of the Third World is not only an essentially "necessary" response to the crisis—an expression of inherently weak bourgeoisies in the Third World and the power of foreign capital over those States—but may foreshadow the institutionalization of militarism in the periphery. Frank observes that "the militarization of the state, and indeed of the economy, society, culture, and ideology is also penetrating beyond and below the immediately visible surface in one Third World country after another" (Frank 1979, 42).

The dependent State, for Frank and the other world system analysts, is different from metropole States because it is organized in significant part to meet the needs of a powerful international bourgeoisie and because local bourgeoisies are relatively weak. It is inherently less democratic because it is much more difficult for Third World bourgeoisies to establish hegemony and thus for bourgeois democratic regimes to be legitimate. The availability of distributable resources appears to be the exception rather than the rule. The typical Third World State may be headed for long-term authoritarianism as the world capitalist crisis continues and militarism is institutionalized. Amin sees the inability of the local bourgeoisies to impose their hegemony and the pressure on them to impoverish the Third World masses in order to extract more surplus as leading inexorably to socialist revolutions. But Frank is much more pessimistic in the face of metropole capitalist power, and Amin has not provided us with a very extensive analysis of class structure and class struggle in the Third World. The weight of outside influence on the local State in world system dependency theory, as Warren (1980) has noted, takes the emphasis off local capitalist development, domestic class struggle, the autonomy of the State, and the shift of struggle to the State. For an analysis that establishes that emphasis, we must turn to the work of Cardoso and Faletto (1979).

HISTORICAL-STRUCTURAL DEPENDENCY

Cardoso and Faletto's theory of dependency leads to a view of the dependent State that places it more in the context of local class struggle. Because of that, popular movements play a more important role in the form of that State, there can be rapid and sustained local economic development even with the important influence of foreign capital, and the long-run tendency of the State is toward the democratic form. Thus, the pressure of popular groups may not be revolutionary, but the people ("*el pueblo*") have an undeniable power that constantly forces the State in a democratic direction. Furthermore, the dichotomy between the "dependent capitalist State'' and the ''revolutionary socialist State'' inherent in the Amin formulation is replaced by the possibility of a continuous class struggle that may produce many forms of popular victories, including social democracy. As in Poulantzas's (1980) analysis of the metropolitan State, the dependent State becomes a primary arena of class conflict, and the whole issue of expanded democracy as a principal goal of struggle comes to the fore.

Cardoso and Faletto develop an approach to the condition of periphery societies that they call historical-structural: ''It emphasizes not just the structural conditioning of social life, but also the historical transformation of structures by conflict, social movements, and class struggle'' (Cardoso and Faletto 1979, x). They agree with Frank and Amin that the existence of an economic periphery cannot be understood without reference to the economic hegemony of the metropole, which was responsible for the creation of that periphery and for the global dynamic of international capitalism. They also agree that imperialist penetration of the periphery is the result of external social forces, and the nature of those forces has to be understood to analyze the development process in the periphery (1979, xvi-xvii). But unlike Frank, who points out the self-perpetuating structural mechanisms of dependency, or Amin, who introduces into these structural mechanisms general possibilities for anti-imperialist resistance (based on bourgeois bargaining and the impoverishment of the masses) and reconstruction, Cardoso and Faletto argue that the expansion of capitalism in different countries (as well as the different periods outlined by Frank and Amin) did not have the same history or consequences. The differences, they claim, are rooted not just in the natural resources available (Frank's argument), nor just in the different period of expansion in which the economies were incorporated into the international system. Rather (or in addition), the different histories are the result of the different historical instances ''at which sectors of local classes allied or clashed with foreign interests, organized different forms of state, sustained distinct ideologies, or tried to implement various policies or defined alternative strategies to cope with imperialist challenges'' (Cardoso and Faletto 1979, xvii).

Thus, Cardoso and Faletto explicitly reject an analysis of the periphery that derives ''mechanically significant phases of dependent societies only from the 'logic of capitalist accumulation' '' (1979, xv). For them, the system of domination reappears as an internal force, through the social practices of local groups that impose foreign interests ''not precisely because they are foreign, but because they may coincide with values and interests that these groups pretend are their own'' (1979, xvi). ''It is necessary to elaborate concepts and explanations able to show how general trends of capitalist expansion turn into concrete relations among men, classes, and states in the periphery'' (1979, xviii).

Such an analysis diverges in other ways from the Frank and Amin versions of dependency: Although Cardoso and Faletto accept that dependent capitalist economies are not identical to central capitalist economies, they do not subscribe to a theory of dependent capitalist development. They reject, for example, the idea implicit in both Frank's and Amin's work of permanent stagnation due to the narrowness of internal market (wages representing a cost rather than a source of realization) in the periphery. Rather, they argue that the market for goods is more limited (mass consumption goods in the metropole are luxury goods in the periphery), and that industrialization in the periphery enhances income concentration as it increases differences in productivity and income without generalizing increased consumption to the whole of the economy. Frank's assertion that industrial wages have to be kept low in order to export manufactured goods is thus implicitly disputed, on the grounds that these wages *do* form the basis for the expansion of an internal market. The production of transnational firms in Latin America, for example, is almost entirely for domestic consumption, either for production or *final* consumption (1979, xx). The conditions of capitalist development, furthermore, vary considerably among periphery societies.

Nevertheless, when all is said and done, Cardoso and Faletto do subscribe to the idea that capitalist development in the periphery is not a duplicate of capitalist development in the metropole, and that periphery development *is* conditioned by capitalism as a world system. They also agree that there are general statements that can be made about industrialization, for example, in the periphery as compared to industrialization in the metropole. Their primary disagreement with Frank and Amin on this point is essentially on the existence of an internal market and therefore what the contours of dependent economic development are, particularly in the period since 1930.

The significance of Cardoso and Faletto's analysis lies, however, in their concentration on the particular rather than the general, and in that particular on the inter- and intra-class struggles that marked the spread of capitalism into the periphery. This focus on social relations rather than broad economic epiphenomena puts the periphery on the same historical-materialist footing as the metropoles. It recognizes that social struggles took place in the periphery and that these struggles had significance both for the capitalist development process *there* as well as for the development of world capitalism. This puts the dependent State at center stage not only as the bourgeois mechanism for appropriating local resources for capital export, but also as a mechanism of consolidating and reproducing bourgeois hegemony. Once resistance to the imperialist project is assumed, the State therefore becomes much more than the instrument of imperialist penetration. It *is* the instrument of that penetration but only on the condition that the exporting bourgeoisie can organize hegemonic blocs that overcome resistance to deepening dependency. The way to such successful organization varies.[7]

Even so, Cardoso and Faletto agree with Frank and Amin that the State in pre-1930 Latin America fundamentally expressed the interests of the exporting bourgeoisie and landholders and had acted as an agent for foreign investment especially in primary-good exporting, unindustrialized (enclave) economies (Cardoso and Faletto 1979, 129). But with the crisis in world capitalism in 1929, the periphery State (in Latin America) intervened to set up protective tariffs, to transfer income from the export to domestic sector, and to create the infrastructure needed to support the import-substitution industry. Cardoso and Faletto see this change in terms of the formation of new alliances—a new hegemonic bloc—during the previous period, and the response of these new alliances with the demise of the export sectors. Crucial to their explanation are the *differences* in response to the crisis depending on whether foreigners controlled the export sector (enclave economy) or whether exports were controlled by a national bourgeoisie. In the latter case, there are also important variations: in some countries, one of the agro-exporting sectors would assert its dominance not only over the nation but also over the other producing groups; in other countries, there was only tacit agreement among the exporting groups— no one of them could assert its hegemony, but the "alliance" did define the sphere of internal influence of the State.

In each case the response to the Great Depression was different. There had already been diversification in the nationally controlled export economies before 1929; once the slump was over, the agro-exporting groups believed that they could become prosperous through formation of an industrial sector, although only as a supplementary source, and through an expansion of the domestic market. Development changed fundamentally after 1929 in these economies, not because of the economic crisis itself, but as a result of pressure on the political system by new social groups and the reaction by groups linked to the export sector (Cardoso and Faletto 1979, 100-101). Because of the potential for growth of the internal market, middle classes could be incorporated into the hegemonic bloc, and in fact

[7] But as Frank points out, and Warren (1980) ignores, failure to participate in the imperialist project could also have disastrous effects on a periphery society—for example, the case of Paraguay in Latin America which, with British support, was invaded and decimated by its neighbors.

the speed with which this was done largely determined how quickly the economy industrialized.

On the other hand, in the enclave economies, national dominant groups were linked to foreign enterprises more as a politically dominant class rather than as one that controlled the means of production. In this sense, the enclave State had some of the characteristics of the colonial State, particularly since its main function was the maintenance of internal order that would ensure a supply of labor and natural resources needed by the enclave. The enclave State was also "independent" of the enclave, and the oligarchy that controlled it had its own economic base in the latifundias that produced food and other products for the domestic market. This system of domination was much more closed than in the case of nationally controlled export economies; middle classes could gain entrance to the political bloc only by using enclave workers and peasants as allies to overthrow the entire structure. The Great Depression did not, in and of itself, change this system, but the recession in the enclave caused severe unemployment, which generated radical movements, in turn met with armed force by both dominant oligarchy and enclave. Creating a domestic market required using the State, taking income generated by the enclave sectors and investing it in urban industrial sectors. The State, in this case, was already controlled partly by a landed, *hacienda*-based oligarchy, so the post-1930s period is marked by a sharing of power between a new national bourgeoisie and the old oligarchy.

These examples show how Cardoso and Faletto's analysis has the political consequences of the world economic crisis depending on the class structure and class conflict within each country. According to them, development changed fundamentally in character after 1929 as a result of pressure on the political system by new social groups and of the reaction by groups linked to the export sector, either agro-export groupings or *hacienda*-based oligarchies. The struggle in each case was over control of the State, or at least access to it, since the State apparatuses determined how State revenues would be used and the relation of the national economy to foreign economic interests. Cardoso and Faletto see the world capitalist system and its division of labor as the structure in which a series of alternatives emerge based on local sociopolitical conditions. Dependency is a generic term that frames a number of different possibilities. Changes in the world system (e.g., the Great Depression) obviously change the framework, but previous history in each country (the class structure and the structure of domination) conditions the response to the changed condition. These different responses also change the world system as a whole, as Amin points out.

The dependent State is set in this context of conditioned class struggle—

conditioned by crises and developments in the world system and by the role of export sectors in the national economy. It is this State that is primarily responsible for organizing the internal market and the local accumulation of capital, based in large part on revenues from export industries. In countries that had an important industrial sector before 1929, further industrialization was based on the expansion of private enterprise. But even in those economies, the State created new areas of investment concentrated around heavy industry and infrastructure works. In the pre-1929 enclave economies, groups not directly tied to the import-export system tried to create an urban-industrial base through State direction. In some of those countries the State apparatus was used to form an industrial class, which eventually shared entrepreneurial functions with State-owned enterprises (Cardoso and Faletto 1979, 128). The industrialization movement, in turn, created population movements toward the cities and mass urban societies, composed of a wage-earning proletariat and a non-wage earning popular sector. Different alliances of dominant groups in the State had to deal with this growing urban mass in order to continue the industrialization process. The dependent State took on many of the attributes of the capitalist State in the advanced countries, except that the industrial base was not developed, and its development still depended on economic conditions set in the world capitalist system. Even so, in the larger countries the State was the arena of ideological attempts to achieve a reasonable consensus and to legitimize a new power system based on an industrialization program offering benefits to all.

The distinctive features (in the post-1929 period) of industrialization policies in each country depended on how the roles of the State and the industrial bourgeoisie were reconciled (Cardoso and Faletto 1979, 132). In complete disagreement with Frank and Amin, Cardoso and Faletto argue that the masses were needed for the process of industrialization as a labor force but also as an integral part of the consumer market. They also had to be taken into account by the groups in power to the extent that they ensured or rejected the latter's hegemony (1979, 132). But, unlike the advanced countries, whose dominant groups had been able to incorporate essential elements of the working class through domestic capital accumulation (particularly through increased agricultural productivity) and the exploitation of Third World resources (including labor), the previous and actual position of dependent societies in the world system *limited* the possibilities for the economy to incorporate the masses through industrialization, and for the State to incorporate them politically. The industrialization and incorporation process could only function if export prices were maintained or even increased, so that broader industrial sectors could be increased without the profit level being lowered. According to Cardoso and Faletto, the State as distributor (setting wage levels of the urban working class, tariff levels, and following expansionary or restrictive monetary policy) and investor (borrowing abroad, investing directly) played much the same role as in the advanced countries, but all this was set within the limits of continued export dependence and the difficulty of sustained economic and political incorporation of *"el pueblo."*

THE NEW AUTHORITARIANISM IN LATIN AMERICA

The early phase of substitutive industrialization in Latin America required extensive State participation and control but was based largely on internal accumulation. In the 1950s this began to change with the search for new markets by foreign industrial capital. The new investment by foreign capital was not, for the most part, intended to exploit Third World labor to reduce consumption goods costs in metropole markets, although there was that too. Rather, metropole capital was seeking to expand output by increasing the extent of its market primarily for production goods in the Third World itself. So, although foreign investment intensified the "exclusive social system characteristic of capitalism in periphery communities, it nonetheless promoted capital accumulation and increasing complexity in the production structure" (Cardoso and Faletto 1979, 158-159).[8]

The new industrialization, tied to the transnational corporations and considerable foreign borrowing, concentrated on industry that produced for domestic consumption, particularly producer goods and consumer du-

[8] Warren (1980) makes a much stronger argument, contending that the countries of Asia, Africa, and Latin America are increasingly playing more independent roles in the world economy, in large part as a result of foreign investment and the development of the productive forces in those countries. The recent world debt crisis, however, weakens many of Warren's claims. In retrospect, economic gains in the Third World in the 1960s and 1970s relied heavily on increasing borrowing and exports, and increased borrowing in the 1970s relied on increased oil money funneled through U.S. and European banks. Since so many different economic strategies, from Mexico's and Brazil's state capitalism to Chile's "open" economy, seemed to have "misused" their borrowing, Warren's contention that internal inefficiency rather than "dependency" is to blame for development problems is considerably less convincing. But Warren's argument has even more profound problems. In addition to his assumption of the rapid development of the forces of production under capitalist development, he assumes that this development is democratic, and that only under such democracy can worker consciousness reach the necessary levels to achieve socialism. But it may very well be, in the absence of a strong local bourgeoisie, that democracy is crushed and replaced by authoritarianism, and that the subordinate group struggle against this authoritarianism (the struggle for democracy) is the basis of consciousness formation. Warren therefore assumes that the basis for worker consciousness can only be found in the development of forces of production under the conditions of bourgeois democracy, conditions that are inherently unstable in the Third World.

rables. That created a demand for trained labor and increased local labor productivity. But even with higher growth rates, the advent of transnational corporation industrialization accentuated a pattern of development that is "highly dependent on the wholesale importation of consumption patterns, production processes, technology, institutions, material inputs, and human resources, adding new *internal* economic, socio-cultural, and political dimensions to the old patterns of external dependence, and aggravating the structural tendency toward increasing external imbalance" (Sunkel and Fuenzalida 1979, 68).

Just as important from the point of view of this analysis, the new industrialization generated popular pressure for increased social spending and greater mass political participation. In Latin America, the nation was used to mediate mass movements rather than to isolate the individual from his class through citizenship rights (as described by Poulantzas 1980). In the 1950s and 1960s, the new industrialization was accompanied by the political activation of the previously marginal popular sectors, an activation in which they were treated much more as mass movements striving for greater equality than as citizens (O'Donnell 1979). These mass movements were legitimized by the concept of nation that had developed earlier in the century, but crystallized in the expansion of State spending and the electoral success of popular political parties during the postwar period.

Yet within slightly more than a decade (1964-1976), a number of democratic regimes in Latin America (Brazil, Peru, Uruguay, Chile, and Argentina) fell to military coups that were different from the former *caudillo* (military dictator) type, and did not correspond to the European fascist "political" dictatorships of the 1920s and 1930s. These more recent coups represented, rather, a brand of technocratic terrorism that attempted to "depoliticize" society in the name of economic efficiency, the nation, and social order. The democratic representative regime, which in one form or another survived in the previous period of industrial development, was converted into the authoritarian corporatist regime, through "rebellions in which large national organizations like the army and the public bureaucracy (rather than the national or internationalized bourgeoisie) take action and organize" (Cardoso and Faletto 1979, 166-167).

Two conceptions of the dependent State emerged to explain its non-democratic nature and its increasing intervention in the national economy. The first is the State capitalist model. It emphasizes the increased role in production of the Third World State. We have already discussed the nature of the State capitalism concept as applied to the developed countries, and how this concept was revised by the derivationists and Offe (see Chapter 5). In the dependent economy context, the existence of a weak bourgeoisie creates even more propitious (and necessary) conditions for State expansion into production (Fitzgerald 1979). For State capitalist analysts, this role of the State is characteristic of a particular stage of the accumulation process, a process that is in crisis because of the relation of dependent economies to the metropole centers (Evans 1977; Fitzgerald 1977). The contradictions in this role go beyond those articulated by Offe (1973) in his theory of the advanced capitalist State. For not only is the State involved in the distribution and production of goods, but as a dependent State, it must interact with powerful foreign bourgeoisies and their supporting metropole States.

Probably the most important argument made by the State capitalist school centers on the role that State intervention plays in creating a State bourgeoisie—a new class whose interests are connected with *power* over resources rather than their direct ownership. The model tries to show how this bourgeoisie has interests in the State as the State itself rather than as a bureaucratic representative of class interests in civil society (Canak 1983). There is *correspondence* and *antagonism* between the interests of the State bourgeoisie and the interests of national and international capital. Equally important, the State, by taking on production to stabilize and shore up the accumulation process, weakens its independent political base and thus reduces the relative autonomy required for the restructuring of capital (Fitzgerald 1979).

The second model—bureaucratic authoritarianism—has its roots in the class struggle view of Cardoso and Faletto. Bureaucratic authoritarianism is, first and foremost, "guarantor and organizer of the domination exercised through a class structure subordinated to the upper fractions of a highly oligopolized and transnationalized bourgeoisie" (O'Donnell 1979, 292). It politically excludes the previously activated popular sectors by imposing a particular type of "order" through extreme coercion, including the "depoliticization" of the society, and economically excludes them by shifting State social spending to infrastructure that promotes foreign investment, and, above all, to the State bureaucracy itself—military spending, State capital investment, and the employment of highly paid civil service technocrats (Cardoso 1979). Furthermore, capital accumulation is skewed to benefit large national and foreign units of private capital and State corporations. Labor unions and mass organizations are tightly controlled. The regime eliminates political access to the State through political parties, mass organizations, or interest groups, and essentially limits that access to individual contacts between persons outside and inside the bureaucracy. There is a distinct separation between the State and the civil society. Legitimacy vis-à-vis national and transnational capital and the middle class (heavily subsidized by State employment) depends on economic growth and increasing material consumption—a legitimacy of technocratic efficiency—while the working and peasant classes are kept acquiescent through the coercive apparatuses (Stepan 1978, 76-77). In bureaucratic authoritarianism, the public sector, the transnational corporation, and the modern capitalist sector of the national economy are joined. The State sector of the economy comes to act as a public entrepreneur, no longer as implementor of a populist policy of income distribution through wage increases (Cardoso and Faletto 1979, 165).[9]

There is general agreement on these characteristics, but is bureaucratic authoritarianism rooted in some inherent economic condition of dependent societies—in the *structure* of dependent development—and therefore a structurally necessary form of the dependent State, or is it a "historical" response to particular political conditions in the capitalist dependent State? Frank, as we have seen, argues that these regimes were necessary to increase capital accumulation (to increase the exploitation of labor) in the face of a world economic crisis. O'Donnell (1973) contends that the import-substitution process encountered difficulties in the 1950s and early 1960s that, it was thought, could only be solved by "deepening" industrialization through vertical integration, and that this deepening could only be accomplished by attracting foreign capital. To do this required increasing the rate of investment, therefore freezing or reducing popular consumption *and* achieving institutional stability and political order—a favorable long-term investment climate for foreign and domestic capital. O'Donnell argues that bureaucratic authoritarianism is a "type of authoritarian State" (1979, 291), in the sense that this type of regime corresponds to a particular "stage" of accumulation in dependent economies.

But both Cardoso (1979) and Stepan (1978) disagree with this formulation for similar reasons. Stepan considers that rather than the crisis of import substitution, political exigency—specifically the threat to "elite" hegemony by popular movements—is the unifying theme of exclusionary corporatist regimes. He places the Salazar regime in Portugal and the Franco regime in Spain in this same category. Bureaucratic authoritarianism is not a type of State but a type of corporatism, specifically an antipopulist corporatism. Cardoso argues that the dependent capitalist State, even in the face of the world capitalist crisis and the difficulties of import-substitution industrialization, has coexisted with many different political regimes, including nonmilitary corporatist (Mexico, for example), inclusionary military (Peru), exclusionary military (Argentina, Brazil, Chile, Uruguay), and even democratic (Venezuela, or Brazil during the time of Kubitschek, for example). The military regimes themselves have varied considerably

[9] For more detail on the development of this entrepreneurial State in the Brazilian context, see Cardoso (1979).

in the version of orthodox economic policies they have followed—the difference is especially clear in comparing Brazil with Chile. Serra's (1979) empirical work also tends to undermine the idea that there are strict structural-economic bases for bureaucratic authoritarianism. Thus, Cardoso considers it to "refer, not to the form of the state as such, but to a type of political regime" (Cardoso 1979, 40). It is a response to the crisis provoked in the State by political movements and social struggle before the military takeover. Cardoso writes: "It is better . . . to recognize frankly the ambiguous character of historical situations than to proclaim nostalgia for the logic and coherence of explanations which ignore the unexpected and contradictory aspects of real political life and thus reinforce the image that authoritarian military regimes are likely to cope successfully with new demands" (1979, 57).

But, as Hirschman (1979) makes clear, we should also consider that there are important ideological factors involved in assessing these "historical situations": although the authoritarian military regime as a political form is, to a large extent, inconsistent with a noncoercive corporatist ideal (see Chapter 1 above, and Stepan 1978), it does include many corporate forms and—apart from its use of torture and extralegal assassination—is consistent with transnational corporations' organizational ideology. We could argue that the emergence of the entrepreneurial authoritarian State corresponds in form and operation to the growth of the large corporations as the dominant form of capitalist organization.[10] In an ideological sense, the bureaucratic authoritarian State is much more suited to be the local partner of transnational capital than are other forms of the bourgeois State. Together, the two attempt to continue the process of capital accumulation and the development of the productive forces in dependent economies: there exists a relationship of "mutual indispensability" between the bureaucratic authoritarian State and transnational corporations, a partnership

[10] There is even a question of what constitutes the "local dominant class" when the State controls such a significant percentage of domestic investment. Since the appearance of Berle and Means's book (1935) on the corporation in the United States, there has been a long discussion on whether or not capitalists control capital any longer and on the whole meaning of the term "bourgeoisie" (see Fitch and Oppenheimer 1970; Sweezy 1970). Monopoly capitalism has certainly been marked by the growth of a managerial class, which makes an increasing share (if not the totality) of decisions in capitalist society. Transnational enterprises are large, bureaucratic organizations—a far cry from the individual nineteenth-century entrepreneur. In some countries, like Tanzania or Guyana, the State bureaucracy, for all intents and purposes, controls the economic decision-making process (and "owns" the means of production) even though there exist in those countries small and politically weak fractions of producer and merchant bourgeoisies. Do these bureaucracies incorporate and reproduce bourgeois culture, including their relations in production, accumulation patterns, and consumption habits? This seems the crucial issue, but the answer is not altogether clear.

that allows the transnationals to penetrate local economies in return for the technological and financial expertise that they possess, which is so crucial to deepening industrial development and to increasing economic growth (Warren 1980).

Where does this all leave us? Is the dependent State inherently different from the metropolitan State because of the domination of the periphery's economy by foreign capital? Does this domination create different *forms* of the State in the periphery than in the metropoles? The more instrumentalist views represented by world system theory imply that the dependent State *tends* toward authoritarian forms: the dominance of the world system has historically kept local bourgeoisies weak; the weak local bourgeoisie cannot establish its hegemony, hence cannot maintain power (and guarantee access to its economy for foreign capital) through democratic forms of the State. At the same time, the strength of foreign capital and metropole States and their unwillingness to allow popular, anti-imperialist control of democratic States pushes and helps the local bourgeoisie to back the military in establishing bureaucratic authoritarian regimes—regimes that are much more beholden to the "real" power of foreign than to local capital. The form of the dependent State is therefore a function primarily of external capital and its need to extract surplus from the periphery. The fact that bureaucratic authoritarianism may ultimately not be in the interests of the local bourgeoisie and middle class is less important than its necessity to capital accumulation on a world scale.

Cardoso and Faletto and other more "political" dependency theorists (see Collier 1979), including O'Donnell in his latest writings, place much more emphasis on local struggles in their analysis of the dependent State.[11] They tend to see the dependent State as subject to many of the same forces as in world system theory, but also subject to national class struggle and hegemonic crisis. In that sense, the bureaucratic authoritarian form is subject to popular pressures and internal contradictions similar to any capitalist State's. But although in a bourgeois democratic regime, the State is able to mediate economic domination through the concept of citizenship or nation—the nation and either "the people" or the individual citizen are embodied in an externally legitimized State (legitimized by political participation)—in the authoritarian regime, the State institutions must "statize" the meaning of nation. The general interest or identification with the State must be subsumed under the establishment of "order" and "ration-

---

[11] In O'Donnell's words, "the implantation of BA [bureaucratic authoritarianism] is the result of a frightened reaction to what is perceived as a grave threat to the survival of the basic capitalist parameters of society" (1979, 295). This is a significant addition to the more structuralist O'Donnell of 1973, who based his explanation for authoritarianism on the crisis of capital accumulation in the dependent economies.

ality" and an increased rate of economic growth (O'Donnell 1979, 295). The State must rely on tacit consensus, coercion, fear, and the support of "the least national fractions of its society" (1979, 300)—the upper bourgeoisie—whose interests are intimately connected with the transnationalization of the economy.

Tensions appear in this combination of economic domination and coercion, and the bureaucratic State is subject to them, just like any other. These tensions are inherent in the very project of the State—to maintain order and increase economic growth within the context of an alliance between the upper bourgeoisie and the military. One of these tensions, as Cardoso (1979) emphasizes, is between the military State and its bourgeois civilian social base. The authoritarian State in some countries, such as Brazil, is a producer, and the State bureaucracy considers itself more efficient than local entrepreneurs and even transnational corporations. It is in the national interest of the State to produce as much of its own military supplies as possible, rather than importing or depending on strategic production by transnational firms. The less the national State must depend for its production on transnational enterprises, the more control it has over mediating conflicts between capital accumulation and popular demands. Certainly, "independence" from metropole dictates in the foreign policy of countries like Argentina, Brazil, and Mexico is one means by which these countries' States present to their masses an ideology of national sovereignty in the face of economic and cultural dependence. And national State bureaucracies will attempt to negotiate better international economic terms not necessarily for their national bourgeoisies vis-à-vis transnational enterprises, but for the State bureaucracy itself. Once the curator of the monopoly of violence (the armed forces) in a country controls the State apparatuses and dominates the political system as well, the question can be raised whether the transnationals are the dominant economic actor in that national context. The autonomy of the State and even its "independence" from the dominant class in civil society become crucial issues in such periphery societies.

The second major tension is between the authoritarian State and the "silent void" of civil society. One option for the State is to expand its social base by an expansionary economic policy, abandoning the International Monetary Fund and local economic orthodoxy. Can the authoritarian State achieve such expansion? O'Donnell (1979) claims not, largely because any expansionary fiscal policy or increased investment in State enterprises conflicts with the interests of the upper bourgeoisie. But, as Warren (1980) argues, it *is* in the interest of both transnational corporations and the entrepreneurial State to stimulate domestic capital accumulation and the growth of internal markets. Increasingly, the TNCs (transnational corporations) are looking at semi-industrialized countries as consumption goods outlets. Even if this capital accumulation process depends on exports and foreign investment, the fact is (as Cardoso and Faletto note) that many State enterprises are profitable and are themselves a source of capital accumulation. Similarly, under bureaucratic authoritarian regimes there has been growth of local consumer goods industries, which are also accumulating capital.[12]

Nevertheless, O'Donnell may be correct. The current debt crisis bears out that much of the growth that did occur in the 1970s was financed by international borrowing (including by State enterprises), and this raises serious questions about this growth as a means of incorporating important fractions of the working class into the dominant-class development project, that is, in significant increases in consumption for these groups. Just as important, the current crisis exposes yet another aspect of authoritarian State's economic project: its extreme reliance on the metropolitan financial bourgeoisie and States for whatever growth has occurred, and the concomitant power of that bourgeoisie and those States over the national economy. This undermines mass identification with the authoritarian State as the carrier of national culture.

Thus, in O'Donnell's terms, the State is fragile because of its limited options for expanding its social base. Ultimately the authoritarian State has to face its own illegitimacy and the "nostalgia for democracy" (O'Donnell 1979, 314).

> The issue of democracy is important not only because it contains the Achilles heel of this system of domination, but also because it contains a dynamic that can be the unifying element in the long-term effort to establish a society that is more nearly in accord with certain fundamental values. . . . The proposal for a limited form of democracy . . . is not the gracious concession of a triumphant power, but the expression of its intrinsic weakness. (O'Donnell 1979, 317)

The importance of the struggle for democracy as an underlying "tendency" even in the periphery introduces a third tension: the relationship of the class conflict and expansion of democracy in the metropoles (see Chapter 6) and that expansion in the periphery. Frank and Amin in a very general way, and Cardoso and Faletto and O'Donnell in a more specific way, tie local hegemony of the independent State to metropole *capital*, and in this form, to crises in the metropole capital-directed world economic system. But this formulation makes a crucial assumption about the relation

---

[12] Even though, as Serra (1979) points out, the economic growth record of the BA regimes has been no better than their "chaotic," more socially oriented predecessors.

of the metropole bourgeoisie (or transnational corporations) to the metropole States. It supposes that the State is the instrument of the metropole dominant class. The repressive apparatus of the metropole State is at the service of that bourgeoisie to protect and extend its economic activities in the Third World. Amin specifically argues that increased accumulation of capital in the metropoles promoted by capitalist imperialism prevents social conflict in those countries, and that, therefore, socialist revolutions of an anti-imperialist nature are the most likely kind of radical change in the present period of capitalist development. This leaves subordinate groups in the metropoles out of the theory of the dependent State. Even Cardoso and Faletto assume metropole State hegemony and hence a set of possibilities for transnational corporations that only fluctuates in terms of (1) competition among metropoles; or (2) U.S.-Soviet relations (e.g., see Cardoso and Faletto 1979, 188-199). The metropole working class is implicitly viewed as an ally of transnational enterprises in their relationship to the Third World State and civil society.

Although metropole working-class passivity in the face of and even support of imperialism seemed to be prevalent in the 1950s and early 1960s, the events of the late 1960s and 1970s show that transnational expansion has difficulty mediating the contradictions of capitalist development in the periphery *and in the metropoles*. It is generally recognized that struggle over surplus in the metropoles drives both financial and productive enterprises to seek higher profits in the periphery. But whereas this results in low-priced consumer exports coming back into the metropoles (which subsidizes working-class consumption), such "runaway shops" also create metropole unemployment and put downward pressure on metropolitan working-class incomes. Also, nontransnational capitalists—mostly smaller, domestic, competitive enterprises—in order to compete with the transnationals, reduce labor costs by inducing new sources of domestic cheap labor (women) out of household work into low-wage production and service jobs and by hiring illegal aliens. These pressures on wages generate increased conflict both in production and the State. Transnationals' operations become increasingly "high profile," which subjects their economic power to serious questioning. This creates opposition to the unconstrained freedom of transnationals to destroy domestic metropole jobs. Finally, struggles emanating from the super-exploitation of metropolitan women, minorities, and aliens are accentuated by the intensified use of these groups in the labor force.

But the most important resistance comes at another level: the "bought-off" working class in the metropoles is less and less willing to fight and die for the maintenance and expansion of transnational investment, especially when that expansion becomes fraught with difficulties. It was the resistance of an important fraction of this post-World War II middle class that finally made the transnationals put pressure on the American State to abandon the war in Vietnam. The legitimacy of the State and transnational hegemony eventually became more important to the transnationals than defeating communism in Indochina. They acceded to exacerbated conflict at home in the early seventies by adding their pressure on the Nixon government to withdraw. American intervention in Angola was also prevented by mass resistance to "getting involved." Successful revolution was aided in Nicaragua by American hesitation to intervene within the context of President Carter's "human rights" policy—a policy that was again a response to the delegitimization at home of U.S. foreign policy.

These details serve to illustrate that transnationals continue to be dependent on metropolitan nation-State repressive apparatuses for the military power necessary to enforce their expansion, even though in some of the countries, local militaries can usually fulfill the direct repressive role. Nevertheless, if the willingness of the metropole State to use military power to support transnationals is reduced by working-class resistance within the metropole, the power of the transnationals to control development in the periphery is also reduced. And since the options of the bureaucratic authoritarian State in the periphery are so closely linked to that foreign capital and the military power of the metropole State, a change in the willingness of the metropole to support military regimes in the periphery economically and militarily certainly figures both in the periphery investment climate for metropole capital and in the capacity of authoritarian regimes to resist democratic pressures. The degeneration of bureaucratic authoritarianism, therefore, is intimately tied to democratic expansion in the metropoles.

It is to recent theories of the State in the United States and a discussion of that democratic expansion that we now turn.

CHAPTER EIGHT

Class and State in Recent American Political Theory

WE HAVE NOW COME full circle. In Chapter 1, we reviewed dominant currents in American views of the State, currents directly opposed to an important European Marxist tradition. The basis for those American views lies largely in the works of John Locke and Adam Smith, adapted to the changing conditions of capitalist societies, but always supportive of the fundamental relations of capitalist production, and denying the existence of antagonistic social classes inherent in such production. Now, in this chapter, we return to American political and social theory, but this time to recent works that try to unify—from a class-analysis perspective—the U.S. experience with the European Marxist historical tradition, especially as that tradition has developed since Gramsci. There are several keys to understanding this unifying effort. First, American research on the State is concerned primarily with capitalism and social movements in America— with a rather decentralized State, large minority populations, a populist tradition, the capitalist world's most powerful military, and, in some sense, the most "successful" historical example of the free enterprise system. The United States also has a long, uninterrupted, democratic tradition; therefore, the issue of democracy itself is an important element in any discussion of the American State.

The success of the free enterprise system and the growth of democracy in America frame the analysis of the State, for because of these elements, the very notions of class and class struggle are much less clearly defined than in Europe and social mobility has resulted in a more porous upper class (a power elite, in C. Wright Mills's terms) and a working class that has difficulties seeing itself as such. This seeming contradiction between the existence of classes that are not clearly defined and a class-analysis perspective forms a basic theme in recent theory: What is the relation between the capitalist class and the State? What is the nature of class struggle and its relation to the State? The new American political analysis is also concerned with the American State itself, a State that is seemingly not very powerful in the face of powerful private corporations, but one that has become the focus of consuming political struggles during the last two decades.

A second key to understanding this analysis is the effect of American political realities on its discussion of democracy. Previous chapters suggested that Italian and French Marxists are increasingly concerned with the role of democracy in the transition to socialism. This reflects the real and present strength of socialist and communist political parties and the politicization of workers' movements in those countries. Socialist politics and the role of a socialist State in a bourgeois democracy are not distant theoretical issues. In contrast, and largely because there is no significant socialist movement in the United States, democracy for the American Left is more important in terms of the contradictions it poses for capitalist development—that is, analysts ask whether there is an inherent conflict between capitalism and democracy, and if there is, how it is reflected in the capitalist State.

A third key is that research on the American State is being done by social scientists, as in Europe, but social science research in the United States is heavily influenced by an American brand of empiricism. Even class-perspective work on the State, therefore, tends to build on European theories through empirical analysis (either historical or observational-analytical) rather than attempting to develop an entirely new way of looking at the State. At the same time, Americans writing in the European Marxist tradition have felt compelled to respond to the dominant forms of social science research on the relation between State and society. Neoclassical economic theory, Parsonian social theory, and empiricist-pluralist political theory are so pervasive in U.S. intellectual circles, particularly in universities, that anyone who does not employ them as the basis for research is required to couch theoretical and empirical work in terms of a response to that dominant formulation. Concomitantly, almost all American social scientists writing from a class perspective are initially trained largely, if not entirely, in empiricist, positivist epistemology.

For example, Erik Olin Wright tells us in the methodological introduction to his essays on Marxist theory (1978):

> As a graduate student in sociology I constantly confronted the hegemony of an empiricist, positivist epistemology in the social sciences. In virtually every debate over Marxist ideas, at some point I would be asked, "prove it!" To the extent that Marxist categories could be crystallized into "testable hypotheses," non-Marxists were willing (sometimes) to take these ideas seriously; to the extent that debate raged simply at the level of theory, non-Marxists found it relatively easy to dismiss our challenge. (1978, 9)

According to Wright, American Marxists in the social sciences reacted to these pressures either by (a) rejecting the concept of "testable hypotheses," contending that they were inimical to Marxist methodology of historical and dialectical explanation, (b) trying to generate empirical studies that would prove Marxist arguments (for example, power structure research, discussed below, which demonstrated the existence of a governing U.S. upper class)—empirical studies that, however, lose the dialectical character of Marxist theory in the research process, or (c) attempting to develop empirical research agendas rooted not only in the categories, but the logic, of Marxist theory.[1]

American class-perspective writers on the State emphasize the empirical. This attempt to engage the hegemony of empiricist, positivist epistemology while simultaneously developing an empirical approach to Marxist phenomena within a Marxist theoretical logic provides new insights into understanding the State in advanced capitalist society. There has been a surprisingly abundant literature on this subject in the United States.[2] In this chapter, some of this research—more as a representative survey than as a definitive bibliography—is organized under three areas of particular interest for class-perspective American scholarship on the State: (1) the relation between the capitalist class and the State—who rules and how the American class State reproduces capitalist relations of production; (2) the relation between the logic of capital and State policies—in which the class State itself is the focus of research, but class is not an historical subject; and (3) the class struggle and the State, in which the primary emphasis is on the nature of social conflict and its relation to the State and State policies. The first theme includes G. William Domhoff's power structure studies (inspired principally by C. Wright Mills's earlier work), Adam Przeworski's more structuralist notions of class compromise and social democracy (indirectly related to Samir Amin's view of capitalist economies discussed in the previous chapter); and the post-structuralist critique of both these views by Fred Block and Theda Skocpol. (Although Skocpol does not have a class-perspective view per se, her critique is so relevant to the analysis that it is included.) In the second theme, we review James O'Connor's work on the fiscal crisis of the State and Alan Wolfe's analysis of its ideological counterpart, the legitimacy crisis. In the third theme, we turn to the class struggle-focused analysis of the current economic and

---

[1] For a review of American Marxist writings in the social sciences, see Ollman and Vernoff (1982).

[2] Three journals have published extensively on the State during the seventies and these represent the best source of American research in this field: *Kapitalistate*, a joint German-American effort, heavily influenced by Claus Offe and James O'Connor, but publishing a wide range of international research on the State; *Politics and Society*, a source for "alternative" U.S. political science and sociology research; and *Socialist Revolution* (now *Socialist Review*), another important source for "alternative" views.

political crisis by Manuel Castells, Erik Olin Wright, and Samuel Bowles and Herbert Gintis.

RELATIONS BETWEEN THE CAPITAL CLASS AND THE STATE

Power Structure Studies

G. William Domhoff's power structure research is not, in and of itself, a study of the State.[3] But the implications of his results are important to a discussion of many of the questions raised in previous chapters, particularly those on the relation between the economy and the State that is, the reproduction of capitalist relations in production. The work is based in part on C. Wright Mills's 1956 work, *The Power Elite*, although Mills talked of "elites" and "institutions" rather than "classes." He also rejected the revolutionary role claimed by Marxists for the working class. Nevertheless, Mills flew in the face of dominant pluralist models by discussing an American power structure, and this is the spirit of Domhoff's research. In *Who Rules America* (1967) and later works (1970, 1978, 1979), Domhoff spells out his main thesis that there not only exists an upper class in America, but that it is a *governing class*. He argues that the American upper class is different from the upper classes of European countries in that it is made up exclusively of successful businessmen and corporation lawyers. Coincident with the rise of the national corporate economy in the last half of the eighteenth century, this class gradually dropped its sectional bases and itself became national in scope.

Domhoff's formulation of the American upper class is interesting on two counts. First, it includes the possibility of social mobility by non-members into a ruling group and describes the mechanism through which that social mobility occurs:

> this social group, whether its members are aware of it or not, has well-established ways of "training" and "preparing" new members. This point must be stressed because it is certainly the case that people are moving into (not to mention out of) this group all the time. . . . Social mobility can be looked at from many points of view and in terms of many different questions, but the important thing to keep in mind in understanding this phenomenon in a sociological study of the upper class is the process of "co-optation." For our purposes, we will mean by co-optation the processes whereby individuals are assimilated and committed to the institutions and values of the dominant socioeconomic group. In studying co-optation we want to know which institutions select

[3] For similar power structure research in France, see Birnbaum (1978, 1979).

and prepare those who are assimilated, as well as the ideas and values that make a person acceptable . . . the co-optation of bright young men into the American upper class occurs through education at private schools, elite universities, and elite law schools; through success as a corporation executive; through membership in exlusive gentlemen's clubs; and through participation in exclusive charities. (Domhoff 1967, 4-5)

Second, Domhoff's formulation describes the lines and nature of conflict within the class, a conflict that often sets the State "against" elements of the power elite while representing its interests as a whole (see Domhoff 1967, 28-31 and 138-156). According to Domhoff, the most important antagonisms within the upper class are due to the clash of business interests, the existence of religious antagonisms, and differences between liberals and conservatives. He argues that this does not contradict the evidence that the upper class is a governing class: there may be disagreements and even conflict over long-range strategies and short-run tactics, but the primary goal of that class to protect the private property system as a whole and to reproduce its own control over major institutions of society remains intact.

How does Domhoff demonstrate that this upper class, with its internal conflicts, is a governing class? First, he defines "governing class" as "a social upper class which owns a disproportionate amount of the country's wealth, receives a disproportionate amount of a country's yearly income, and contributes a disproportionate number of its members to the controlling institutions and key decision-making groups of the country" (1967, 5). Then he goes on to show that the upper class indeed meets these criteria. Their disproportionate ownership of wealth and income earnings implies economic interests different from other socioeconomic groups, and their vast overrepresentation in directing key institutions gives them significant control over them. Specifically, he shows that the American upper class controls the major banks and corporations, the foundations, the elite universities, the largest mass media, such important opinion-molding organizations as the Council on Foreign Relations, the Foreign Policy Association, the Committee for Economic Development, the Business Advisory Council, and the National Advertising Council, and that it controls the executive branch of the federal government, the regulatory agencies, the federal judiciary, the military, the CIA, and the FBI. On the other hand, he argues, the governing class does not control, but merely influences, the legislative branch of the federal government, most state governments, and most city governments.

Domhoff's analysis gives us a picture of an upper class based on business wealth, which is open to newcomers but prepares (coopts) them for class loyalty through educational and membership institutions. This class actively controls the major means of capital accumulation, the private ideological apparatuses, and important State agencies. It has different interests from other social groups because of its disproportionate wealth and income, and it is able to ensure the promotion of its interests through its governance. The upper class, then, selects and trains the governing group and participates directly in the major institutions of American society; indeed, to a large extent, it comes to define *what* the major institutions are. This is the "power elite." "[The] power elite serves these interests by maintaining a profitable business system whose dividends, salaries, and expense accounts are the basis of the style of life and political power of the American business aristocracy" (1967, 62).

For all intents and purposes, Domhoff shows that Marx's—or better, Gramsci's or Poulantzas's—conception of a dominant class, exhibiting hegemony over economic and social institutions, really exists in the United States, and that this class is a corporate bourgeoisie, cohesive and with clear definitions of who is and is not a member, but at the same time in conflict and disagreement about how best to run the society to protect its particular interests. Domhoff does not argue that this class's power is in any way unlimited or that it is only used for its own interests:

> We would also agree that there are restraints on the power of the governing class, for the governing class is part of a system which includes other nation-states as well as other socioeconomic groups. We would even agree that members of the power elite often try to anticipate the reactions of other groups when they make their decisions. The potential power of angry, organized masses is well known in twentieth-century America thanks to foreign revolutions, the battle over women's suffrage, labor strikes, and the civil rights movement. (1967, 152)

So he acknowledges that there is a struggle for power among social groups, but at the same time tries to show how the power elite primarily serves an upper class, who that upper class is, and how it reproduces itself.

We have already discussed the debate between Poulantzas and Miliband, a debate in which Miliband is seen as an exponent of the power structure approach to the State. Poulantzas argued that whether or not there is direct participation of the capitalist class in the State apparatus and the government is not the important issue; rather, analysis should focus on the *objective* relations between the bourgeois class and the State. "This means that if the *function* of the State in a determinate social formation and the *interests* of the dominant class in this social formation coincide, it is by reason of the system itself: the direct participation of members of the ruling class in the State apparatus is not the cause but the *effect*, and moreover a chance and contingent one, of this objective coincidence'' (Poulantzas 1969, 73). Gold, Lo, and Wright (1975) incorrectly classified this as a debate between ''instrumentalists'' and ''structuralists'' and found both theoretically wanting. The instrumentalist view is characterized as one where government is a committee of the ruling class, directly manipulated by members of that class. The view, they argue, is under the influence of an overly simplistic ''economistic'' Marxism that does not take account of the relative autonomy of the State. Domhoff is seen as attempting to show that the American upper class controls the State directly and is able to make that State do its bidding.

But a careful reading of *Who Rules America* suggests that Domhoff's work is far from an attempt to demonstrate that the American State is a committee of the ruling class. Rather, if anything, he moves away from narrow Marxist conceptions of class struggle between capitalists and workers, to show how a dominant class is able to maintain its dominant position without completely restricting entry into such a group and without completely controlling the State apparatuses. Domhoff describes a State that represents the interests of the corporate class while at the same time opposes the interests of individual capitals or fractions of the business elite. And he makes quite clear that control of the executive branch does not mean control of the government or of public policy.

A more significant critique of power structure research is its absence of dialectical explanation—its empiricism to ''prove'' Marxist categories and relations simultaneously abandons Marxist logic (Wright 1978). It is in this spirit that Poulantzas's critique should be taken seriously.

Class Compromise and Social Democracy

For Adam Przeworski (1979; also Przeworski and Wallerstein 1982), the persistence of capitalist-class relations is not necessarily explainable by direct capitalist-class control of the State's reproductive mechanisms or, for that matter, the activities of the autonomous State. The necessity for a capitalist State to perpetuate capitalism assumes a model of conflict in which the interests of classes are ''irreconcilably opposed to each other, a model that implies that workers should always be hostile to capitalism and capitalists'' (Przeworski and Wallerstein 1982, 215). But Przeworski argues that the interests of workers and capitalists may not be irreconcilable under all circumstances. Rather, workers in democratic capitalist societies may, under some economic and political conditions, *choose* capitalism because of what it can deliver materially (high growth rates and improved material conditions for the working class) and politically (parliamentary democracy). This is the Keynesian or social democratic compromise, and, in some crucial ways, is closely related to the Panitch (1980) view of corporatism discussed in Chapter 1.

Put another way, Przeworski asks whether, if workers living under capitalism seek to maximize their material well-being, they will be led rationally to opt for socialism as the social organization that will best meet their material needs. His answer, developed in terms of a mathematical simulation model, confirms the historically observable social democratic compromise: "The compromise consists of a trade-off between workers' militancy and capitalists' consumption. Capitalists agree to invest at a high rate and workers agree to moderate their demands with regard to profits" (Przeworski 1979, 32). The existence of such conditions, he argues, is sufficient to "break the necessary implication between the short-term material interests of workers under capitalism and their preference for socialism" (ibid.). Capitalists are awarded concessions by the State to stimulate investment (and profits), while workers are accorded wage increases from profits. Corporatist arrangements protect the worker-capital compromise for the workers, ensuring for them that capitalists will not change the compromise in the future under different political conditions; the arrangement also specifies that investment uncertainty will be shared by both workers and capitalists.

Przeworski's and Wallerstein's analysis is interesting because it shows the conditions under which workers could *choose* to compromise with capital, on material grounds, giving up militant action in return for institutionally guaranteed arrangements for wage participation in profit. They also argue that if workers enter worker-capital negotiations with a high degree of militancy, they would be better off to "go all the way" to the conquest of power, assuming that they have the political power to transform economic relations. If they do not, an economic crisis from capitalists' disinvestment—a decline in business confidence, in Block's (1977) words— occurs, and workers would be much worse off than on any other grounds, including cooperating with capitalists at low levels of worker economic demands (Przeworski 1979, 34). And even if a structural transformation is accomplished, the flight of private capital and degree of social dislocation entails high economic costs: "Under democratic conditions—and today one cannot envisage any other ones—the support for socialist transformation is likely to be eroded if this support is sought in terms of economic demands and economic promises" (Przeworski 1979, 35). Przeworski suggests that the immediate material interest of workers under capitalism— given the threat of private capital disinvestment at any time—is not necessarily to opt for socialism (a choice that almost certainly will lead to a decline in their material well-being), but to compromise with capital in some form that will guarantee worker participation in profits. The social democratic compromise is "an expression of the very structure of capitalist society" (1979, 36), and the policies of the social or liberal democratic State are not the actions of an autonomous State facing the threat of a militant working class; rather, they reflect a compromise that expresses the interests "of a class coalition which includes important segments of organized workers" (1979, 37). The compromise reproduces capitalist relations because "crises of capitalism are not in the interests of workers, who bear their cost," and because the "socialist alternative is a costly one even when capitalists behave simply as profit motivated, rational individuals" (ibid.).

Such a compromise gives an entirely different significance to the activities of the State than ascribed to it by functionalist analyses. In the class-compromise model, the State institutionalizes, coordinates, and enforces compromises reached by a class coalition that encompasses both workers and capitalists.

> The State must enforce the compliance of both classes with the terms of each compromise and protect those segments of each class that enter into a compromise from non-cooperative behavior of their fellow class members. The State must induce individual capitalists to make the decisions required by the class compromise, shifting the terms of choice which they confront to produce the requisite aggregate effects as capitalists compete with each other. Finally, since the state of class compromise is a democratic state, it must see to it that the class coalition that forms the compromise can win popular support in elections. (Przeworksi and Wallerstein 1982, 236)

The essence of this approach is relative political power and how it is used by capitalists and workers (Przeworski and Wallerstein 1982, 233). The result may not be class compromise at all, but a tug of war between capital and labor (a prolonged crisis). Conditions may change and the class compromise may deteriorate. For example, the corporate accord can begin to break down under certain conditions where the capitalist class is unable to deliver higher wages. It may be in the interest of the coalition to find a capitalist production-preserving solution to the crisis, but the solution may be so costly to workers, particularly in terms of the *previous compromise*, that changes in the structure become more attractive. Furthermore, the capitalist accumulation process itself may produce such a high level of worker income that stability of material consumption and general security (community ties, full employment, absence of crime) become more important to the working class than immediate material gains. As the corporate accord appears to be breaking down, confidence in capitalists and the "compromise" State to deliver stability and security may erode.

This is Gramsci's hegemonic crisis, and it leads us to a second issue. Przeworski well understands that the assumptions of workers wanting increased material gratification, and their belief that capitalism can deliver higher wages (and solve economic crises) are a mixture of reality (people need to eat and shelter themselves; historically, capitalism has been very successful in accumulating capital; revolutions have resulted in economic hardship) and ideology (capitalism *creates* wants and controls the communication media—hence its view of itself and of alternatives is dominant). But does class compromise and a "worker-capitalist compromise hegemony" reflect working-class political power in institutional arrangements and in the ideology inherent in those arrangements? For example, do the ideological apparatuses of the State become class-neutral? When Przeworski argues that workers consent to capitalism and capitalists consent to democracy, the democracy capitalists consent to is defined in the State, which is not just the guarantor of the compromise, but also embodies the rules of the game, and—as Gramsci and the Italian debate make clear— it is these rules that are as much a part of the class struggle as is the distribution of material gains. In principle the Przeworski-Wallerstein model can deal with such "imponderables," and the class-compromise State, such as in today's Austria or Sweden, is a useful concept. But does the compromise take place through the capitalist State itself? If so, at what point does that State operate as an *ideologically* unbiased representative of capitalists and workers?

Panitch's (1980) discussion of the corporatist literature (see Chapter 1) suggests another problem with the Przeworski analysis. What Przeworski characterizes as class compromise could, in fact, begin as such a compromise but then ossify institutionally to State-induced collaboration of the working class with the capitalist class. The officially recognized trade unions are, after all, the institutional basis of the class compromise. But the very nature of that compromise and the trade union organizations that develop to enforce it can transform the capability of the working class to wage class struggle. As in the United States after World War II, the unions themselves can serve to integrate the working class into the capitalist State.

Post-Structuralist Critique

Fred Block (1977) presents us with a third interpretation of the State based on a critique of Domhoff and Poulantzas and a combination of Offe's theories with Poulantzas's greater emphasis on class struggle. Block argues that structuralist relative-autonomy theories (see our discussion of Marx in Chapter 2 and Poulantzas in Chapter 4) still assume that the ruling class will respond effectively to the State's abuse of that autonomy; they assume that the ruling class must have "some degree of political cohesion, an understanding of its general interests, and a high degree of political sophistication" (Block 1977, 9), all the things that Domhoff claims it *does* have, at least in the United States. But even accepting capitalist influence in the political process, Block bases his own view on the contention that neo-Marxists must "reject the idea of a class-conscious ruling class" and start instead from the concept that there is "a division of labor between those who accumulate capital and those who manage the State apparatus" (Block 1977, 10). According to this analysis, capitalists do not directly control the State, for the State is under the direction of "State managers." The capacity of capitalism to rationalize itself is not in the hands of capitalists, but is the outcome of a conflict between the capitalist class, the managers of the State apparatus, and the working class. In this framework, "the central theoretical task is to explain how it is that despite this division of labor, the state tends to serve the interests of the capitalist class" (Block 1977, 10). Block, of course, rejects Domhoff's assertion that an important way capitalists do this is by placing members of the upper class in key positions throughout society, including the State. "For one thing, ruling class members who devote substantial energy to policy formation become atypical of their class, since they are forced to look at the world from the perspective of state managers. They are quite likely to diverge from ruling-class opinion" (Block 1977, 13).[4]

Block uses Offe's argument that State managers reproduce capitalist relations not because they are directly answerable to the bourgeoisie, but because those who manage the State apparatus are dependent on some level of economic activity. The dependency exists both because economic activity produces State revenues and because public support for a regime will decline unless accumulation continues to take place. State managers willingly do what they know they must to facilitate capital accumulation. Given that the level of economic activity is largely determined by private investment decisions, such managers are particularly sensitive to overall "business confidence." This is not instrumentalism, he argues, not ruling-class consciousness, but "an evaluation of the market that considers political events only as they might impinge on the market" (Block 1977, 16). Capitalists are acting here out of self-interest, but the net result of any State reforms that capitalists perceive as "anticapitalist" or "antibusiness" is a decline in private investment and hence a decline in economic activity, a decline that makes the State less legitimate. Yet, if the State is "unwilling to risk a decline in business confidence, how is it then that the

---

[4] This critique is certainly less evident under the Reagan administration than it was when Block wrote it.

state's role has expanded inexorably throughout the twentieth century?'' (Block 1977, 20). Block argues that it is class struggle that pushes forward the development of capitalism, speeding the process by which capitalism advances the development of the productive forces. "Class struggle is responsible for much of the economic dynamism of capitalism" (1977, 21). It is this struggle, carried over from production to the State itself, that has expanded the role of the State into economic regulation and the provision of services. "The major impetus for the extension of the State's role has come from the working class and from the managers of the state apparatus, whose own powers expand with a growing state" (1977, 22).

According to Block, the expansion of the State, occurring more rapidly in periods of depression and war, when capitalists are not as powerful compared to working-class pressures and State managers, depends on the State's response to pressures from below. "The capacity of the state to impose greater rationality on capitalism is extended into new areas as a result of working-class pressures" (1977, 22), but the way the State uses its resources as a result of this expansion depends on the inherent necessity to facilitate a smooth flow of private investment. Even so, the tendency to rationalize capitalism occurs with a great deal of friction and the possibility of other outcomes. State managers can make mistakes, giving too much to the working class, and they have no special knowledge of what is necessary to make capitalism more rational. They grope, Block says, "toward effective action as best they can within existing political constraints and available economic theories" (1977, 26). And once the critical or "special" period is over, the restored business community is likely to demand concessions in *its* favor. But these demands come up against the interests of both the State managers and the working class.

Theda Skocpol, in a recent (1981) paper on the New Deal, generally supports Block's conception of the State. For her, that conception, much better than either instrumentalism or structuralism, explains both the reforms and the process of reform during the first two Roosevelt administrations. In addition to providing the dimension of a State not only relatively autonomous from the ruling class but behaving as a third *agent* in the class struggle, Block alone, she argues, alludes to ways in which transnational structures and conjunctures affect the course of domestic politics in advanced capitalist economies. Yet even Block, "fails to accord such transnational factors the systematic explanatory weight they deserve. It is not only the interplay of capitalists' economic decisions, working class pressures, and state managers' initiatives that shapes political conflicts and transformations in advanced capitalism. International economic and politico-military relations also matter" (Skocpol 1981, 197-198).

Skocpol goes further. "No existing neo-Marxist approach affords sufficient weight to state and party organizations as *independent* determinants of political conflicts and outcomes. . . . so far, no self-declared neo-Marxist theory of the capitalist state has arrived at the point of taking state structures and party organizations *seriously enough*'' (Skocpol 1981, 199-200). There is, she contends, a systematic assumption that politics in capitalist society always works for the reproduction of capitalism and thus in favor of capitalists, and almost all neo-Marxists ''theorize about the 'capitalist state' in general'' (1981, 200), deriving politics directly from some conception about the capitalist mode of production as such. But capitalism in general ''has no politics, only (extremely flexible) outer limits for the kinds of supports or property ownership and controls of the labor force that it can tolerate'' (ibid.). This implies that there can be no theory of the capitalist State or even a theory of the State in advanced capitalism. She calls for analyses that consider each historical case in its own right, with historically specific political institutions as key explanatory variables. From such studies it becomes clear that classes do not act as classes, only as groups and organizations in particular class-structured social situations. Domestic problems intersect with transnational economic and political-military relations, and States and political parties within capitalism have cross-nationally and historically varying structures that have independent histories, ''shaped and reshaped through the struggles of politicians among themselves, struggles that sometimes prompt politicians to mobilize social support or to act upon the society or economy as part of the pursuit of political advantages in relation to other politicians'' (Skocpol 1981, 200). These struggles in turn shape State interventions in the economy and the way class interests and conflicts get organized in the political arena.[5]

In Block's view, the relations of production are important, but ''state power is *sui generis*, not reducible to class power''[6] and ''each social formation determines the particular way in which state power will be exercised within that society,'' including the limits imposed on State power by class power (Block 1980, 229). This assumes that State managers are, in Block's words, ''collectively self-interested maximizers, interested in maximizing their power, prestige and wealth,'' and that even where these managers come directly out of corporations and the upper class to serve temporarily in the State, they behave as self-interested State managers rather than as members of a corporate upper class (1980, 229). It is the pattern of class relations, which places private investment decisions in the

---

[5] Bob Jessop, in England, makes many of these same points (1977), but Skocpol, much more than Jessop, makes political *institutions* themselves (and everything else) so important that she courts the danger of falling into an ex post facto empiricism that is atheoretical and explains nothing.

[6] Perhaps, to be consistent, Block should say, ''not reducible to *conscious* class power.''

hands of capitalists rather than workers that limits State managers, but the interests of these managers and of capitalists are often in conflict, so much so that it is crucial to understand the nature of political institutions as much as the underlying class structure and class struggle.

For Skocpol, the most important conflict for understanding social change appears to be the one between the dominant economic class and the State (Skocpol 1981); for Block, the capitalist class-State conflict is rooted in class struggle, but the State clearly has a life of its own, independent of the pressures that might or might not come from the working class. That is, even if there were no militancy, demands from subordinate classes, or other potentially disruptive threat, State managers' interest in expanding the State would threaten capitalists. Put another way, in ordinary times, the exercise of State power has generally served the capitalist accumulation process, but State managers are under constant pressure to ameliorate the economic injustices and costs generated by capitalist production. These interventions may tend to save capitalism but are opposed by large sections of the capitalist class because they are seen as threats to class privilege. The growing State is opposed as such by capitalists, according to Block (1980, 234).

The problem with this new view lies in two quite different assumptions. First, neither Block nor Skocpol provides us with evidence that members of the capitalist (upper) class have no class consciousness, or that those serving in the government break with the interests of their economic class to become collectively self-interested State managers. It would certainly be a mistake to confuse disagreement on strategies with differences in class interests, or intraclass conflict with lack of class consciousness. There is little doubt that more than in any other industrialized country, America has an upper class founded on business wealth, one that participates directly in the directorships of executive-branch State agencies. In no other country do business leaders and lawyers who serve major corporations occupy cabinet positions (even a majority of cabinet positions in some administrations), and occasionally the Presidency. Obviously, in a parliamentary democracy, such direct participation can raise serious questions about the "legitimacy" of the State. It could even be suggested that those corporate leaders most likely to be brought into government are those most approved of by the corporate leadership as a whole, and that this approval is based on the appointees' image of separation from particular interests and capability to represent broader capitalist ("national") interests. Furthermore, there is little doubt that the legitimacy of the executive branch *is* an important concern of business leaders (this was most evident during the Watergate scandal).

Second, it seems evident from both Block's and Skocpol's work that the underlying threat to capitalism as such from working-class, black, and women's dissatisfaction with social organization, the division of labor, and of course, the State's handling of economic and social problems, is the primary basis of conflict between State managers and capitalists in the private sector. If it were not for the inherently antagonistic relations between the interests of the upper class and the subordinate classes, even though Block and Skocpol can claim that they do not act consciously as classes, there would be no conflict between State managers and capitalists. As Block shows (1980), we can conceive of a State that, with its monopoly on violence, moves beyond a reliance on the capitalist class for its economic base and moves on to dominate both capitalists and workers, even while it preserves the capitalist-class structure—Hitler's Germany was such a case. The much more common example of the authoritarian State, however, is one in which, as we discussed in Chapter 7, the military takes State power and suppresses *working-class* dissent in the name of capitalist accumulation. As long as that dissent can be kept at bay and *State policies are successful in promoting accumulation*, there is little conflict between capitalists and the State. Our point is simple: the conflict between State managers and capitalists is rooted in the class struggle (as Block also argues), and although some capitalists may be in conflict with State managers, it is questionable whether the conflict can be attributed to the aims of the State itself, or to the interests of State managers as such, except when those managers give in "too much" to the working class or other subordinate groups. Later, when we discuss the present crisis, we will summarize Castells's, Wright's, and Bowles and Gintis's views of the relation between State and class struggle, a view that brings us back to the joint articulation of the *structures* of capitalist production and the liberal democratic State, and away from the independence of political structures.

One of the interesting side effects of Offe's and O'Connor's influence on American radical analysis of the State is the relative suppression of hegemony as an important variable in explaining the limits placed on class struggle and the relationship of classes to the State (Przeworski's work is a notable exception). Block discusses hegemony briefly (1977, 14) but then passes on to Offe's and O'Connor's economic explanations (Block 1977, 15) for structural mechanisms behind State managers' behavior. For one thing, hegemony implies some organization of capitalist-class consciousness, not allowable in the Block-Skocpol model. For another, the discussion of hegemony must focus on the class or group struggle itself and how it is articulated in the nature of the State, State policy, the role of ideology, and State crisis.

Another interesting effect of Offe's and O'Connor's influence and also of American (and, to a lesser extent, German) political reality, is the discussion of democracy in the American radical literature. The relative absence of Left politics makes the transition to socialism less of an issue than the issues of the role democracy might play in creating contradictions for American capitalism and whether democracy will prevail in its inherent conflict with capital accumulation. Even in Przeworksi's formulation, the trade-off in the class compromise is between capitalism and democracy. In that sense, Przeworski's "State as the guarantor of the compromise" is still an arena of class struggle, but of a class struggle in temporary resolution. Democracy, as the right to contest capitalist development, is guaranteed in return for the continued right of capitalists to make profits. For Wolfe (as we shall show below), democracy guarantees that the capitalist State responds to citizen rights (legitimacy) and this constrains an inherently exploitative capitalist development. Again, the State is the principal arena of struggle and democracy is the basis of the struggle.

The Relation Between Capital Accumulation, Legitimacy, and the State

We have already encountered in the "derivationist" approach and in Joachim Hirsch's work (see Chapter 5) a theory of the capitalist State in which the State is shaped by the "logic of capital"—a tendency, through class struggle, for the rate of profit to decline. The State's principal function is to offset that tendency. We have also shown how Claus Offe focuses on the class State as an organizer of capitalist-class interests in the context of maintaining its legitimacy vis-à-vis mass demands on it. Like Hirsch and Offe, influenced by the Frankfurt School, and like Offe, particularly influenced by Habermas, James O'Connor developed in the U.S. an analysis of the American State in the context of class struggle and the "logic" of capital. But in his analysis, the economic crisis is the result of the underproduction of capital (not its overproduction, as in traditional Marxist analysis). The crisis of the State is not derivative of the general crisis of capitalism (as in Hirsch), but rather develops in accordance with its own logic, which is "reciprocally and dialectically related to the general economic crisis" (O'Connor 1981, 42).

O'Connor, again like Hirsch and Offe, emphasizes the economic role of the State. He argues that growing State intervention is both necessary for continued capitalist development and is laden with contradiction. In Chapter 5, we showed how Offe concentrates on the State's role as a collector and spender of vast revenues to promote capital accumulation and legitimation. O'Connor independently developed a similar framework to analyze the fiscal activities of the American State. But unlike Offe, he concentrates less on the internal contradictions of State administrative apparatuses (allocative versus productive functions) and more on (a) the contradictions inherent in extracting taxes to subsidize capital accumulation and legitimate capitalist development, and (b) the contradictions in the labor process within the State apparatuses. O'Connor superimposes the logic of capital argument (as the determining force behind the nature of the capitalist State) onto the Poulantzas argument that State intervention displaces class struggle from base to superstructure, and onto the Offe-type analysis of the State apparatuses themselves. O'Connor argues that "the fusion of economic base and political superstructure in the current era has extended the class struggle from the sphere of direct production to the sphere of state administration, and transformed the forms of the struggle . . . the state is unable to contain these struggles in formalized relations among labor unions, workers, clients, and state agencies such as welfare institutions" (O'Connor 1974, 105).

Significantly, the American State is hardly involved at all in direct production. Trapped by the enormous power of private corporations and the sanctity of corporate-State "free enterprise" ideology, the American State must rely on taxation and debt creation to finance growing expend-itures. This eliminates the possibility of surplus-producing public enter-prises (rather, the State takes over highly unprofitable services, such as passenger trains, mail delivery, and urban mass transit) and forces the State to raise taxes or debt in order to subsidize private capital accumulation or pay for the worst injustices of capitalist development. It is on the contradictions in this process that O'Connor focuses, contradictions that are explicitly (rather than implicitly, as in Offe's work) rooted in the class struggle. The State intervenes, he argues, to bureaucratize, encapsulate, and administer class conflict by regulating the relations between labor and capital, between organized labor and the unemployed and poor, between big capital and small capital, between capital based in different regions, and between capital in expanding sectors of the economy and capital in contracting sectors (O'Connor 1974, 113). These aspects of State power are expensive, and it is the increasing expense of monopoly capitalist development, according to O'Connor, that creates the fiscal crisis of the State.

Like Offe, O'Connor divides the government budget into that spending which subsidizes private capital accumulation (social capital expenditures) and that which covers the social costs of private production (social expenses of production). In the first category, there are those expenditures that are valuable to a specific industry or group of related industries: these increase the productive forces, providing facilities without which private projects would be unprofitable, or providing incentives for private capital accu-mulation. The most important investment of this kind in the United States is highway construction: from the standpoint of private capital and of commuters getting to work, availability of good roads is crucial to location decisions and in both cases is a giant subsidy. It has also provided the main stimulus to the auto and related industries. But at the same time, as O'Connor shows, road transport has a very high social cost: once roads are constructed, the demand for them grows as congestion increases simultaneously. The cost to urban areas also increases, since with better roads, property-tax payers move out of the cities to reenter only as day-users of city services. O'Connor's argument is straightforward: the principal means of subsidizing specific industries, highway construction, serves those industries and workers with automobiles, but create costs to taxpayers as a whole and put cities into increasingly difficult financial conditions.

Also in the first category, O'Connor includes public spending for economic infrastructure, expenditures on education, general business subsidies, credit guarantees and insurance, social consumption, etc. These expenditures do not serve specific industries, but corporate capital as a whole.

> The development of the production relations has also compelled corporate capital to employ state power in its economic interests as a whole, and socialize production costs. The struggles of the labor movement, have reinforced the general tendency for the rate of profit to decline, and have thus compelled corporate capital to use the state to mobilize capital funds from the liquid savings of the general population. And, finally, the onset of the general realization crisis has forced large scale business to use the budget to subsidize the demand for commodities. (1974, 126)

For O'Connor, the most expensive of these general economic needs, particularly after World War II, have been the costs of research, the development of new products, and the development of new production processes, including the training and retraining of the labor force. These costs, he argues, have been *socialized* by private capital in the form of public education, the subsidization of research in universities, and through government expenditures on military projects and space exploration. Finally, among the types of State intervention to subsidize private capital as a whole, the most extensive is solving the problem of realizing private profits. "In the absence of regular increases in private commodity demand, which in the current era require fresh state subsidies, accumulation comes to a halt" (1974, 130).

The second category of State spending attempts to cover the social costs of capitalist development—in essence, to maintain bourgeois hegemony and the legitimacy of the capitalist State itself. Although it is not clear from O'Connor's explanation, the social costs of private production only become social costs when the voters demand that something be done about them. He argues rather that costs such as pollution, for example, are damaging not only to the ecological structure, but to continued profitable accumulation itself. Therefore the State intervenes, it is implied, because profits are at stake. By and large, however, the public has demanded that private corporations themselves bear the costs of cleaning up at least their own pollution. Even though these costs may be passed on in the form of higher prices, the State's role until the Reagan administration was to enforce increasingly strict controls on corporations not only regarding pollution but also regarding hazards for workers in production. The second major category of social expenses of production, according to O'Connor "consists of the expenses of stabilizing the world capitalist social order: the costs of creating a safe political environment for profitable investment and trade" (1974, 131). These include controlling the proletariat at home and abroad, the costs of keeping small-scale, local, and regional capital at home, and the costs of maintaining favorable governments in power abroad. It is here that O'Connor sees the income transfers to the old, unemployed, and the welfare poor as keeping the proletariat in check. Such expenses also include the police and military expenditures required to suppress populations in revolt. "The political containment of the proletariat requires the expense of maintaining corporate liberal ideological hegemony, and where that fails, the cost of physically repressing populations in revolt" (1974, 132).

These expenses are large, especially as capital expands abroad and puts pressure on the State to develop the military capability and commitment to ensure foreign investment and markets. And as O'Connor points out, military expenditures not only serve to protect investments abroad, and U.S. corporate hegemony at home and abroad, but also subsidize the development of civilian technology and even serve as a means of increasing employment. Indeed, one of the interesting points about the expansion of the American State into the economy (directly) is that it has done so through subcontracting to private firms and has done so for military ends. The fusion of economic base and political superstructure that O'Connor describes is tied profoundly, in the United States, to military production and expansion. All this places an enormous burden on the State budget without corresponding direct access to the profits that might accrue to military production (arms, aircraft, and high-tech sales to private firms or other governments).

There are two major contradictions that arise from the increasing burden. First, according to O'Connor, the State must raise this increasing budget from taxes and it is the working class that must pay these taxes. Since monopoly capital dominates the State budget and socializes various production costs and expenses but resists the socialization of profits, the working class bears the burden of subsidizing capital accumulation through corporate profits. The fiscal crisis, O'Connor argues, consists of the "gap between expenditures and revenues, which is one form of the general contradiction between social production and private ownership. The severity of the fiscal crisis depends upon the production and social relations between corporate capital, local and regional capital, state employees and dependents, and the taxpaying working classes at large'' (1974, 142). Well before California's Proposition 13 or the Reagan administration's move to cut taxes (while increasing military expenditures), O'Connor predicted that taxpayers would resist higher taxes—that they would organize a tax revolt. This resistance to rising taxes ''both reflects and deepens the fiscal crisis,'' he argued (1974, 142), an analysis that not only applies to the United States but to all welfare States. But in the U.S., the nature of tax priorities make the issue particularly complex, since a large fraction of taxes goes for military expenditures, and these military expenditures are heavily oriented toward maintaining investment and markets abroad: ''foreign economic expansion and imperialism are required to maintain corporate liberalism by *expanding* national income and material wealth, thus muting domestic capital-labor struggles over the *distribution* of income and wealth. And the growth of social and welfare expenditures (and the establishment of class harmony) at home are preconditions for popular acquiescence in militarism and imperialism abroad. The 'welfare-warfare state' is *one* phenomenon, and military and civilian expenditures cannot be reduced significantly at the expense of one another'' (1974, 145).

The second contradiction is that partly as a reflection of the tax revolt, and partly as a reflection of the deepening crisis that is producing the tax revolt, State employees organize and agitate against State administrators for higher wages, and dependents of the State do the same for higher payments (social security, welfare, higher quality education, and so forth). Like private employees, those who work for the State have accepted traditional modes of organization and conflict: economistic labor union activity, designed to protect the living standard and work conditions in the State sector.

O'Connor sees significant problems with both these contradictions in terms of class struggle. The fiscal crisis, he argues, will continue to divide State workers from State dependents (teachers from parents, social workers from welfare and unemployment-assistance recipients) and State employees and dependents from private sector workers (teachers and students from taxpayers as a whole). Tax issues are rarely seen as class issues, ''partly because of the general absence of working class unity in the United States, and partly because the fiscal system itself obscures the class character of the budget'' (O'Connor 1974, 142-143). Tax issues are seen as interest group or community issues, and act to divide the working class. And it is conservatives who have been best able to exploit this issue, because they have organized around the *size* of government spending, around reducing taxes per se and balancing the budget, and have played down priorities in the budget and the structure of taxation. Furthermore, agitation by State employees and dependents for higher wages and payments also divides the working class because labor struggles in the State sector are generally opposed by the taxpaying working class as a whole, and as a result, "the traditional conduct of these struggles tends to *worsen* the condition of state employees precisely because the struggles worsen the fiscal crisis itself" (1974, 147). Unlike private corporations, which pass higher wages on to consumers in the form of higher prices, the State can only provide higher wages or welfare payments by increasing taxes or debt, both opposed by the working class as a whole.

There is a division between State and private workers that makes wage-raising activities by State employees a "losing struggle." There is, O'Connor tells us, "no general understanding that the growing antagonism between state employees and state administration conceals an objective antagonism between wage labor and private capital" (1974, 148). This leaves employees particularly vulnerable to strong resistance and retaliation by the executive branch of federal and state governments, as well as the mobilization of parents at the local level to resist teacher strikes.

The strength of O'Connor's analysis is that it brings a new dimension to our understanding of class struggle and the role of the State both in displacing that struggle and changing its nature. As part of this displacement, workers are simultaneously taxpayers and increasingly employed directly and indirectly by public expenditures. But although O'Connor focuses so clearly on this new aspect of crisis and struggle, he does not analyze the role of increasing the State debt and how that mechanism, substituted for raising taxes, creates its own contradictions for capitalist development, especially by increasing inflation and tending to use that inflation to redistribute income. And, although arguing that class struggle is displaced into the superstructure, and that pressure from the grassroots increasingly forces the State to provide services that are not supplied by private investment, he emphasizes the inherent logic of monopoly capitalist development—an inevitable logic—in creating the fiscal crisis. It is monopoly capital that needs the State to cover the social costs of private production. Social movements have a place in O'Connor's work (working-class struggle creates contradiction in capitalist production, and tax resistance contributes to the fiscal crisis) but movements are not, in his analysis, *historical subjects.*[7]

[7] Recently, O'Connor has claimed that *Fiscal Crisis* (1973) "lined up in favor of the position that the modern State is 'an object of class struggle . . . (and thus) social policy

Furthermore, O'Connor's focus on the economic aspects of struggle in the State apparatuses only implicitly touches on the ideological base of State power. State legitimacy for O'Connor, as for Offe, is a question of material benefits accruing to the voting masses (the commoditization of labor power). It is Alan Wolfe—starting from a similar notion of inherent tendencies in capitalist development (the logic of capital)—who analyzes historically the political (or ideological) crises of the American State.

The State, Wolfe claims, is subject to contradictions (resulting from class struggles and the logic of capitalist development) and attempts to resolve them, but instead only intensifies the contradictions themselves. The late capitalist State is the product of this process, and Wolfe considers the "liberal State" as having exhausted available methods of resolving contradictions between liberal needs and democratic desires—between, indeed, capitalism and democracy. The "growth in the potential power of the state is matched by a decline in the options that the state has at its command" (Wolfe 1977, 258). For Wolfe, the primary contradiction is between the necessities of capitalist development (capital accumulation, world order, and so forth), and a set of broad mass demands, some specific, some vague, including mass political participation (economic and political democracy). The State cannot resolve this contradiction. The public sector grew in response to it, but this "increased activity of the state reflects, not an expansion of alternatives, but the exhaustion of them" (ibid.).

> Class struggle is thus the root cause of the political stagnation of the capitalist state. . . . The decline in the ability of the private accumulation system to generate capital necessitates that the state play more of a role in the accumulation process, granting subsidies to giant corporations, helping multinationals subdue populations, supporting research and development costs, and warping the tax structure to help private companies increase their profits. Then, *if the balance between class forces is not to be disrupted*, welfare and repressive functions must continue to be increased. And as hegemonic powers lose control, their arms budgets, searches for new weapons, and corresponding state expenditures go up also. Inertia pushes one way while necessity pushes the other. . . . This implicit point throughout this discussion is that the late capitalist state is incapable of working its way out of the contradictions that both the conditions of production and the expectations of political life have imposed on it. (1977, 259; italics added)

(is) the contradictory result of the compromise between capital and a powerful labor movement' " (O'Connor 1981, 43). The elements of such a position may have been there, but "revealed" O'Connor is much more "automatic" and "capital logic" than class struggle. The derivationist overtones are clearly there.

The essence of Wolfe's argument hinges on the balance of class forces in advanced capitalist society (also Offe's implicit assumption)—neither the masses nor the capitalist class is able to seize State power; hence, the inherently capitalist State, tied to reproducing capital accumulation, is pushed into a corner despite its increased size and potential power.

"Liberal democracy," says Wolfe, "loses respect because it is not democratic enough, because its liberalism is maintained at the expense of its popular component" (1977, 328). At the same time, he goes on—and this is the second key to understanding his model—"structural factors inherent in the capitalist mode of production bring about a crisis of disaccumulation, best reflected in the economic troubles of the 1970s" (ibid.). The State has to intervene increasingly to keep the system afloat and, just as O'Connor suggests, this merely shifts the problem from production to the State—from one area to another. But for Wolfe, the shift is not primarily incorporating into the State the economic contradictions inherent in private production ("the fiscal crisis"), but more an ideological confession of the failures of capitalism. It "reinforces public cynicism toward government," because of the "basically correct" analysis that the State only helps the rich (1977, 329). "In other words, the problem of legitimacy and problems of accumulation reinforce each other. . . . The legitimacy crisis is produced by the inability of the late capitalist state to maintain its democratic rhetoric if it is to preserve the accumulation function, or the inability to spur further accumulation if it is to be true to its democratic ideology" (ibid.). The political conditions of late capitalist society, he claims, "have locked state action into contradictions from which there is no easy escape" (ibid.), and it is under those *structural* conditions that inherent tensions between liberalism and democracy appear.

Since the State cannot deliver satisfactorily either to the capitalist class or workers, one way out is to resort to ideological subterfuges (reification) in an attempt to restore legitimacy, particularly among the working classes. Wolfe's analysis, although it seems at times to assign a high degree of autonomy to the State apparatuses, rests on the class nature of the State.[8] In other words, it is the capitalist class that is interested in legitimizing the State, largely because no other institution is capable of reproducing its rule.

The ambiguities, confusions, and irrationalities of the late capitalist state adversely affect the quest for legitimation. In order to continue to rule without challenge, late capitalist elites need an institution that can make it appear that the political contradictions of society either do not exist

---

[8] Wolfe's dominant class—"capitalist elites"—are, in late capitalism, quite loosely defined as businessmen.

or are being resolved . . . the only institution that can be called upon
to resolve the contradictions taking place within the state is the state
itself. . . . Only the state, the object of class struggle, can appear to be
above class struggle. The self-proclaimed spokesmen for each class,
businessmen as well as labor leaders, wish the state to be both partisan
and non-partisan, to serve their specific interests and to serve the general
interest at the same time. Hence the late capitalist state can satisfy its
class interest only by being universal and can be universal only by
fulfilling its class character. The state is part of the problem and part of
the solution at the same time. (Wolfe 1977, 278)

Simultaneously, it appears that leaders of the working class also want a
State that solves problems (this certainly could be viewed as Przeworski's
class compromise, even though Przeworski and Wallerstein [1982] would
disagree with Wolfe's subsequent analysis), and this, combined with dominant-class needs, leads to a *reification* of the State—assigning it extraor-
dinary powers, not in order to fulfill a cause, such as justice (as it was for
Plato), but as an end in itself. Reification is necessary because of both
social conflict (the need to gain acceptance of government authority) and
legitimation in the face of democratic ideology (Wolfe 1977, 280). Reification takes many forms (personification, objectification, epicization),
but all represent this need to reestablish control and legitimacy by the
increasingly powerless State.

The opposite of State reification is the political theory of *resignation*—
the reaction to the impossibility of reifying accomplishments that are increasingly meager. "The reification of the state turned into its opposite,
and public philosophers became as skeptical about government power as
they once were enthusiastic" (Wolfe 1977, 285).[9] Now, these philosophers
call for reduced expectations and a "retreat from objectives" (1977, 286)—
in other words, the "reprivatization" of the economy and society rather
than new public intervention. This is the Reagan administration policy—
according to Wolfe, a reflection of the politics of exhaustion characteristic
of late capitalism, and also another form of attempting to legitimate the
class State. In this case, the State ideology argues that the State *cannot*
solve the problems of capitalist development; to the contrary, State intervention is to *blame* for capitalism's problems. The growth of the State
must be reversed; it must be withdrawn from its previous liberal role as
social mediator and socializer in order (allegedly) to restore individual
liberty and the optimization capabilities of the free market.

[9] See also Carnoy (1980) on neoconservatism. There I argue that the corporate neocon-
servatives of the late seventies, such as Irving Kristol, Patrick Moynihan, and those associated
with *Commentary* magazine, were proponents of big government in the early sixties.

Previously pro-statists therefore turned against the State. But more is at stake here than inconsistency or a simple reversal of position. ''The fact is that state spending is popular . . . as it affects specific individuals. Welfare spending is democratic; some want to eliminate or substantially reduce it; those who do become undemocratic. *The attack on government has become, in other words, a not particularly disguised attack on democracy itself'* (Wolfe 1977, 331). Thus, Wolfe says, the resignation theory is an expression of undemocratic attitudes, especially prevalent among businessmen (ibid.).

Wolfe also tries to show that not only the State, but the *political process* changes in late capitalism. Political parties have become transformed. At one time parties had a clear mobilizing function, but twentieth-century experience with parties is ''a history of depoliticization'' (1977, 306). The importance of such depoliticized parties to late capitalism cannot be overestimated, Wolfe argues (in agreement with Miliband), since ''an active state requires a passive citizenry, and the party system, by default, becomes the best available means for ensuring that passivity'' (1977, 307). Again, it is the capitalist class that is directly responsible for this changing party role. ''A capitalist class that found competition intolerable in the economic sphere was no less inclined to view it with disdain in the party sphere. The politicizing character of party systems began to disintegrate as capitalist elites no longer found it to their advantage'' (1977, 306).

But he also contends that this depoliticization contains its own contradictions: as the parties substitute technocratic solutions for politicization, they ''shed their historical preoccupation with mobilization and take the chance of losing support''; in other words, ''as parties drop their mediating role and move closer to the state, they inevitably move farther away from the citizen'' (Wolfe 1977, 308). Thus, they are increasingly illegitimate, and become less the vehicles for expressing conflict than *sites* of conflict: ''In late capitalism struggles take place not between the parties but over them'' (1977, 309). ''The most striking political fact about late capitalism is the absence of politics. The rigidity of the late capitalist state . . . would be a solvable problem if the political process were capable of generating new sources of political energy. But the opposite takes place'' (1977, 321).

The exhaustion of the political process and the State as mediator of class conflict leads to yet a third antidemocratic ideological view in the dominant class (through its intellectuals). In this third view, the attack is on liberal democracy itself, not simply an emphasis on the undemocratic aspects of the State (reification) or an assault on the State's democratizing social expenditures (resignation). The exhaustion of alternatives raises the question of whether ''the capitalist state can continue to exist with minimal legitimacy and, if it cannot, what new forms it is likely to take'' (Wolfe

1977, 328). This view in the dominant class emerges, according to Wolfe, in response to an observed decline in public faith in government combined with increased political participation outside of elite-controlled party structures by especially preoccupied and politically alienated groups. It is fear among business leaders that democracy might really begin to work that leads them to conclude that perhaps too much democracy is not a very good thing. The disaccumulation crisis of the 1970s intensifies feelings among the dominant class that if capitalism is in trouble, "democratic demands will have to be curtailed" (1977, 333). This point of view goes further than, and indeed disagrees with, the resignation theory. It is not *less* government intervention that is called for, but a different *kind* of intervention. It is not just an attack on programs that raise the value of labor power, but an attack on the very concept of democracy and the way it has developed.

The reduction of participation leads quite logically to a brand of corporatism, as discussed in Chapter 1. The important elements of a corporatist organization of society include domination by monopolies making private investment decisions, but working closely with a State planning apparatus that helps them make investment decisions and investments, and also with responsible unions, which enforce wage-fixing decisions (combined with price fixing). Corporatism restricts freedom of speech and assembly as part of a general depoliticization of social life, but these restrictions are offset by increased welfare programs and income polices that increasingly reduce the role of the market as a distributor of work and income. Transnational political units extend the corporatist framework to all capitalist countries (Wolfe 1977, 338). Significantly, these are corporate-led reforms, and this is what makes them inherently antidemocratic. They share with both reification theories the attempt to solve the legitimation crisis in a way that keeps political and economic power in dominant-class hands. And furthermore, "given the priorities of late capitalism, planning proposals that originate from the left could easily be adopted by the right and turned into an authoritarian direction" (1977, 339).

Wolfe's analysis expands O'Connor's crisis from an almost purely economic one to a much broader relation between the material bases of contradiction and the ideological foundations of the liberal State. The logic of capital (the disaccumulation crisis) accentuates the already existing historical tension between accumulation and democracy. The source of this tension, for Wolfe, is the pressure of the masses' "democratic dreams." "Pressure from below has constituted a driving force in the adoption of new solutions to the political contradictions of capitalism and has constituted the major reason for the obsolescence of solutions once adopted. Without that pressure, no tension would be present, for then there would be nothing to prevent the capitalist state from serving as a mechanism of accumulation pure and simple. Democratic dreams have come and gone. . . . But even though they may be suppressed momentarily, their existence can never be discounted'' (1977, 341). He identifies struggle not so much as a conflict over economic or political power per se, but as a struggle between capitalists' economic interests (capital accumulation) and working-class limits placed on that accumulation process by the democratic dreams of subordinate, oppressed groups (which are expressed in part as increased State social expenditures)—in other words, a struggle between class interests within an ideological framework. Democracy itself comes into question when capital accumulation is threatened. Then the struggle over political rights and prerogatives becomes central to the legitimation crisis and its results.

This conflict, with its roots in the logic of capital, shares an important conceptual basis with O'Connor's work: the crisis of legitimation, like the fiscal crisis, has its origins in the *structural* process of capitalist development. Wolfe's history of crisis is a history of State development in the context of contradictions in production. The State is a living, breathing entity in his model, but the class struggle that shapes the State is a set of mechanistic contradictions. The nature of conflict for Wolfe is one of ideas—representations of classes, rather than workers and capitalists, blacks and whites, women and men. At best, the struggle of the working class is based not on their day-to-day work, consumption, and family reality, but on an abstract democratic vision. Materialism, therefore—particularly as it shapes social movements—also becomes abstract, appearing only at the edges of capitalist development (and the development of the capitalist State). So Wolfe's State is much less a site of class and group struggle than it is a State dominated by a ruling class but limited by abstract ideologies—a State over which no class can establish its hegemony, giving State bureaucracy power to create policies within the limits established by dominant material needs and subordinate ideological visions.

These criticisms are not meant to imply that Wolfe is ''wrong'' in his analysis. He does add a very important dimension to O'Connor's and Offe's work—the role of democratic vision as ideology and the contradictions that emerge in the liberal democratic State as capitalism develops. Yet, the historical nature of class struggle, particularly in advanced capitalism, which shapes both the fiscal and legitimation crises, is absent (as in O'Connor's and Offe's writings, and, to a large extent, also in Hirsch's). Other writers, influenced by O'Connor and Wolfe (Bowles and Gintis's analysis of the crisis seems especially influenced by Wolfe), but moving in approximately the same direction as Poulantzas in his last work (1980), deal with the State much more directly from a class struggle perspective.

CLASS STRUGGLE AND THE STATE

The view that emphasizes social struggles' role in shaping the State and its policies is best exemplified in America by the work of Manuel Castells (1980),[10] Erik Olin Wright (1978), and Samuel Bowles and Herbert Gintis (1982). For them, the contradictions in the State are not the "logical" outcome of the conflict between its capital accumulation function and a "democratic vision" and legitimation constraints (the commoditization of labor, for example), but the result of direct action by dominant and subordinate groups, acting in both the production sector and the State to maintain or extend material gains and ideological influence.

The origins of the present crisis in America are, for Castells, in the process of capital accumulation, and the crisis results from "contradictions that are an expression of social relations of production, distribution, and management" (Castells 1980, 138). But the policies that the American State will use to deal with the crisis will be "determined less by structural requirements than by the political process of American society (even if the possible alternatives and the specific problems are structurally conditioned)" (ibid.). Castells poses a State whose alternatives are *conditioned* (the capitalist State is still a class State), but whose policies are subject to political action by subordinate groups: "This political process will be largely determined by the interplay of political and ideological factors with the structural positions of difference social groups in the process of production and consumption" (ibid.).

What we have, then, is a *relatively autonomous* State, not independent from the dominant class, yet not its pure instrument. The State in advanced capitalism has been shaped by contradictory class struggle, "where both the dominating and dominated classes have produced effects . . . the state is shaped by contradictions of the society and continuously affected by changing power relations" (Castells 1980, 153). Nevertheless, the historical process that produced the capitalist State is characterized by the "continuous domination of capital. . . . Therefore, the state is the crystallization of this class domination, and its institutions will reflect fundamentally the interests of the bourgeoisie, although the purity of this expression will vary according to the historical capacities of contradictory classes" (ibid.).

Now it becomes clear how Castells's analysis differs markedly from the "logic of capital" argument: O'Connor, specifically couching his analysis in the underlying social relations of production, views the State as responding to the needs of monopoly capital, particularly through an eco-

[10] We have included Manuel Castells's work here (even though many of his writings are in French) both because it is relevant to the kind of research being done on the State in the United States and because he now teaches permanently at an American university.

nomic intervention that stimulates capital accumulation. And for both O'Connor and Castells, (a) the capitalist State intervenes to offset the tendency for the rate of profit to fall and to contribute to capitalist accumulation (in this way monopoly capital successfully socializes costs while privatizing profits); (b) class struggle displaced into the State requires increased expenditures to cover the social costs of production (the legitimation of capitalist development and the capitalist State); and (c) resistance by workers to increased taxes on personal income and by capitalists to increased taxes on profits, creates the fiscal crisis. But Castells develops this analysis more fully and at the same time emphasizes that State intervention is necessary to overcome the contradictions of capitalist production that emanate from class struggle. The declining rate of profit and the necessity of covering the social costs of production are the direct result of a mobilized working class, and civil rights and community movements for greater economic participation in capitalist development. The State intervenes within "the structural rules of capitalism for the purpose of overcoming the historical contradictions that arise during the latter stages of its development" (Castells 1980, 130). It is the American class structure and class struggle over State policies responding to crisis that are of special interest to Castells, because it is through the analysis of that class structure and struggle that we can understand the dynamic of the relationship between monopoly capitalist development and the State.

Castells does agree with O'Connor that the expansion of the State under monopoly capitalism is organized to stimulate the accumulation of capital and to legitimate social order: the State, he argues, "has become the center of accumulation and realization in advanced capitalism" (Castells 1980, 130). Does this change the mode of production? No, Castells responds, for "the intervention of the state takes place within the structural rules of capitalism for the purpose of overcoming the historical contradictions that arise during the latter stages of development. The crucial mechanism that reveals the capitalist logic of public policies is the fact that we can observe a systematic trend toward the socialization of costs and the privatization of profits" (ibid.). A major contradiction of this process is that expanded intervention reduces the State's revenue base: the monopoly sector produces more value but distributes less income. In the absence of profitable public enterprises (the reason for that absence is discussed at length by O'Connor), the State can either increase taxes or increase debt, as we have seen. Castells accepts the difficulty of collecting more taxes on profits or personal income, a difficulty that became even more evident in the late seventies than ten years earlier. He shows that despite increasing income taxes resulting from inflation (with a progressive tax, inflation continuously throws taxpayers into higher marginal tax brackets), the primary form of covering government expenditures since the late 1960s has been through the creation of public debt. The U.S. government, he argues, has been increasing the public debt and money supply without a corresponding increase in actual levels of production. "The structural gap between the socialization of costs and the privatization of profits has led to the fiscal crisis of the state" (Castells 1980, 132).

For Castells cutting off the possibility of raising tax rates quickly enough to cover increasing demands on the State by corporate capital pushes the State into debt financing, avoiding the tax revolt but producing inflation. Since his latest data are circa 1975, however, he does not fully capture the effect, within the U.S. class structure, of inflation ultimately reducing real wages (as a means of shifting income to profits), contributing to the realization problem, delegitimating the liberal State, and resurrecting supply side economics. Inflation is turned into a tax on wage income, but even so does not end debt creation, since the increased severity of the realization problem (as real wages decline) requires continued increases in government expenditures. Just as important, the continued inflation and erosion of real wages makes of inflation and one of its causes, increased debt creation,[11] major political issues: so much so, that the Reagan government is severely constrained in its capability to finance both the accumulation of capital and the social expenses of production, and therefore, as Castells argued well before Reagan was elected (1980, 215-254), cuts the latter sharply, hoping to mobilize middle-class taxpayers against the welfare poor and the unemployed. The State begins reducing its role in bearing the social costs of capitalist development.

"People," Castells says, "make their own history, but they do so within the framework of given social conditions" (1980, 245). Thus, "the political consequences of the current crisis will develop through the interaction of its effects on two related levels of the social process. On the one hand, the economic class struggle and grassroots mobilization; on the other, the mediation of social protest and structurally dominant interests by the political system" (ibid.).

A member (along with O'Connor) of the *Kapitalistate* group and a leading American writer on the State, Erik Olin Wright presents another version of the class struggle model of the advanced capitalist State (Wright 1978). Like Hirsch, Wright views the State in terms of the changing forces

---

[11] Castells identifies debt creation as a major (and perhaps the major) cause of inflation in the U.S. He qualifies this by arguing that the monetarist finding of correlation between inflation and the expansion of debt/money supply must be put into the broader context of accumulation dynamics in advanced capitalism, and tends to underplay the argument that the increased monopolization of advanced capitalist economies and monopoly pricing are key factors in explaining inflation (see Wachtel and Adelsheim 1976; Kurz 1979).

and relations of production. These changes occur as a result of class struggle and capitalist competition (but not, as they are for Hirsch, necessarily expressed as the declining rate of profit), which gradually make a given organization of accumulation less and less productive and typically, lead to a restructuring of the forms of accumulation themselves, "restoring at least a minimal compatibility of the forms of accumulation with the forces/ relations of production. . . . It is such structural solutions which define the essential character of the different stages of capitalist development" (Wright 1978, 165-166). The organization of the State and the role it plays are part of the structural solution to constraints on accumulation.

So, for Wright, in the rise and consolidation of monopoly capitalism stage of capitalist development, the central constraint on accumulation is an underconsumption-realization crisis and a growth of a more militant labor movement. The State takes the form of Keynesian intervention designed to expand aggregate demand, and this and other forms of structural change and the expansion of markets into the periphery, leads into "advanced monopoly capitalism." The central constraint on accumulation in this stage is the "ever-increasing reproductive costs of the system as a whole stemming from the contradictions of the accumulation and legitimation functions of the state, resulting in stagnation and chronic inflation. These tendencies are considerably exacerbated by the continued growth of monopoly capital and the internationalization of capital. Raising the rate of exploitation [is difficult] because of the strength of the working class, and because the effectiveness of the reserve army of the unemployed has been reduced by social reforms" (1978, 169). This requires the extension of State intervention, Wright argues, from the simple "Keynesian manipulations of effective demand to active involvement in the production process itself; state policies geared directly to increasing productivity ('post-industrial' state policies)" (ibid.), and in turn leads into State-directed monopoly capitalism and the emergence of a full-fledged, repressive "state capitalism."

While recognizing that the "immediate response to the problem of the ever-expanding reproductive costs of monopoly capitalism relative to the growth in productivity has been an attempt at cutting back many Keynesian policies, especially in welfare programmes, education and various public services," Wright argues that the long-run solution to the present crisis will be to move from Keynesian interventions to active State involvement in the production process itself. This increasingly makes the economic conflict between capital and labor a political conflict; while the "erosion of market rationality means that those political conflicts will more directly pose the class content of state interventions within production itself" (1978, 237).

Wright also recognizes the difficulty of this kind of intervention in the United States (O'Connor precludes it). In order to intervene in production directly, even through planning measures (such as during World War II), the State would have to increase its capacity to control and discipline individual capitalists and the working class. This means being able to eliminate unproductive sectors of capital and constraining wage and employment demands for an extended period. Small and medium capital will oppose such moves, and labor, given the fact that all this would occur within the continued capitalist social relations and the reproduction of those relations through the State, would be wary of such proposals (although in Sweden, labor is generally cooperating with similar measures, albeit under different political conditions).

Wright's, Castells's, and O'Connor's views clearly place much more emphasis on the structural conditions imposed by class struggle in order to understand the nature of State response to the crisis than the Block/ Skocpol/Wolfe approach, which is much more politics-specific. Block, for example, criticizes the contention that there will be a drift toward corporatism and more authoritarian forms of rule. The underlying problem with this argument, he argues, "is its failure to recognize that the core of the capitalist offensive has been an attack on the state itself" (Block 1980, 237). He presents the principal struggle in the present crisis as one between capitalists and State managers. On the one hand, capitalists realize that an increase in State power might well push the State past the "tipping point" (where the State is so autonomous, it won't return to control by capitalists), depriving them of the their leverage over State managers; on the other, the underlying problems that generated stagflation, he claims, "require serious forms of restructuring, including direct challenges to some of the major corporate actors in the 'free market' " (ibid.). The failure of conservative political solutions to the economic crisis will make it increasingly in the interest of State managers to extend State power and to pursue more Statist policies, as Wright predicts will be necessary. Block contends that this will bring to the surface "more direct conflict between state managers and capitalists" (1980, 238), but that because the two parties are evenly matched, the conflict will be long and divisions will grow even wider.

There is not as much disagreement between Block and Wright as might first appear. Both think that greater State intervention is the logical structural change required to resolve the present structural constraints on accumulation, and both agree that this will be politically difficult in the United States at this time, Wright because it means eliminating unproductive capital and constraining wage demands and Block because capitalists are inherently pitted against an expanding State. The difference lies in Wright's emphasis on class struggle and capitalist competition (some capitals will be eliminated in order to save capitalism; labor distrusts the capitalist State) and Block's emphasis on a State "independent" of the capitalist class, hence in conflict with it.

Bowles and Gintis (1982) make a different argument. They suggest that the State is neither just an effective agent of intervention in an accumulation process set by capitalist relations alone, nor a factor of cohesion in the social formation, an instrument predominantly functional to the reproduction of the social relations of production (as argued by Castells and O'Connor). For Bowles and Gintis, the liberal democratic State is an articulation of social struggle that has "quite fundamentally altered the accumulation process" (1982, 52). Thus, the nature of State intervention is such that it may worsen the conditions of capital accumulation and hence simultaneously delegitimate the State. "[This articulation] remains contradictory and, under current conditions, has contributed substantially to the persistence of relative economic stagnation and inflation" (ibid.).

In this contradictory articulation of the social relations of liberal democracy and the social relations of capitalist production, the State performs the two functions of accumulation and legitimation as claimed for it by O'Connor and Castells, but the two functions come into conflict. Moreover, Bowles and Gintis posit that the liberal democratic State and capitalist production are distinct structures whose articulation may be described as a contradictory totality. Thus, the liberal democratic State is in inherent conflict with capital accumulation. The tendency toward crisis therefore not only originates in the capital accumulation process responded to by the State more or less effectively (and generating new contradictions), but the State is part of the problem as well as part of the solution. Bowles and Gintis thus argue that the State can alter the relationship between capital and workers (the rules of the game can change), and also even alter the relative influence of capitalists over the pattern and pace of investment.

The primary difference between the two "sites" (economy and State) is that the political practices in them are divergent: in capitalist production political participation (relative power) depends on property alone, while the liberal democratic State vests rights both in citizens and property (Bowles and Gintis 1982, 61). These rights are not only distinct, they are in potential conflict. Sites do not only interact by delimitation along common boundaries (capitalist production sets the boundary of State practices by use of what Block [1977] calls business confidence, but what others have called the capital strike) but by the "transportation of practices across site boundaries" (Bowles and Gintis 1982, 63). Indeed, it is this transportation of practices that can bring pressure for transformation of one site due to practices in another site. For example, rights vested in persons (as in the liberal democratic State) may result in demands by workers for greater political participation in decision-making in the private corporation (Carnoy and Shearer 1980). "Having struggled to attain the principle of person rights in the state in the course of the 19th and 20th centuries, workers and others have often disagreed over how much these rights might take precedence over property rights in the economy itself. The structure of interpenetration of person and property rights in this totality is thus central to an understanding of the contemporary crisis of U.S. capital" (Bowles and Gintis 1982, 63-64).

For Bowles and Gintis, the major period of rearticulation of the State with the site of capitalist production was in the 1930s and early 1940s, when a series of legislative acts redefined the relationship of workers to workers, of capitals to capitals, and of capital to the working class. The State became a major locus of class struggle, political discourse was limited to the language and demands encompassed by person and property rights, and the major vehicles for expressing working-class interests became the Democratic Party and the bureaucratic trade union structure of the labor movement. But, as Bowles and Gintis point out, this version of liberal social policy, and its definition of the distributional struggle as the primary axis of class struggle, depended critically on the integration of workers into the political process and particularly on the capability of the State to pay off materially a series of worker interest groups, a pay off made possible by rapid economic growth. This resulted in significant distributional gains by workers not so much in confrontation with capital over the bargaining table but with the state. Bowles and Gintis show that the growth rate of average weekly earnings in the postwar period was only 1.5 percent annually (to 1977), while the estimated weekly social welfare expenditures (including transfer payments, health, education, housing, veterans' programs, and child nutrition) rose at a 5.6 percent rate. By 1977, these social welfare expenditures represented 75 percent of average take-home pay for a single worker with three dependents (Bowles and Gintis 1982, 73). In addition, wage and salary workers' consumption expressed as a fraction of gross national product gradually but significantly increased in this period. The entire increase may be attributed to the growth of social wage expenditures (social spending by all levels of government) from 8 to 19 percent of total output (1982, 76). Capital's share of output, on the other hand, gradually declined in gross terms during the same period, and taking account of depreciation and government costs not related to social welfare expenditures, the decline was very rapid, net capital share falling from 16 percent of output in 1948 to 5 percent in 1972 and rising again to 7 percent in 1977 (1982, 77).[12]

[12] Although Bowles and Gintis do not pay much attention to the different periods implicit

The main argument here is that the redistributive programs won by workers in the struggle within the State site, as well as regulatory programs such as the Occupational Health and Safety Act of 1970 and the Clean Air and Water Act of 1971, were costly to capital. ''We do not wish to argue that these regulatory programs and the redistributive programs described above, are the sole or even primary cause of the slowdown in the capitalist growth process experienced not only in the U.S. but also in most advanced capitalist countries. But we believe that they have made a significant contribution to the slowdown. More importantly, these programs, and the political configuration which they represent, pose a major barrier to the familiar reconstitution-through-crisis of the accumulation process'' (Bowles and Gintis 1982, 77-78).

Secondly, Bowles and Gintis argue that the capital-labor accord struck during the thirties and forties significantly changed capital's possibility of using the reserve army of unemployed as a means for disciplining labor and lowering wages. There are three parts to this change: first, unemployment itself has become much more of a political issue since the high rates of the 1930s and the concomitant (even if temporary) radicalization of the labor movement. A high unemployment rate represents a failure of the State in managing the economy (full employment, growth, and stable prices). Second, the increased segmentation of the labor market may mean that a high overall rate of unemployment does not measure the threat of job loss to all workers, but just to blacks, women, and teenagers. Third, and most important, a high unemployment rate has meant the deproletarianization of the wage-labor force, through its exercising its right of citizenship and gaining a substantial part of its standard of living from the State. This last element attenuating the effects of the reserve army is even enhanced by the fact that the level of social welfare expenditures is designed to move anticyclically, to compensate for movements in the unemployment rate and the level of wage income. Thus, these results of the class struggle have, at one and the same time, tamed the struggle but also profoundly altered the accumulation process and limited the options open to capital.

It is this analysis of the State that Bowles and Gintis use to understand the current economic crisis. ''The liberal democratic state has affected the

___

in their data, it is worth noting that in 1948-1965, both spendable average weekly earnings and social welfare expenditures increased rapidly, the former at a 2 percent rate and the latter at a 5 percent rate. Between 1965 and 1977, however, spendable earnings increased negligibly (3 percent in 12 years), while weekly social welfare expenditures more than doubled. Similarly, the increase in workers' share of consumption as a percentage of total input is concentrated in the period 1965-1975 (more specifically, probably 1969-1973, if Bowles and Gintis's data were more detailed) and the severe drop in capital's net share of output occurred in that same period.

capitalist accumulation process in two, quite substantial ways: a gradual redistribution of the total product away from capital and a decreased ability of the reserve army to discipline labor. These effects have played a critical role both in producing and in prolonging the current period of economic stagnation and rapid inflation'' (1982, 84). As a result, they argue, the current economic situation is a crisis, rather than a cyclical downturn, because a restoration of the rapid and stable expansion of capital will require a ''structural reconstitution of the accumulation process'' (1982, 89). The liberal democratic State has become a problem for the capitalist class, particularly the labor-capital accords developed as a response to the last accumulation crisis, and the effect that they had on the ability of capital to discipline labor. Bowles and Gintis think that the reserve army will never again play the same role that it did in the past. This limits capital's options in emerging from the present crisis. Capital's search for a solution to the crisis has therefore focused primarily on the State, on the one hand to cut regulation and business taxes, increasing profits directly, and on the other, to cut social expenditures, both to drive wages down by increasing the size of the reserve army, and to reduce the cost to capital of social welfare expenditures.

But Bowles and Gintis's characterization of the liberal State as a cause of capital's problems is based on a questionable interpretation of events in the late 1960s and early 1970s. More important, they overestimate the control of labor over liberal State policies, and underestimate corporate hegemony and its resultant capability to undo previous accords in the name of increased stability and economic growth.

A reanalysis of the profit decline in the late 1960s (Carnoy, Shearer, and Rumberger 1983) suggests that State spending in an already tight labor market made it possible for the wage bill to increase to historically high postwar levels as a percentage of GNP—this, and not the increase in State spending per se, is what ate into profit rates. From the early 1970s onward, business has apparently moved away from the New Deal accords, contributed to inflation by attempting to raise prices even during recession to restore ''normal'' profit rates, and reduced productivity-raising investment—instead, speculating in real estate, investing abroad (until the late 1970s) or in ''better business climate'' regions such as the South and West, and shifting into high-profit industries like oil and gas (Bluestone and Harrison 1982. The result of this anti-organized labor strategy has been to lower real wages drastically (average real weekly incomes fell 16 percent between 1973 and 1982 [Carnoy, Shearer, and Rumberger 1983, 63]) and increase profit rates slightly, at least until the Reagan recession. Although productivity has also increased at a much lower rate, falling real wages have more than made up for this slowdown. The State has indeed been a battleground between labor and capital, with labor first trying to recover declining real wages through increasing social spending (contributing to inflation) and then the less-organized part of labor pushing for lower taxes and lower inflation when the first strategy made labor as a whole worse off. Now it is clear that the lower tax rate and lower inflation strategy is also not working in labor's favor. Inflation itself has become the political issue around which the State's role of increasing social expenditures is being dismantled, with the accord of a significant part of the working class, at least in the short run. The working class misgauged the degree to which reduced demand, unemployment, and union-busting would be used by a conservative administration to put downward pressure on prices. In each of these phases of the 1970s and 1980s, a labor movement that operates from a position of class compromise was pushed back, showing its weakness rather than its strength and the State has shifted away from enforcing the compromise to playing a more "traditional" capitalist-reproductive role.

Whether the liberal democratic State can be dismantled is still questionable. But to argue that the State has a power of its own, as does Block, or that as the working class gained increased control over the State, the State itself became the *cause* of crisis, as do Bowles and Gintis, does not seem to lead us very far in understanding the present situation. Przeworski's analysis is more helpful: it tells us that once capital's confidence in the class-compromise State eroded in the late 1960s and early 1970s, capital moved to reassert its power over the State, and use its profits for its own purposes. What the Przeworski analysis fails to tell us is that once the capital-labor accord is struck and capitalism is preserved, capitalist hegemony tends to use the accord itself to undermine, through what Gramsci termed "passive revolution," the willingness or ability of workers to take anticapitalist positions in the future. The very success of capitalism under the New Deal allowed capital to take an increasingly antilabor position, and made labor decreasingly militant. The compromise was indeed between capitalism and democracy but, as Wolfe shows, democracy (expressed as legitimation) undergoes change if the compromise succeeds.

In the early 1980s, despite record unemployment, the majority of the working class—the nonunionized, nonminority portion particularly—can still be convinced that sharp increases in profits are necessary for future higher growth rates and stable prices (and wages). This means, under capital's solution to the crisis, a decline in the citizen wage (wages plus social benefits), and even that may be an acceptable compromise. But the State bureaucracy advocating such a policy on behalf of capital must show that it works. The problem for the State in increasing capital accumulation does not necessarily reside in the manifest political power of the working class, although that would certainly increase the State's problem. Rather, it lies in past accords that shaped capitalist economic expansion into a dependence on an increasing citizen wage and increasing productivity. This is not a State that causes the capitalist crisis; it is part of the crisis and will, in any democratic reform, necessarily be part of the solution. It is a State marked by a struggle that, even under Przeworski's class compromise, attempts to shape the way the compromise is carried out.

CHAPTER NINE

Whither Theories of the State?

POLITICS IN THE United States is now at center stage at the very moment that political participation seemed to have lost all momentum. The reason for this is clear: the world capitalist crisis, emerging from the tumultuous 1960s, heralds the decline of the welfare State—of the "solution" to the previous crisis, fifty years ago. But this time around, it is not only the economy's performance that is called into question, but also the State's. The very public sector that was instrumental to the previous solution is now part of the new crisis. This is not to say that the crisis has become more "ideological," whereas in the 1930s, it was more "economic." As Althusser argues, ideology is at the very basis of every social formation, and thus every contradiction in the formation's development is ideological. The crisis of capitalism in the 1930s was no less or more ideological than the present one. But the 1970s and 1980s differ for another reason: the nature of capitalist hegemony has changed substantially.

All recent writings recognize this profound alteration. Some claim that the major change is in the dominant form of capitalism—from national competitive to transnational oligopolistic. In addition, capitalism has come to depend on State subsidization in direct and indirect forms, a subsidization that is larger than the amount paid by corporations in direct and indirect taxes. Others emphasize the change as a "victory" of the working class within the context of a class society: hence, a redefinition of personal rights in society, personal rights that the State is committed to uphold (in order to maintain its legitimacy under the new conditions), often in conflict with the fundamental property rights inherent in capitalism. The focus is less on the State's ability to provide resources that maintain or improve monopoly capital accumulation than on its ability to deliver its commitment to the citizenry which, broadly speaking, comprises the working class— thus a focus less on the relationship between the State and the falling rate of profit that causes a fiscal crisis, and more on the relationship of crisis to social movements and, in turn, their effect on the State.

There are also those taking a nonclass perspective who see the crisis in terms of "too much State" or "too much democracy." Both these views regard the problem as not residing at all in the nature of capitalism but in the extent to which the State, either as an autonomous entity with its own power, or as a representative of the masses, "irrationally" interferes with capitalist development. The two different reasons for such irrational behavior, however, are crucial to the political response prescribed by each view: in the first case, where the State is autonomous and "irrational," the response is to reduce the State in all spheres, "reprivatizing" the economy and society; in the second case, where the State's irrationality results not from its autonomy but from its responsiveness to "irrational" masses, the response is to increase the State's role but increasingly to separate it from mass influence.

Theories of the State, then, are still enormously varied. Some of the differences among them are not subtle, such as research that either supposes the State to reflect, in some way, the general will and only the general will, unconditioned by economic power relations, or supposes the State to be completely autonomous from civil society, and research that analyzes the capitalist State in the context of a class society marked by inherent economic *and* political inequalities. But within these two categories, there exist shades of difference that have important implications for political strategies and outcomes. The differences have been the focus of this book, and it is now appropriate to summarize where we are in the debates surrounding them. It is these debates that reflect both the present crisis and the political options before us.

LIBERAL AND CORPORATIST THEORIES OF THE CAPITALIST STATE

Our main focus is on class-perspective theories of the State. But the predominant view of the State—at least in America—is rooted, as we have shown, in a tradition of "liberal" rather than Marxian thought. What is this "liberal" position in the present crisis? In fact, there appear to be two. The first is Adam Smithian, but "adapted" to the new context of monopoly capitalism. Insisting that the "invisible hand" of the free market still operates even in the new context (Friedman and Friedman 1979), and that therefore a welfare optimum (the greatest good for the greatest number) can be reached only by allowing the invisible hand to operate as unencumberedly as possible, this view sees the State as acting not only independently of both capitalists and the general will, but even against the public interest, general and specific. The State bureaucracy is its own power base, advised by intellectuals and inhabited by technocrats who wish to extend their power by increasing the size of the public sector for objectives specific to that power, not to public needs. According to this theory, the liberal State, brought into being by the 1930s crisis and greatly expanded by the exigencies of World War II, never receded when it was no longer necessary to meet such unusual circumstances. Instead, the State steadily infiltrated further and further into the free market, spurred by lobbies working through a self-aggrandizing government bureaucracy.

In this Smithian utilitarianism, the production sphere stands on its own and organizes society. The State *should be* the perfect expression of men's wills, working only to invest in those goods and services that the free enterprise system finds unprofitable but the public demands (defense, roads, and some forms of education, for example), enforcing the laws, and—as a post-1930s Depression addition—using monetary and fiscal policy (ideally only a constant, average GNP growth-based, increase in the money supply) to smooth out the business cycles inherent in free-enterprise development. The "best State" is one that is the "least State": for Adam Smith and this version of liberal theory, the State is in constant tension between being part of a civil society defined in opposition to the imperfect "state of nature" (Hobbes and Locke), thus a "perfect" expression of collective will, and interfering with the perfection of civil society (the invisible hand). The more the State is independent of the general will (and material needs as expressed in the economic sphere), the more it is likely to act imperfectly and corruptly. It was not very much later that Bentham and Mill saw a completely other side to that corruption, only hinted at in Smith: if the State really becomes the instrument of the general will, a will that included the collective interests of the nonpropertied working class, it could also be posed against the bourgeois civil society. For the utilitarians, the "masses," in fact, were an even greater danger to the bourgeois civil society than a partly feudal State because, rather than just interfering with it, as might a corrupt, bureaucratic State, the "masses" might use the collective means of violence residing in State power to replace bourgeois civil society with a different social order.

Since Bentham's and James Mill's day, the working class has, indeed, proved itself sometimes disposed to use its rights of suffrage to make substantial changes in civil society. However, in the advanced capitalist economies it has rarely *voted* to dismantle capitalism, although there have been some cases that might be interpreted as moving in this direction, such as Swedish social democracy, the Communist vote in Italy, and the recent Socialist Party victories in France, Greece, and Spain. The United States working class has certainly been notable in its support of capitalist development. With such empirical data in hand, the present-day, "pure" Smithian version of State theory, which we can call populist conservatism, assumes that the general will favors the free market and even the minimum State. The theory uses this assumption to argue for the elimination of a host of social programs (including government employment) that may benefit the working class but also increase the size of government at the expense of the free enterprise system and individual liberty. More mainstream conservatism, still based in Smith's general propositions regarding the State and civil society, is less trustful of the popular consensus. This brand of conservatism wants to believe that the voting public is pro-free market and anti-State bureaucracy, but is also well aware that the same public is anti-large corporations and *for* many welfare-State social programs (e.g., Kristol 1977). It is in this sense that Smithians see the popular consensus itself as corrupt—irrational enough to sacrifice its own liberty for short-run material gains.

The second of present-day versions of utilitarianism emerges directly from Bentham's and James Mill's distrust of direct democracy. Pluralism sees the State as reflecting the majority will of those who are concerned enough with State policy to get involved on one side of an issue or another. In its most elementary form, pluralist theory is just an explanation of political behavior, analogous to Kenneth Arrow's work on the economic theory of public choice (1951). But as a practical political science, pluralism has been used to rationalize as functional observed lower participation rates among those with less formal education or less "knowledge" about the issues. The masses have been viewed, implicitly and explicitly, as compulsive, easily swayed, and lacking the information to make informed political judgments (Lipset 1963).

Social corporatism is a logical countertheory to pluralism for those who think that liberal democracy cannot survive in modern society but are fearful of authoritarian alternatives from the Left and Right. For them, a progressive, humane, but powerful State decision-making mechanism, separated from mass participation, is necessary in a complex, modern world. Too much democracy interferes with economic and political efficiency, and this may lead to an irrational mobocracy. A rational State run by correct-thinking leaders is a logical way to run the country's economy, foreign policy, and social policy, for the citizenry's own good.

Corporatism seeks to save the liberal State from the limits democracy places on the State's economic role. Rather than reducing independent bureaucratic (technocratic) power, corporatism seeks to increase it; the oligopoly corporation and corporate trade union, rather than the invisible hand, are not only accepted as capitalist economic reality in today's America, but as the most *efficient* available economic reality. Smith's axiom concerning the relation between individual action and social welfare translates into one where the pursuit of corporate interests (including the executive branch of the government) leads to the greatest good. In this model, meritocracy plays a key role in allocating power in the society, on the assumption that power should be allocated more to *knowledge* rather than to property (as in the classical liberal model). The meritocratic concept is carried to its logical conclusion in corporatism. Since, in modern capitalist society, corporate and union leaders and State high-level technocrats are the most "successful" of its members, they are the most knowledgeable, and should be given the responsibility for solving national (collective) problems, with much less restriction on their activities by the less-knowledgeable, less-capable public. Corporate planning is more rational than democratic, participative decision-making.

In corporatism, the State takes a central role in capitalist development, and democracy is reduced in the name of economic growth and national order. The State is seen not as interfering with the efficiency of a free market economy, but as *essential to its rationalization*. Democratic politics, always mistrusted by the utilitarians, is, in order to achieve the society's material and security aims, placed at a second level of social importance. The State becomes a *subject* of power rather than an object, this apparently with the citizenry's consent. In other words, the populace is asked, for its own good, consciously to turn over its power to a class-neutral State.

CLASS-PERSPECTIVE THEORIES OF THE STATE

Theories of the State rooted in a Marxist, class-perspective analysis differ fundamentally from liberal theories in that they posit a State that is an expression, or condensation, of social-class relations, and these relations imply domination of one group by another. Hence the State is both a product of relations of domination and their shaper.

As we have tried to demonstrate, class-perspective theories have come a long way since Marx, Engels, and Lenin, and athough one can find much in Marx's (and Engels's) abundant writings, it is fair to say that today's Marxist writers develop a political theory that was incomplete in Marx's work.

Today's Marxian analyses can be characterized by two features. First, they are generally opposed to Lenin's view of the State: the State is not regarded simply as an instrument of the ruling class. Second, they challenge the idea of a universal theory of the State: rather than proposing a single version of the capitalist State, they argue for specific historical analyses within universalistic conceptions relating the State and capitalist society. Who rules the State *is* an important issue, but few, if any, current writers claim that the ruling class controls the State directly. Most argue rather (a) that the State's class nature is expressed through the "structure" of capitalist development or relations of production, and (b) that dominant-class control of the State is contested in the political apparatuses by subordinate classes and social movements.

The various versions of these anti-Leninist Marxian views are derived from Marxist epistemology rather than any specific political theory in

Marx's writings. They fall into three principal categories: (1) the "logic of capital" theory, which argues that the contradictions of capitalist development, following universal historical tendencies (derived from Marx's *Capital*), shape the capitalist State and its contradictions; (2) the independent State theory, which introduces Weber's notions of the State as a power subject, and poses the class State against both civil society-dominating capitalists and subordinated labor—a State that reproduces capitalist relations of production *independently* of any conscious class interests; and (3) the "class struggle" theory, which views the capitalist State as a product of the fundamental characteristic of capitalist society—class struggle—and therefore as a class State, but one that necessarily incorporates working-class demands. The reproduction of class relations is therefore conditioned by the *internalized* contestation of power in the State apparatuses.

The *logic of capital theory* has been identified, in recent years, with the "derivationists" in Germany and England. As suggested in Chapter 5, according to this theory the principal characteristic of capitalist development is the tendency for the rate of profit to fall. Class struggle is expressed through surplus extraction and is reflected in declining profits. The State emerges as a necessary response to this tendency and is historically shaped by it. As a class State, its principal role is to provide countertendencies to the falling rate of profit—to maintain and stimulate capital accumulation in the face of its "logical" and unavoidable tendency toward decline. Capital logic argues that the form of the capitalist State and its functions (including its crises) are totally derived from the general crisis of capitalism, and the general crisis is a function of the overproduction of capital.

The *independent State theory*, as Offe's contribution to the debate, implies that the State is an "independent" mediator of the class struggle inherent in the capital accumulation struggle, independence hinging on the inability of both capitalist and working class to organize themselves as classes. Offe makes politics the focus of contradictions in capitalist economy and society. It is the State that is responsible for organizing capitalist accumulation within the limits imposed on it by legitimacy in the eyes of the working masses, where Offe defines legitimacy largely in material terms. Capitalist crisis in advanced economies is, inherently, State crisis in Offe's analysis, for it is in the State that reproduction takes place, and it is bureaucratic conflicts and contradictions that shape reproduction alternatives. Block, Skocpol, and Wolfe take this analysis to its logical conclusion: in the absence of coherent class positions in the civil society, the State is an independent political power, and the State's power is posed between capital's and labor's fractionalized interests. Crisis is resolved (or not resolved) by a State situated between antagonistic positions, trying to promote the contradictory goals of capital accumulation (in the cause of raising revenue for bureaucratic growth) and legitimacy (also for self-preservation). Conflicts within the State itself become very important in understanding the way this tension is resolved, for obviously there are a number of possibilities, including abandoning the "traditional" capital accumulation process for a more "socialistic" one. The innovator for these possibilities in the "independence" model is the State bureaucracy and its intellectual advisors. The crisis is present and the bureaucrats and politicians respond. New contradictions occur, but they occur in terms of the alternatives proposed and implemented either not working, or working but leading to a new crisis and new proposals for resolution. This is why Skocpol argues for more detailed analyses of crisis situations like the New Deal, where the research should focus on the *politics* (the decision-making process and struggles *within* the State) of the crisis and its "resolution." All this is based on the assumption that class struggle in the civil society has little to do with what the State decides to do and how it does it.

O'Connor wrote his major analysis at the same time as the derivationists and Offe. He begins with the economic crisis of the capital logic view, but argues that the falling rate of profit is rooted, not in the overproduction of capital, but its underproduction, and that this underproduction comes from working-class demands for State social spending. The State subsidizes capital in part (providing a countertendency to the falling rate of profit) but also must pay social expenses to achieve political consensus and legitimation.

O'Connor develops this concept to include contradictions in the State's functions that interfere with their profit-maintaining role. These emerge from the increasing demands of capital for infrastructure investment for *specific* capitals (roads, for example), for capital in general (technology subsidization through military expenditures, for example), and for the socialization of capitalist development costs, such as pollution, unemployment, urban blight, and so forth. The fiscal crisis is not strictly derivative of the general crisis of capitalism, but also develops in accordance with its own logic. Contradictions appear in trying to raise the public funds to cover these subsidies and capital's social costs. O'Connor argues that as capital's demands grow, the State is obliged to increase taxes to the point where the public resists paying. The State becomes unable both to maintain capital accumulation and to finance social programs needed to maintain capitalism's legitimacy. Although he does not discuss it in his early work, the way the State can (and does) finance both accumulation and legitimacy is through increasing public debt. But as Castells points out, this way also leads to contradictions: increased debt in the 1970s has led to increased inflation with only small decreases in unemployment, and increased inflation is directly associated in recent years with falling real wages, obviously another important issue of working-class resistance to increased public spending.

So although Hirsch sees the State shaped by its capital accumulation-subsidization role, O'Connor suggests that major contradictions emerge from demands by the working class on State revenues and the resultant State role of covering capital's social overhead costs (O'Connor and Offe agree here). As it tries to meet these *economic* needs of capital and the working class, the State itself becomes the source of contradictions for capitalist development. For O'Connor, the "logic of capital" is a principal shaper of the State; it is the expression of class struggle, which is relevant to understanding what the State does and how it does it. But the State is also shaped by the need to remain legitimate, and this legitimacy orientation is defined by the State's spending to maintaining labor's value in the face of decreasing relative possibilities for employment in the private sector and of the degenerating work and physical environment.

When all this appeared in the early seventies, it made the fiscal crisis seem almost as "automatic" and deterministic (functionalist) as the derivationist's capital logic or Offe's independent State. In O'Connor's work, contradictions in capitalist development and in the State mediation process appeared inevitable. The specific-historical part of his analysis is more related to the tax revolt and public sector unions than to the struggles of various social movements in the economy and over revenues in the State itself. Yet, O'Connor now claims that *Fiscal Crisis* portrayed the modern State as an object of class struggle in general. The elements of this position may have been there, but it was Wolfe's analysis, following O'Connor's inspiration and focusing on the relation between working-class struggles and democracy, that brought out the State as an object of struggle, a position only vaguely implicit in O'Connor's work.

In that sense, Wolfe's analysis has much in common with Ingrao's and Poulantzas's (last) State theory in which the crucial social dynamic is *class struggle*. The capitalist State, rather than being "independent" from the dominant capitalist class, is relatively autonomous from it. This means that the dominant class is a conscious class and attempts to influence and control the State as an object of its socioeconomic power, but at the same time, because of the existence of class struggle, the State must appear to be autonomous from dominant-class power in order to retain its very legitimacy as a State. The development of political forms is couched in the class structure, where the dominant class exerts powerful influence and control over the State through its dominance in civil society, and class struggle, where to be legitimate with the dominated working class the State must appear independent of the capitalist class, and each worker must appear to have the same political power as each individual capitalist.

Relative autonomy incorporates class struggle into *the heart of the State itself*. The State becomes, in Poulantzas's words, the "materialization and condensation of class relations." Even as the relative autonomy of the State is necessary for its legitimacy as an authority above class struggle, this autonomy creates the contradiction of bringing the class struggle into the political apparatuses, and creates the possibility of subordinate classes and groups taking over these apparatuses, thereby interfering with the class-reproductive functions of the capitalist State. Democracy for Ingrao is therefore the growth of subordinate-class power in the State apparatuses as well as in the institutions of civil society. It is the victories of improved material conditions, extension of suffrage, increased worker control, the growth of a working-class party, and so forth.

In this class struggle view, class relations inside and outside the State both emerge from struggles for material gain *and* are shaped by them. Such relations, in turn, describe the nature of society and hence the role of the State in it. It is only through a theory of this kind, where the State is a condensation of class relations, that we can understand how the State can, at one and the same time, represent the interests of a conscious dominant class and still be a site of class struggle, a site where the working class can win increased democracy yet be out of power. It is only through such a theory that we can understand how the State can appear—indeed must appear—to be above class struggle, yet be a class State. State "independence" implies that the State bureaucracy depends on capital accumulation for its own survival. Relative autonomy means that in order to represent class interests—that is, to be legitimate in the context of class and group conflict—the State bureaucracy must appear to be autonomous from the dominant class. Contradictions, "independence" theory, occur within the State apparatuses, and are the result of struggles in the State to mediate the inherent tension between the necessary State functions of capital accumulation and legitimation. But this conceptualization captures neither the effect of social movements on social change nor the resulting relationship between contradictions in the civil society (especially the production sector), the mediating role of the State, and contradictions in the State itself.

These are the principal current controversies surrounding theories of the capitalist State, and the crises and contradictions they emphasize. Each has its own appeal. The logic of capital model, its dynamic situated in the tendency toward historical-particular crises—that is, crises that are the reflection of a universal economic tendency (the falling rate of profit), but whose manifestations are specific to particular historical conditions—provides an alternative to the ahistorical structuralism of Althusser and early Poulantzas, an alternative that also emphasizes the economic role of the

State rather than the ideological. The independent, or "political" model, its dynamic situated in the tension (contradictions) between the State's role as promoter of capital accumulation and its legitimacy from the voters' (labor's) view, provides an alternative in which the State bureaucracy makes decisions that reflect its own interests as well as those of conflicting groups in civil society, an alternative that also emphasizes economic rather than ideological State functions, and argues that capitalist-class consciousness is organized within the State. The class struggle model, its dynamic situated in the inherent class conflict characterizing capitalist development, provides us with an alternative where social movements, both class-based or nonclass-based, form the context in which economic and political change takes place, including the shaping of crisis and the State's reaction to it. Like the logic of capital model, the class struggle analysis is structural-historical. The historical element in both models is the particular economic and social conditions (the product of previous struggles) that shape the nature of class conflict and the State's responses to that conflict. Yet, the structural dynamic in the class struggle analysis is not governed by the tendency for the rate of profit to fall, but by the relations of production and the resulting class structure and conflict. And unlike both the logic of capital and independence models, the class struggle analysis stresses ideological as well as economic aspects of hegemony and crises, and it is in that ideological-economic context that the relation of class struggle to democracy or authoritarianism is analyzed.

All three of these theories of the State tend, in one degree or another, to challenge the idea of a *universal* theory of the State and replace that notion with the call for specific historical analyses within a set of universalistic "rules" about the relation between State and society. This means that there is such a thing as a capitalist State (as opposed to a feudal or bureaucratic authoritarian State), but the functions of that capitalist State (its particular role in capitalist development) vary according to the historical conditions in which it is situated, specifically the nature of its class struggle, or structure of production, or previous State interventions to resolve previous crises. The capitalist State is at any moment in history, therefore, the product of its previous history, including its relation to previous struggles in civil society. Those conflicts, in turn, at least in the class struggle model, are shaped by previous State interventions. This implies that theories of the State can only be seen in terms of their specific historical applicability, totally contrary to either Althusserian structuralism or Leninist instrumentalism. Cardoso and Faletto's major contribution is exactly this point: the peripheral State is an historical instance of the structure of class relations in world capitalist production; each peripheral State has to be analyzed separately in the unifying context of world development. From a methodological perspective, their analysis is perfectly consistent with later work in metropole societies, which comes to the same conclusion.

The very development of the theories of the State we have discussed is subject to this same analysis. They are the product of historical conditions themselves. Gramsci's emphasis on superstructure was an attempt to explain the failure of socialist revolution in post-World War I Italy; Althusser's structuralism was an attempt to develop in the context of French intellectual thought (particularly that of Lévi-Strauss and Sartre), a modern Leninist alternative to the inapplicability of instrumentalism to Western Europe of the 1960s; Offe's and Hirsch's work was an outgrowth of a previous intellectual history, in turn heavily influenced by German political conditions in the 1920s and 1930s, and their own work, especially Offe's, conditioned by the apparent subject power of the post-World War II German governments; Ingrao's ideas were developed in the Italian Communist Party's strategies and successes in organizing inside and outside the State; Cardoso and Faletto's theories (as well as Amin's and Frank's) were heavily influenced by the subordinate relations and economic conditions of the periphery; and finally, the American preoccupation with democracy and conflict, in the absence of traditional "class" struggle and at the center of the empire, was also heavily influenced by the intellectual hegemony of American social science empiricism. It is logical that these different historical conditions should affect the way that researchers see the State and theorize about it.

The relationship between history and political philosophy is, in and of itself, a complex topic. It has been the object of a heated debate over Althusser's theories, specifically because Althusser claimed that a theory of society had to transcend history.[1] Yet, theories of politics can only with great difficulty be separated from the practice of politics. Hobsbawm (1982) notes that Marx was less concerned with politics than political economy because civil society seemed so dominant in shaping mid-nineteenth-century European history. Gramsci's emphasis on the political, he adds, stems in part from his participation in the proletarian revolutionary activity of post-World War I Italy and the subsequent rise of a strong fascist State. Even the changes in dependency theory from the more structuralist analysis of Amin and Frank to the much more historically specific work on bureaucratic authoritarian regimes reflects a change in political and economic realities: economic growth has taken place in the periphery, social movements have challenged capitalist development in the context of increasing standards of material life for the masses, and liberal democratic regimes

[1] See Thompson (1978) on Althusser, and Anderson's (1980) response to Thompson.

have been overthrown by military coups. Political analysts have to be influenced by the time and place in which they live.

However, it would be a mistake to attribute all differences in theories of the State to historical conditions. There are different analyses of the American State, for example, even among U.S. Marxists at the same historical moment. These differences lead in different political directions, and it is crucial to understand precisely what those are.

POLITICAL IMPLICATIONS OF CLASS-PERSPECTIVE THEORIES

Orthodox Leninist theory argues that the only good bourgeois State is a dead one: the transition to a mass-based society can be achieved only through the destruction of the capitalist State and its replacement by the dictatorship of the proletariat. Since Gramsci's time, there has been a gradual movement away from this position. But it has certainly not been a total rejection of the previous position, in large part because of the vitality of armed revolution in the Third World. The new, more extensive "overthrow" view is one that discusses the world capitalist system and the need to change that entire system in order to make possible the transition to socialism.

It is not difficult to understand the logic of this position. In many countries of the world, the class State seems intransigent, immutable, and willing to use increasingly sophisticated repressive instruments to reproduce capitalist relations and to "advance" capitalist culture. Frank's and Amin's world system position is also perfectly conceivable. The hegemony of world capitalism allows it to maintain the "structure" of metropole and dependent periphery development, and even to incorporate the bureaucratic authoritarian socialist economies into that system. Frank particularly finds it difficult to imagine socialist development in any country without the radical alteration of U.S. transnational hegemony. His point is well taken, but politically it is not very useful. There exist social movements in the periphery, in the secondary metropoles, and in the socialist bloc. Should these movements cease their activities because they are "structurally determined"? To the contrary, as Amin points out, the very "partial" successes of Third World revolutionary movements have an effect on transnational hegemony. They correspond on a national level to a successful factory takeover or the election of a progressive city council, except that a progressive national government has much more control over resources, schools, the army, the police, and national development policy. On the other hand, smaller-size national progressive economies are severely constrained by their insertion into a world economy organized materially and ideologically to make socialist development difficult.

The rest of Amin's argument regarding periphery versus metropole political action is not as persuasive, however. Social movements in the metropole, even if not revolutionary, can have important implications for the nature of transnational capitalist hegemony and hence for social progress in the periphery. The State in the metropole is crucial to social movements in the periphery. Therefore, political activity in the United States, Europe, and Japan (and in the Soviet Union as well) has worldwide importance.

Much of our review of State theories is a discussion, implicitly, of what such political activity should be in the capitalist metropoles and in industrializing periphery countries like Brazil, Mexico, South Korea, and so forth. The Marxian discussion has shifted away from the armed overthrow of capitalist States to the accentuation of contradictions within capitalist States and the development of social movements that aim to control State apparatuses or to win reforms in production, particularly through the State.

This is an important shift, because it emphasizes political action through and within the State as well as action through civil society against the State. Poulantzas in France, Offe in Germany, Ingrao and Bobbio in Italy, O'Connor, Castells, Wolfe, and others in the United States all argue for one form or another of change *through* capitalist democracy to expand mass power over resources already controlled by the State, and to expand mass political power itself through the contradictions implicit in the democratic process. Given the extensive involvement in the economy by the welfare State—even if that involvement is not necessarily in direct production—this kind of politics makes eminent sense. Since the State has become increasingly the primary source of dynamic for the monopoly-dominated capitalist economies, it is the State rather than production that should and will be the principal focus of class conflict. And given the emphasis on expanding democracy, the State necessarily becomes the arena for that conflict.

Yet, there are significant differences in the political strategies implied by the various class-perspective theories. The capital logic theory suggests that continued class antagonism in production plus competition between capitals will lead to an economic crisis that will necessarily embroil the State. In O'Connor's response to and transmutation of capital logic, the State is increasingly brought in to offset falling profit *and* must simultaneously remain legitimate by responding materially to working-class demands for more social benefits. O'Connor shares with Hirsch an emphasis on class struggle in production as the important political action, because it is that class conflict which accentuates economic crisis and forces the State to intervene further in the economy. O'Connor further emphasizes the importance of labor struggle in the State sector as the State expands more and more into this production role. Offe's and O'Connor's analysis, carried forward in the United States by Wolfe in one direction and Block and Skocpol in another, emphasizes contradictions and conflicts in the State apparatuses themselves. For example, Wolfe argues that different groups in the executive branch attempt to resolve the ever-deepening legitimacy crisis in the U.S. federal government. The cause of the crisis is mass demands for greater social justice and a democratic society, but its articulation, for Wolfe, is in the State apparatuses themselves. Block and Skocpol also focus on this same aspect of the crisis. It is the State's ability to resolve the economically-based legitimacy crisis that is crucial to social change itself. Essentially, social change is organized by the "independent" State bureaucracy under pressure from groups of capitalists and a need to be reelected (legitimacy). If the bureaucracy fails, and only when it fails, class or group struggle will result. The political strategy implied is pressure of State apparatuses, the election of representatives to various levels of government who will push more progressive social reforms, and so forth. The State is not really a class State in the Block-Skocpol model; rather it is posed *between* capitalists and the masses. If the STate is biased toward capitalists' interests, it is because the bureaucracy depends on capital accumulation for revenues.

In the class struggle view, the class State can be moved against capitalists' interests by the development of movements inside and outside the State to force it to move against its fundamental role as reproducer of class relations. This position suggests that such political action has already been successful and can continue to be so. The State is shaped by such movements: its functions are expanded and it takes increasing responsibility for capital accumulation and social peace. But the State will not reform in a progressive direction without such movements pressing it. In other words, the capitalist State is inherently class-based and will act in that way unless pressured by mass organizations. The correct political strategy is to organize at the base, both outside and inside the State, bringing those organizations to bear on society's dominant institutions to reform them.

SOME DIRECTIONS FOR FUTURE RESEARCH

We are faced with an unresolved debate in the midst of important economic changes in advanced industrial societies. However, this very lack of resolution should promote increased study of the capitalist State both in advanced capitalist societies and in the Third World.[2] Our analysis of

[2] We have not discussed the State in Eastern European societies, but there was, even before the flourishing of the Polish Solidarity movement, some significant writing coming out of Eastern Europe on the authoritarian communist State (e.g., see Djilas 1962, 1972; Bahro 1980).

different theories suggests some theses and specific directions for such research.

First, the concept of expanded democracy is central to any Marxist theory of politics. But in conceptual and strategic terms, what is the meaning of expanded democracy? How is it reflected in the actions of the State? When does a capitalist State become a socialist State? At one extreme, we have Skocpol's (1981) notion of studying politics in crisis periods, such as the New Deal, to determine exactly what configuration of forces and processes within the State produce responses to such crises, on the assumption that all political action takes place in the State and all political results can be measured by State policies. But such a notion does not take us very far, whatever its empirical usefulness in understanding the details of State behavior in crisis periods. Since Skocpol deemphasizes the class nature of the State, there is no way for such an analysis to distinguish between a weakened hegemonic class's attempts at "passive revolution" and the reforms resulting from subordinate groups exhibiting their own hegemony. Understanding expanded democracy demands the study of—in Gorz's terminology (1968)—"non-reformist reforms," both inside and outside the State, or, as Buci-Glucksmann has suggested (1982), the meaning of an "anti-passive revolution" strategy. This includes more research on the institutions that have developed as part of passive revolution in the past, trade union organizations especially.

Second, as the State has expanded in the context of and in response to social conflict, the traditional separation between civil society and the State has changed. As a result, it is the State rather than production that should and will be the principal focus of class struggle. Yet, have the traditional concept of class struggle and the question of *who* will be the articulators of counterhegemony also changed? That is, once the site of conflict is amplified to include the State and even the family, does the conflict change to include not only workers against capitalists but also citizens against their government, youth and parents against their school, and wives against husbands? The nature of the conflict changes as well, since *rights* (ideology) are at stake as well as material gains. Even though the struggle over these rights may have its roots in economic relations,[3] its articulation in these other sites is manifested differently than in production.

Serious questions about the State's functions and nature emerge from such a formulation. If the conflict is not just seen as a shift of working-class conflict with capitalists in production to the capitalist State (Poulantzas

---

[3] This is the structuralist argument (Althusser 1971), but many feminists (e.g., see Hartmann, in Eisenstein 1979) contend that the domination of women by men, which is certainly an important element of precapitalist, capitalist, and postcapitalist societies, has its origins in biological reproduction and is only *shaped* by production relations.

1980), but as a struggle of social movements whose roots are not directly in production but in national identity, position in patriarchical relations, consumption of public goods, or community, then does class-perspective theory change as a result? One example comes immediately to mind: political parties have traditionally been a mechanism through which class political action has been translated into State power, but as parties fail to perform this function, social movements act directly against the State or are manifested in new kinds of political parties (such as the Greens in Germany). When social movements arise on nationalist, patriarchal, eco-logical, or other grounds, and are not easily incorporated into existing political parties, they develop their actions in other forms. Moreover, how do new forms of political, social, and economic conflict relate with other forms, and how does this interrelation shape the nature and functions of the State? Is it possible that the class State degenerates through its own delegitimation to be replaced by other loci of political and economic power?

Third, "national" theories of the State in both advanced capitalist and periphery economies are limited in their understanding of State forms and social conflict. For one, capital is both national and transnational in almost every economy, and production, from the State's and social movements' points of view, has significant international aspects. World system theory has long recognized economic interdependency, but has not applied it rigorously to political analysis. For example, what are the constraints on a transition to socialism in advanced economies situated in a world capitalist system? How does a strategy of anti-passive revolution change under such conditions? What is the relationship of social movements against and within the State in other countries to both the advanced capitalist and dependent State? That is, how does the nature of the State change as a function of conflicts in other societies? Research on the State should point us toward the answers to these questions.[4]

---

[4] The current crisis in the world economy (Frank 1980) that began with the hegemonic crisis of the 1960s in the advanced capitalist societies and Eastern Europe, and of which the State is very much a part, is already proving to be a fertile ground for the investigation of political change (e.g., Buci-Glucksmann and Therborn 1981). The emergence of socialist regimes in France, Greece, Sweden, and Spain, and the general inability of such regimes to transform their societies, or even build socialist institutions, will also provide new insights into the nature of the capitalist State and the class struggle, as will the crisis of bureaucratic authoritarian regimes in Latin America.

Alavi, Hamza. 1912. "The State in Postcolonial Societies: Pakistan and Bangladesh." *New Left Review*, no. 74 (July-August):59-82.

Almond, Gabriel, and Sidney Verba. 1963. *The Civic Culture*. Princeton: Princeton University Press.

Althusser, Louis. 1969. *For Marx*. London: Penguin.

———. 1971. *Lenin and Philosophy and Other Essays*. New York: Monthly Review Press.

Althusser, Louis, and C. Balibar. 1970. *Reading Capital*. London: New Left Books.

Amin, Samir. 1973. *Neocolonialism in West Africa*. London: Penguin.

———. 1980. *Class and Nation*. New York: Monthly Review Press.

Anderson, Perry. 1976. *Considerations on Western Marxism*. London: New Left Books.

———. 1977. "The Antimonies of Antonio Gramsci." *New Left Review*, no. 100:5-78.

———. 1980. *Arguments within English Marxism*. London: New Left Books.

Arrow, Kenneth. 1951. *Social Choice and Individual Values*. New York: John Wiley and Sons.

Avineri, Shlomo, ed. 1969. *Karl Marx on Colonialism and Modernization*. New York: Doubleday.

Bahro, Rudolph. 1980. *The Alternative in Eastern Europe*. London: New Left Books.

Baran, Paul A. 1957. *The Political Economy of Growth*. New York: Monthly Review Press.

Baran, Paul A., and Paul M. Sweezy. 1966. *Monopoly Capital*. New York: Monthly Review Press.

Becker, Carl. 1963. *The Heavenly City of the 18th-Century Philosophers*. New Haven: Yale University Press.

Berle, Adolf, and Gardiner Means. 1935. *The Modern Corporation and Private Property*. New York: MacMillan.

Birnbaum, Pierre. 1978. *La classe dirigeante française*. Paris: Presses Universitaires de France.

———. 1979. *Le peuple et le gros*. Paris: Bernard Grosset.

Block, Fred. 1977. "The Ruling Class Does Not Rule." *Socialist Revolution* 7 (3):6-28.

———. 1980. "Beyond Relative Autonomy: State Managers as Historical Subjects." In *Socialist Register*, ed. Ralph Miliband and John Saville. London: Merlin Press.

Bluestone, Barry, and Bennett Harrison. 1982. *The Deindustrialization of America*. New York: Basic Books.

Bobbio, Norberto. 1977a. "Existe una doctrina marxista del Estado?" In *El marxismo y el Estado*. Barcelona: Editorial Avance.

———. 1977b. "Que Alternativas a la democracia representativa?" In *El marxismo y el Estado*. Barcelona: Editorial Avance.

———. 1979. "Gramsci and the Conception of Civil Society." In *Gramsci and Marxist Theory. See* Mouffe 1979.

Bowles, Samuel, and Herbert Gintis. 1976. *Schooling in Capitalist America*. New York: Basic Books.

———. 1982. "The Crisis of Liberal Democratic Capitalism: The Case of the United States." *Politics and Society* 11 (1):51-93.

Broady, D. 1980. *Critique of the Political Economy of Education: The Prokla Approach*. Stockholm: Stockholm Institute of Education.

Brown, Michael Barrett. 1969. *After Imperialism*. New York: Humanities Press.

Buci-Glucksmann, Christine. 1974. *Gramsci et l'état*. Paris: Feyard.

———. 1979. "State, Transition, and Passive Revolution." In *Gramsci and Marxist Theory. See* Mouffe 1979.

———. 1980. *Gramsci and the State*. London: Lawrence and Wishart.

———. 1982. "Hegemony and Consent." In *Approaches to Gramsci. See* Showstack Sassoon 1982a.

Buci-Glucksmann, Christine, and Goran Therborn. 1981. *Le défi social démocrate*. Paris: Maspero.

Burris, Val. 1979. "Structuralism and Marxism." *The Insurgent Sociologist* 9 (Summer):4-17.

Canak, William. 1983. "The Peripheral State Debate: State Capitalism and Bureaucratic Authoritarian Regimes in Latin America." *Latin American Research Review*. Forthcoming.

Cardoso, Fernando H. 1979. "On the Characterization of Authoritarian Regimes in Latin America." In *The New Authoritarianism in Latin America. See* Collier 1979.

Cardoso, Fernando H., and Enzo Faletto. 1979. *Dependency and Development in Latin America*. Berkeley: University of California Press.

Carnoy, Martin. 1980. "The Ideology of Neo-Conservative Economics." *Journal of Social Reconstruction*, 1 (April-June):58-86.

Carnoy, Martin, Robert Girling, and Russell Rumberger. 1976. *Education and Public Sector Employment*, Palo Alto, Calif.: Center for Economic Studies.

Carnoy, Martin, and Henry Levin. 1984. *The Dialectics of Education and Work*. Stanford: Stanford University Press. Forthcoming.

Carnoy, Martin, and Derek Shearer. 1980. *Economic Democracy*. Armonk, N.Y.: M.E. Sharpe.

Carnoy, Martin, Derek Shearer, and Russell Rumberger. 1983. *A New Social Contract*. New York: Harper and Row.

Castells, Manuel. 1980. *The Economic Crisis and American Society*. Princeton: Princeton University Press.

Chamberlin, W. H. 1965. *The Russian Revolution, 1917-1921*. New York: Grosset and Dunlop.

Chandra, Biban. 1980. "Karl Marx, His Theories of Asian Societies and Colonial Rule." Ch. 14 in *Sociological Theories: Race and Colonialism*. Paris: UNESCO.

Clarke, S. 1977. "Marxism, Sociology, and Poulantzas' Theory of the State." *Capital and Class*, no. 2:1-31.

Colletti, Lucio. 1972. *From Rousseau to Lenin: Studies in Ideology and Society*. New York: Monthly Review Press.

Collier, David. 1979. "Overview of the Bureaucratic-Authoritarian Model." In *The New Authoritarianism in Latin America*, ed. David Collier. Princeton: Princeton University Press.

Dahl, Robert. 1956. *A Preface to Democratic Theory*. Chicago: University of Chicago Press.

Djilas, Milovan. 1962. *Conversations with Stalin*. New York: Harcourt Brace.

————. 1972. *Land without Justice*. New York: Harcourt Brace.

Domhoff, G. W. 1967. *Who Rules America?* Englewood Cliffs, N.J.: Prentice-Hall.

————. 1970. *The Higher Circles*. New York: Random House.

————. 1978. *Who Really Rules?* Santa Monica, Calif.: Goodyear Publishing.

————. 1979. *The Powers That Be*. New York: Random House.

Draper, Hal. 1977. *Karl Marx's Theory of Revolution*. Vol. 1, *State and Bureaucracy*. New York: Monthly Review Press.

Engels, Frederick. [1884] 1968. *The Origin of the Family, Private Property, and the State*. New York: International Publishers.

Evans, Peter. 1977. "Multinationals, State-Owned Corporations, and the Transformation of Imperialism: A Brazilian Case Study." *Economic Development and Cultural Change* 26 (1):43-64.

————. 1979. *Dependent Development: The Alliance of Multinational, State, and Local Capital in Brazil*. Princeton: Princeton University Press.

Fiori, Giuseppe. 1970. *Antonio Gramsci, Life of a Revolutionary*. London: New Left Books.

Fitch, Robert. 1972. "Sweezy and Corporate Fetishism." *Socialist Revolution* 2 (6):93-127.

Fitch, Robert, and Mary Oppenheimer. 1970. "Who Rules the Corporation?" *Socialist Revolution* 1 (4,5,6):73-107, 61-114, 33-94.

Fitzgerald, E.V.K. 1977. *Proceedings of the Cambridge Conference on the State and Development in Latin America*. Cambridge: Cambridge University Press.

————. 1979. *The Political Economy of Peru, 1956-1978: Economic Development and the Restructuring of Capital*. New York: Cambridge University Press.

Foucault, Michel. 1970. *The Order of Things*. New York: Random House.

————. 1978. *Discipline and Punish*. New York: Random House.

Frank, André G. 1978. *Dependent Accumulation and Underdevelopment*. New York: Monthly Review Press.

————. 1979. "Economic Crisis and the State in the Third World." Development Discussion Paper no. 30, University of East Anglia (England). February.

————. 1980. *Crisis in the World Economy*. New York: Holmes and Meier Publishers.

Friedman, Milton, and Rose Friedman. 1979. *Free to Choose*. New York: Harcourt Brace Jovanovich.

Galbraith, J. K. 1967. *The New Industrial State*. Boston: Houghton Mifflin.

———. 1973. *Economics and the Public Purpose*. Boston: Houghton Mifflin.

Giroux, Henry A. 1981. "Hegemony, Resistance, and Educational Reform." In *Curriculum and Instruction: Alternatives in Education*, ed. Henry A. Giroux, Anthony N. Penna, and William F. Pinar. Berkeley: McCutchan Publishing.

Gold, D., C. Lo, and E. O. Wright. 1975. "Recent Developments in Marxist Theories of the State." *Monthly Review* 27 (5,6):29-43, 36-51.

Gorz, André. 1968. *Strategy for Labor*. Boston: Beacon Press.

Gramsci, Antonio. 1971. *Selections from Prison Notebooks*. New York: International Publishers.

Greenberg, Edward. 1977. *The American Political System: A Radical Approach*. Cambridge, Mass.: Winthrop.

Hartmann, Heidi. 1979. "Capitalism, Patriarchy, and Job Segregation by Sex." In *Patriarchy and the Case for Socialist Feminism*, ed. Zillah R. Eisenstein. New York: Monthly Review Press.

Hirsch, Joaquim. 1976. "Woram Scheitert Sladiche Reformpolitik?" *Betrifft: Erziehung* (January).

———. 1978. "The State Apparatus and Social Reproduction: Elements of a Theory of the Bourgeois State." In *State and Capital: A Marxist Debate*. See Holloway and Picciotto 1978.

Hirschman, Albert O. 1977. *The Passions and the Interests*. Princeton: Princeton University Press.

———. 1979. "The Turn to Authoritarianism in Latin America and the Search for Its Economic Determinants." In *The New Authoritarianism in Latin America*. *See* Collier 1979.

Hirsh, Arthur. 1981. *The French Left*. Boston: South End Press.

Hobbes, Thomas. [1651] 1968. *Leviathan*. Ed. C. B. Macpherson. New York: Pelican Books.

Hobsbawm, Eric. 1982. "Gramsci and Marxist Political Theory." In *Approaches to Gramsci*. *See* Showstack Sassoon 1982a.

Hobson, J. A. [1902] 1938. *Imperialism*. London: Allen and Unwin.

Holloway, J., and Sol Picciotto, eds. 1978. *State and Capital: A Marxist Debate*. London: Edward Arnold.

Huntington, Samuel. 1975. "The United States." In *The Crisis of Democracy*, ed. Michel Crozier, Samuel Huntington, and Joji Watanuki. New York: The Trilateral Commission and New York University Press.

Ingrao, Pietro. 1977. *Massa e potere*. Rome: Editori Reuniti.

———. 1979. *La politique en grand et en petit*. Paris: Maspero.

Inkeles, Alex, and David Smith. 1974. *Becoming Modern*. Cambridge: Harvard University Press.

Jessop, Bob. 1977. "Recent Theories of the Capitalist State." *Cambridge Journal of Economics* 1 (4):353-373.

———. 1983. *Theories of the State*. New York: New York University Press.

Joll, James. 1978. *Antonio Gramsci*. London: Penguin.

Keane, John. 1978. "The Legacy of Political Economy: Thinking with and against Claus Offe." *Canadian Journal of Political and Sociological Theory* 2 (3):49-92.

Kolm, Serge. 1977. *La transition socialiste*. Paris: Editions du Cerf.

Kristol, Irving. 1978. *Two Cheers for Capitalism*. New York: Basic Books.

Kurz, Mordecai. 1979. "A Strategic Theory of Inflation." Institute for Mathematical Studies in the Social Sciences, Technical Report no. 283, Stanford University.

Laclau, Ernesto. 1981. "Teorías marxistas del estado: debates y perspectivas." In *Estado y política en America Latina*. *See* Lechner 1981.

Lechner, Norberto, ed. 1981. *Estado y política en America Latina*. Mexico City: Siglo XXI.

Lenin, V. I. [1917] 1965. *The State and Revolution*. Peking: Foreign Language Press.

———. 1978. *On Socialist Ideology and Culture*. Moscow: Progress Publishers.

Lipset, Seymour Martin. 1963. *Political Man*. New York: Doubleday Anchor Books.

Locke, John. [1692] 1955. *On Civil Government*. Chicago: Henry Regnery.

Luxemburg, Rosa. 1961. *The Russian Revolution and Leninism or Marxism?* Ann Arbor: University of Michigan Press.

McLellan, David. 1979. *Marxism After Marx: An Introduction*. New York: Harper and Row.

Macpherson, C. B. 1977. *The Life and Times of Liberal Democracy*. London: Oxford University Press.

Mao Tse-tung. 1954. *Collected Works*. New York: International Publishers.

Marini, Ruy Mauro. 1977. "Estado y crisis en Brasil." *Cuadernos Políticos*, no. 13 (July-Sept.):76-84.

Marx, Karl. [1867] 1906. *Capital*. Vol. 1. New York: Modern Library.

———. [1875] 1972. *Critique of the Gotha Programme*. Peking: Foreign Language Press.

———. [1871] 1978. "The Civil War in France." In *The Marx-Engels Reader*, 618-635. *See* Tucker 1978.

Marx, Karl, and Frederick Engels. [1848] 1955. *The Communist Manifesto*. New York: Appleton-Century-Crofts.

———. [1845-46] 1964. *The German Ideology*. Moscow: Progress Publishers.

———. 1972. *Ireland and the Irish Question*. New York: International Publishers.

———. 1979. *Collected Works*. London: Lawrence and Wishart.

Michels, Roberto. 1966. *Political Parties*. New York: Free Press.

Miliband, R. 1969. *The State in Capitalist Society*. London: Winfield and Nicholson.

———. 1970. "The Capitalist State: Reply to Nicos Poulantzas." *New Left Review*, no. 59.

———. 1973. "Poulantzas and the Capitalist State." *New Left Review*, no. 82:83-92.

Miliband, R. 1977. *Marxism and Politics*. London: Oxford University Press.

Mills, C. Wright. 1956. *The Power Elite*. New York: Oxford University Press.

Mouffe, Chantal, ed. 1979. *Gramsci and Marxist Theory*. London: Routledge and Kegan Paul.

O'Connor, James. 1973. *The Fiscal Crisis of the State*. New York: St. Martin's Press.

———. 1974. *The Corporations and the State: Essays in the Theory of Capitalism and Imperialism*. New York: Harper and Row.

———. 1981. "The Fiscal Crisis of the State Revisited: A Look at Economic Crisis and Reagan's Budget Policy." *Kapitalistate*, no. 9:41-61.

O'Donnell, Guillermo. 1973. *Modernization and Bureaucratic Authoritarianism: Studies in South American Politics*. Berkeley: Institute of International Studies, University of California at Berkeley.

———. 1979. "Tensions in the Bureaucratic Authoritarian State and the Question of Democracy." In *The New Authoritarianism in Latin America*. See Collier 1979.

Offe, Claus. 1972. "Advanced Capitalism and the Welfare State." *Politics and Society* (Summer):479-488.

———. 1973. "The Capitalist State and the Problem of Policy Formation." In *Stress and Contradiction in Modern Capitalism*, Leon N. Lindberg, Robert Alford, Colin Crouch, and Claus Offe. Lexington, Mass.: D. C. Heath.

———. 1974. "Structural Problems of the Capitalist State: Class Rule and the Political System. On the Selectiveness of Political Institutions." In *German Political Studies*. Vol. 1, ed. Klaus Von Beyme. Beverly Hills, Calif.: Sage Publications.

———. 1975. "Theses on the Theory of the State." *New German Critique*, no. 6 (Fall):137-147.

———. 1976. "Laws of Motion of Reformist State Policies." Mimeo.

Ollman, Bertell, and Edward Vernoff. 1982. *The Left Academy*. New York: McGraw Hill.

Panitch, Leo. 1980. "Recent Theorizations of Corporatism: Reflections on a Growth Industry." *British Journal of Sociology* (June):159-187.

Popper, Karl. 1945. *The Open Society and Its Enemies*. London: Routledge and Kegan Paul.

Poulantzas, Nicos. 1969. "The Problem of the Capitalist State." *New Left Review*, no. 58:67-78.

———. [1968] 1974. *Political Power and Social Classes*. London: New Left Books.

———. 1975. *Classes in Contemporary Capitalism*. London: New Left Books.

———. 1978. *L'état, le pouvoir, le socialisme*. Paris: Presses Universitaires de France.

———. [1978] 1980. *State, Power, Socialism*. London: New Left Books, Verso edition.

Przeworski, Adam. 1979. "Economic Conditions of Class Compromise." University of Chicago. Mimeo.

Przeworski, Adam, and Michael Wallerstein. 1982. "The Structure of Class Conflict in Democratic Capitalist Societies." *American Political Science Review* 76 (2):215-238.

Rostow, Walt Whitman. 1960. *The Stages of Economic Growth.* New York: Cambridge University Press.

Rousseau, Jean Jacques. 1967. *The Social Contract and Discourse on the Origin of Inequality.* New York: Pocket Books.

———. 1978. *On the Social Contract with Geneva Manuscript and Political Economy.* New York: St. Martin's Press.

Salvadori, Massimo. 1979. *Karl Kautsky.* London: New Left Books.

Samuels, Warren. 1966. *The Classical Theory of Economic Policy.* Cleveland: World Publishing.

Sardei-Biermann, S., Jens Christiansen, and Knuthe Dohse. 1973. "Class Domination and the Political System: A Critical Interpretation of Recent Contributions by Claus Offe." *Kapitalistate* no. 2:60-69.

Saul, John. 1979. *The State and the Revolution in Eastern Africa.* New York: Monthly Review Press.

Schmitter, Phillippe. 1974. "Still the Century of Corporatism?" In *The New Corporatism,* ed. Frederick Pike and Thomas Stritch. Notre Dame, Ind.: University of Notre Dame Press.

Schram, Stuart R. 1963. *The Political Thought of Mao Tse-Tung.* New York: Praeger.

Schumpeter, Joseph. 1942. *Capitalism, Socialism, and Democracy.* New York: Harper Brothers.

———. 1951. *Imperialism and Social Classes.* New York: Augustus M. Kelley.

Serra, Jose. 1979. "Three Mistaken Theses Regarding the Connection between Industrialization and Authoritarian Regimes." In *The New Authoritarianism in Latin America. See* Collier 1979.

Showstack Sassoon, Anne. 1980. *Gramsci's Politics.* New York: St. Martin's Press.

Showstack Sassoon, Anne, ed. 1982a. *Approaches to Gramsci.* London: Writers and Readers Publishing Cooperative.

Showstack Sassoon, Anne. 1982b. "Hegemony, War of Position and Political Intervention." In *Approaches to Gramsci.* See Showstack Sassoon 1982a.

Showstack Sassoon, Anne. 1982c. "Passive Revolution and the Politics of Reform." In *Approaches to Gramsci.* See Showstack Sassoon 1982a.

Skocpol, Theda. 1979. *States and Social Revolutions: A Comparative Analysis of France, Russia and China.* New York: Cambridge University Press.

———. 1981. "Political Response to Capitalist Crisis: Neo-Marxist Theories of the State and the Case of the New Deal." *Politics and Society* 10 (2):155-201.

Smith, Adam. [1759] 1976. *The Theory of Moral Sentiments.* Ed. D. D. Raphael and A. L. MacFie. Oxford: Clarendon Press.

———. [1776] 1937. *The Wealth of Nations.* New York: Modern Library.

Stepan, Alfred. 1978. *The State and Society: Peru in Comparative Perspective.* Princeton: Princeton University Press.

Sunkel, Osvaldo, and Edmundo Fuenzalida. 1979. "Transnationalization and its National Consequences." In *Transnational Capitalism and National Development: New Perspective on Dependence*, ed. Jose Joaquin Villamil. Atlantic Highlands, N.J.: Humanities Press.

Sweezy, Paul M. 1942. *The Theory of Capitalist Development*. New York: Oxford University Press.

———. 1972. "The Resurgence of Financial Control: Fact or Fancy? A Response to 'Who Rules the Corporations?' " *Socialist Revolution* 2 (2):157-191.

Szymanski, Albert. 1978. *The Capitalist State and the Politics of Class*. Cambridge, Mass.: Winthrop.

Texier, Jacques. 1979. "Gramsci, Theoretician of the Superstructures." In *Gramsci and Marxist Theory*. See Mouffe 1979.

Therborn, Goran. 1978. *What Does the Ruling Class Do When It Rules?* London: New Left Books.

Thompson, E. P. 1963. *The Making of the English Working Class*. New York: Vintage Books, Random House.

———. 1978. *The Poverty of Theory and Other Essays*. New York: Monthly Review Press.

Tucker, Robert C., ed. 1978. *The Marx-Engels Reader*. 2d ed. New York: W. W. Norton.

Vasconi, Tomas. 1977. "Ideología, lucha de clases, y aparatos educativos en el desarrollo de América Latina." In *La educación bourgesa*, ed. G. Labarca, T. Vasconi, S. Finkel, and I. Recca. Mexico: Nueva Imagen.

Wachtel, Howard, and Peter Adelsheim. 1976. "The Inflationary Impact of Unemployment: Price Markups During Postwar Recessions, 1947-70." U.S. Congress. Joint Economic Committee. November 3.

Wallerstein, Immanuel. 1974. *The Modern World System*. New York: Academic Press.

———. 1980. *The World Capitalist System*. Cambridge: Cambridge University Press.

Warren, Bill. 1980. *Imperialism: Pioneer of Capitalism*. London: New Left Books.

Weber, Max. [1904] 1958. *The Protestant Ethic and the Spirit of Capitalism*. New York: Charles Scribner's Sons.

Wolfe, Alan. 1977. *The Limits of Legitimacy: Political Contradictions of Late Capitalism*. New York: Free Press.

———. 1981. *America's Impasse*. New York: Pantheon.

Wright, Erik Olin. 1974-75. "To Control or to Smash Bureaucracy: Weber and Lenin on Politics, the State, and Bureaucracy." *Berkeley Journal of Sociology* 19:69-108.

———. 1978. *Class, Crisis, and the State*. London: New Left Books.

Martin Carnoy is Professor of Education and Economics at Stanford University and the author of works including *Education as Cultural Imperialism* (Longmans); with Derek Shearer, *Economic Democracy* (Sharpe); and with Derek Shearer and Russell Rumberger, *A New Social Contract* (Harper & Row).

LIBRARY OF CONGRESS CATALOGING IN PUBLICATION DATA

Carnoy, Martin.
The state and political theory.

Bibliography: p.
Includes index.
1. Communist state. 2. State, The. 3. Political science—United States. I. Title.
JC474.C37 1984   321.9′2   83-43064

ISBN 0-691-07669-3
ISBN 0-691-02226-7 (pbk.)